DUSTOFF
RECORD CLEANER
J.N. ADAM & CO.
Every Victor Record
"STANDARD" RECORD CLEANER
JOHN R. SIMSON
BUFFALO MUSIC CO.
708 SWAN ST.
BUFFALO, N.Y.
Exclusively Victrolas & Records

I0809246

# ANTIQUE PHONOGRAPH
## GADGETS, GIZMOS, AND GIMMICKS

EDISON
STANDARD
PHONOGRAPH

# ANTIQUE PHONOGRAPH

## GADGETS, GIZMOS, AND GIMMICKS

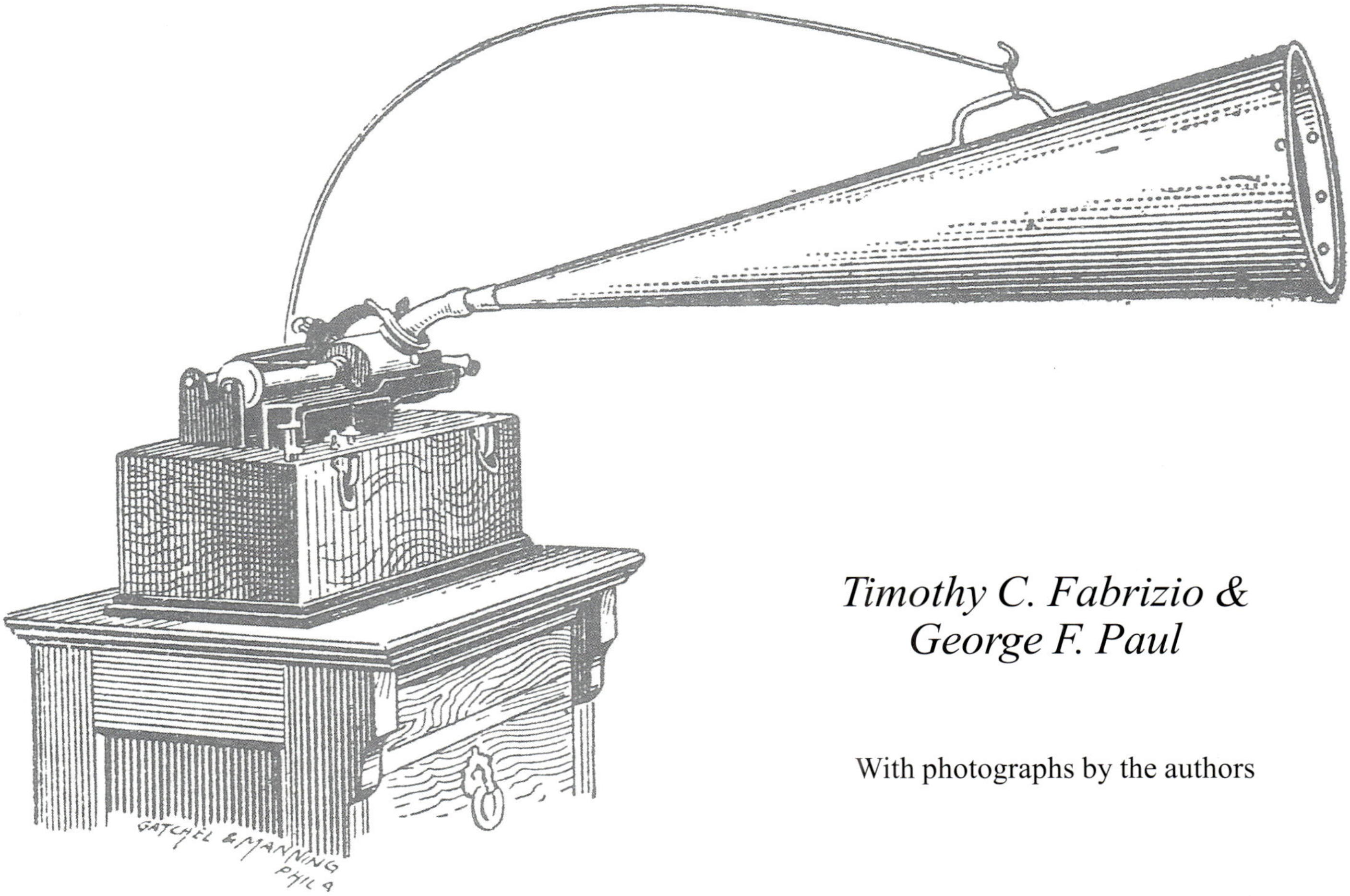


*Timothy C. Fabrizio &*
*George F. Paul*

With photographs by the authors

Schiffer Publishing Ltd ®

4880 Lower Valley Road, Atglen, PA 19310 USA

## Dedication

To Ray Phillips, George "Doug" Anderson and the other gentlemen of the Old School, who mixed their passion for our hobby with altruism and civility.

---

## A Good Phonograph A Treasure

A good phonograph, playing good music, never yet caused a riot. The man who owns it frequently is requested by his neighbors to leave the windows open, so they can participate in the noise, and nobody ever goes gunning for him. The phonograph habit grows on him, and after a while he'd rather hear a song from the machine than from the original human singer.

*–Walt Mason, "The Famous Poet-Philosopher,"* Talking Machine World, *May 1911.*

---

**Library of Congress Cataloging-in-Publication Data**

Fabrizio, Timothy C.
Anitque phonograph : gadgets, gizmos, and gimmicks / Timothy C. Fabrizio & George F. Paul.
p. cm.
Includes bibliographical references and index.
ISBN 0-7643-0733-9 (hc.)
1. Phonograph--Equipment and supplies--History. 2. Phonograph--Collectors and collecting. I. Paul, George F. II. Title.
TS2301.P3F298 1999
621.389'33'075--dc21 98-46570
CIP

---



Designed by Bonnie M. Hensley
Type set in Algiers/Times New Roman

ISBN: 0-7643-0733-9
Printed in China
1 2 3 4

Published by Schiffer Publishing Ltd.
4880 Lower Valley Road
Atglen, PA 19310
Phone: (610) 593-1777; Fax: (610) 593-2002
E-mail: Schifferbk@aol.com

In Europe, Schiffer books are distributed by Bushwood Books
6 Marksbury Rd. Kew Gardens
Surrey TW9 4JF England
Phone: 44 (0)181 392-8585; Fax: 44 (0)181 392-9876
E-mail: Bushwd@aol.com

# CONTENTS

# ACKNOWLEDGEMENTS

The authors would like to express their warmest thanks to the individuals who allowed the items in their collections to be photographed: Jean-Paul Agnard, Julien Anton, Terry Paul Baer, Lynn Bilton, Gary W. Blizzard, Martin F. Bryan, Lou Caruso, Scott and Denise Corbett, Todd Emery, David P. Graber, Howard Hazelcorn, Charles Hummel, Juanita Jones, Pat and Jamie Jones, Michael F. Khanchalian, Philippe LeRay, Robert Lomas, Mark E. Lynch, Charles McCarn, William G. Meyer, Alan H. Mueller, Walter and Carol Myers, Jim Nichol, Ray Phillips, Michael and Suzanne Raisman, Rae Ann Rieping, Steve and Ellie Saccente, Michael Sims, Bob and Karyn Sitter, Norm and Janyne Smith, Chrisopher J. Stephens, Rick Wilkins, and John Woodward.

We also would like to extend our gratitude to those individuals whose items appear without credit. We thank Peter Schiffer, Doug Congdon-Martin and the wonderful staff at Schiffer Publishing, Ltd. for their skill and cooperation.

We wish to acknowledge the following individuals for the succor, support and sanity they have provided one or both of us: Sylvie Agnard, the dilatory Monsieur Jalal Aro, Paul Baker, Freddie and Jeanette Blair, a special word of thanks to W.C. Chin, maestro Carlos Deazevedo, Claire Fabrizio, Kate Fabrizio, Dr. H. Duane Goldman, John and Joan Gresty, Don "Eagle Eye" Gfell, Mary McCarn, Enid Mitchell, Barbara, Jess and Tim Paul, Nancy Phillips, Joe Rieping, Robin and Robin Rolfs, Leslie Rosenfeld (and better luck next time!), Marie-Claude Stéger, Mirek Stehlik, Ray Wile, and last, but assuredly not least, all the wonderful people we thanked in our first book.

# INTRODUCTION

The "turn of the century." Antique collectors are intimately familiar with this term, as it has been used to describe that time, one hundred years ago, when much of what we collect (antique phonographs included) was made. Yet, another century is turning before us, and it gives us pause to contemplate how really archaic early sound machines have become and how much there remains to be learned about them.

Antique phonographs enjoyed a vigorous and viable commercial existence, and the market they inhabited was as filled with options, accessories, gadgets and gizmos as today's late-night television is populated with slicers, dicers, car waxes and beauty secrets. Collectors have acquired, examined and used these peripherals for years. However, little has been written about them beyond the reprinting of an occasional advertisement from the period.

In an effort to reveal more about the fascinating accessories and graphics which surrounded the antique phonograph, we, the authors, have examined nearly 20,000 pages of primary documents and photographed examples from over 35 collections. The results came as a revelation to us, and we hope that you, the reader, will be similarly moved.

It is human nature to cloak our predecessors beneath a veil of industriousness, propriety, and "common sense." Study of these pages will surely confirm the industriousness of those who invented and marketed talking machine accessories. However, the sometimes outrageous claims made for many of these products, coupled with the public's evident willingness to believe these claims and to purchase the items casts occasional doubt on both past propriety and common sense! Nevertheless, most of the items pictured in this book seem to have been grounded in genuine utility. Sometimes, these accessories are also visually stunning, especially in the realms of record cabinets and amplifying horns. The enduring appeal of these products, whether visual, utilitarian or merely frivolous, is our link with those buyers of a century ago. We only need to look at the gadgets and gizmos on our computers, automobiles and digital sound systems to see the parallel.

To finally discover this long-lost aspect of our hobby is something akin to Dorothy's first faltering steps into the Land of Oz. The world is suddenly in Technicolor. What seemed so real before is now pale in comparison. There is suddenly more excitement; more romance; more fun. If our first book, *The Talking Machine, an Illustrated Compendium 1877-1929*, is the cake, we like to think of this work as the icing.

Timothy C. Fabrizio
George F. Paul

Chapter One:

# HORNS

(In the captions, most dimensions are listed width of bell first, followed by length, including nipple. *Value code indicates horn only.*)

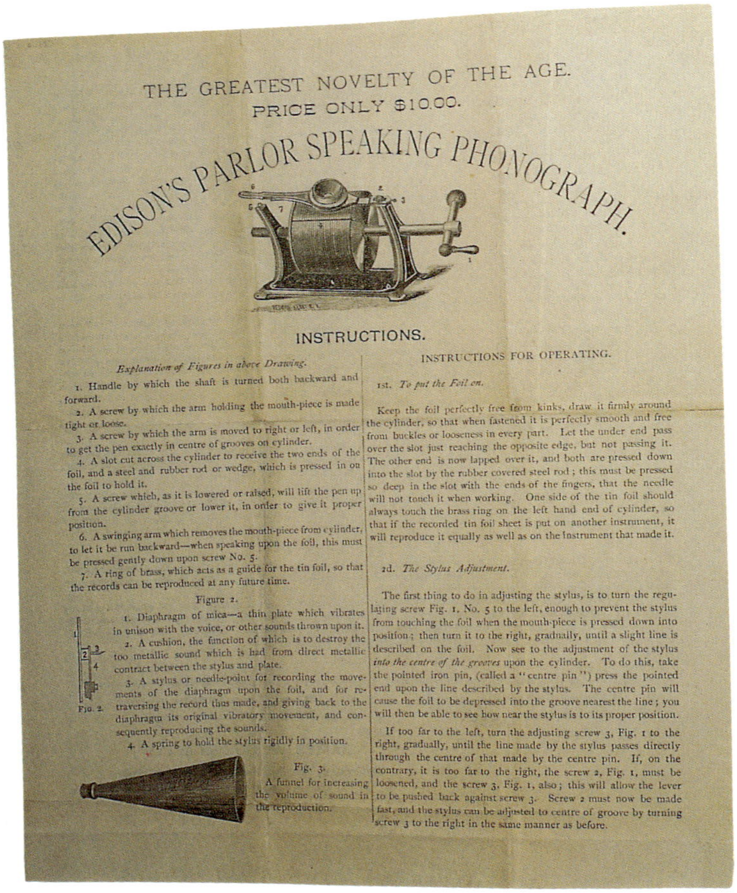

THE GREATEST NOVELTY OF THE AGE.

PRICE ONLY $10.00.

EDISON'S PARLOR SPEAKING PHONOGRAPH.

INSTRUCTIONS.

*Explanation of Figures in above Drawing.*

1. Handle by which the shaft is turned both backward and forward.

2. A screw by which the arm holding the mouth-piece is made tight or loose.

3. A screw by which the arm is moved to right or left, in order to get the pen exactly in centre of grooves on cylinder.

4. A slot cut across the cylinder to receive the two ends of the foil, and a steel and rubber rod or wedge, which is pressed in on the foil to hold it.

5. A screw which, as it is lowered or raised, will lift the pen up from the cylinder groove or lower it, in order to give it proper position.

6. A swinging arm which removes the mouth-piece from cylinder, to let it be run backward—when speaking upon the foil, this must be pressed gently down upon screw No. 5.

7. A ring of brass, which acts as a guide for the tin foil, so that the records can be reproduced at any future time.

Figure 2.

1. Diaphragm of mica—a thin plate which vibrates in unison with the voice, or other sounds thrown upon it.

2. A cushion, the function of which is to destroy the too metallic sound which is had from direct metallic contract between the stylus and plate.

3. A stylus or needle-point for recording the movements of the diaphragm upon the foil, and for re-traversing the record thus made, and giving back to the diaphragm its original vibratory movement, and consequently reproducing the sounds.

4. A spring to hold the stylus rigidly in position.

Fig. 2

Fig. 3.

A funnel for increasing the volume of sound in the reproduction.

INSTRUCTIONS FOR OPERATING.

1st. *To put the Foil on.*

Keep the foil perfectly free from kinks, draw it firmly around the cylinder, so that when fastened it is perfectly smooth and free from buckles or looseness in every part. Let the under end pass over the slot just reaching the opposite edge, but not passing it. The other end is now lapped over it, and both are pressed down into the slot by the rubber covered steel rod; this must be pressed so deep in the slot with the ends of the fingers, that the needle will not touch it when working. One side of the tin foil should always touch the brass ring on the left hand end of cylinder, so that if the recorded tin foil sheet is put on another instrument, it will reproduce it equally as well as on the instrument that made it.

2d. *The Stylus Adjustment.*

The first thing to do in adjusting the stylus, is to turn the regulating screw Fig. 1. No. 5 to the left, enough to prevent the stylus from touching the foil when the mouth-piece is pressed down into position; then turn it to the right, gradually, until a slight line is described on the foil. Now see to the adjustment of the stylus *into the centre of the grooves* upon the cylinder. To do this, take the pointed iron pin, (called a "centre pin") press the pointed end upon the line described by the stylus. The centre pin will cause the foil to be depressed into the groove nearest the line; you will then be able to see how near the stylus is to its proper position.

If too far to the left, turn the adjusting screw 3, Fig. 1 to the right, gradually, until the line made by the stylus passes directly through the centre of that made by the centre pin. If, on the contrary, it is too far to the right, the screw 2, Fig. 1, must be loosened, and the screw 3, Fig. 1, also; this will allow the lever to be pushed back against screw 3. Screw 2 must now be made fast, and the stylus can be adjusted to centre of groove by turning screw 3 to the right in the same manner as before.

1-1. These 1878 instructions for the smaller model of Edison's "Tinfoil" Phonograph already make reference to a "funnel for increasing the volume of sound..." It is interesting to note that small horns of similar shape would be used on talking machines for the next thirty years. (VR)

## BEGINNINGS

The most noticeable feature of early talking machines, the horn, developed slowly at first. Improvements, both real and imagined, were offered by many, but few horn manufacturers enjoyed lasting success. After 1904, horn development accelerated, but changing public taste would doom these efforts to ultimate failure. As the externally-mounted talking machine horn finally achieved its visual and acoustic zenith, the means of its demise had already taken root.

The earliest commercial offering of a talking machine horn was supplied with Edison "Tinfoil" Phonographs. Included in the listing of accessories accompanying the "Tinfoil" Phonograph was "1 Funnel." On page 4 of the 1878 *Instructions for the Management and Operation of Edison's Speaking Phonograph* was an illustration of a small conical horn which was labeled "A funnel for increasing the volume of sound in the reproduction." Another 1878 tract entitled *The Phonograph and its Inventor, Thomas Alva Edison*, offered this advice:

> Now, it is optional with the operator whether he uses the funnel or not, for, like the ladies, *it will speak anyhow*, the funnel only being used to *concentrate the sounds* as they issue forth. This funnel is shaped like a speaking-trumpet, and on putting it to the mouth-piece and turning the crank again, every word which has been spoken into the mouth-piece is exactly reproduced with the utmost distinctness.

We must assume that the "funnel" was in place when the *Instructions* confidently asserted:

> When properly adjusted the Phonograph will speak loud enough to be distinctly heard by an audience of from three to five thousand people.

1-2. Three "dudes" and a "Tinfoil" Phonograph are seen in this 1879 tintype. The machine was an exhibition piece, according to accompanying documents, and the man in the center can be seen holding an amplifying "funnel" in place. *Courtesy of the Charles Hummel collections.* (VR)

The use of horns is notably absent from literature pertaining to the early Bell-Tainter Graphophone. With its 6" long cylinders of ozocerite wax revolving on a tiny diameter of only 1 5/16", neither surface speed nor depth of cut were sufficient to generate volume greater than that necessary for ear-tubes. Not until Graphophones were capable of playing 2 1/8" diameter cylinders were horns mounted on them.

The Edison "Perfected" or Class "M" Phonograph, while employing ear-tubes as a rule, was also used with a variety of horns once its musical possibilities finally began to be exploited. An 1889 booklet published by the Metropolitan Phonograph Company of New York City was virtually silent on the use of horns, having only this to offer: "By means of a small horn or cone, the sound can be thrown out in a room or hall for greater enjoyment of an audience."

An 1892 catalogue of the "Edison Phonograph" issued by the North American Phonograph Company lists but two horns, a "14-in. Tin Horn (for Recording or Transcribing)" for $1.00. An "Ornamented" version cost $1.50. The September 1, 1893 North American catalogue included the two 14" horns listed previously, plus a "26 Inch Tin Horn" for $2.50; a "26 Inch Tin Horn, ornamented on outside" for $3.50; a "26 Inch Tin Horn, ornamented on outside and inside" for $5.00; a "20 Inch Brass Horn" for $4.00; a "20 Inch Brass Horn, Nickelplated" for $5.00; and a "12 Inch Nickelplated Brass Horn" for $2.00. This reflected the virtual explosion in cylinder exhibition during this period, when exhibitors were traveling from town to town with their phonographs. These early horns enabled an exhibitor to sell tickets to one or two daily performances before large groups of people. Otherwise, the exhibitor was obliged to laboriously collect his income all day, a nickel at a time, as patrons listened through ear-tubes.

Ear-tubes were the preferred method of enjoying music as late as September 1897, when the Graphophone catalogue instructed:

> An equipment of a Graphophone for home entertainment purposes should include a rubber hearing tube with two or more branches, and an amplifying horn to be attached to the Graphophone when it is desired to throw the sound out into the room. The wonderful fidelity with which the Graphophone reproduces musical and other sounds can not be fully appreciated unless the reproductions are listened to through the ear tubes, although of course, to entertain many people at the same time, a horn is necessary.

## Innovation

It was at approximately this point that experimenters began to seriously consider what could be done to improve the acoustic qualities of the horn. An 1897 book entitled *A Complete Manual of the Edison Phonograph*, by George Tewksbury, devoted a small chapter to "Horns and Tubes." Tewksbury, a pioneer in the talking machine business, gave an accurate appraisal of the state of the art (broken into paragraphs to aid the reader):

> The horn is still in its experimental stage, although certain definite results have been accomplished, and certain facts are known. One of the chief obstacles in the way is the fact now well proven that other conditions beside material and shape affect the practical action of the horn, especially in recording.
>
> With the Phonograph a speaking tube and a listening tube are provided. The speaking tube for dictation purposes meets the conditions acceptably. The single tube for listening is the best device for the purpose. But for concert use and public entertainment, the sound must be thrown out so that many persons can hear it, and for this purpose numerous types of amplifying horns have been produced. It would astonish the casual reader to learn of the number and thoroughness of the experi-

ments in that direction. Mr. Edison has himself tried a vast number of sizes and shapes, out of all sorts of material. Other experimentalists and enthusiasts have gone over the same ground, and branched out into new paths. Yet all have come back to the main-travelled [sic] road.

Wood, iron, steel, zinc, copper, brass, tin [actually tin-plated steel], aluminum, cornet metal, german silver [that is, nickel alloy], have been tried. Glass, too, and hard rubber, papier-mâché, and probably every other product that nature yields or man contrives. The latitude as to form and shape being greater than the resource in material, there have been almost innumerable attempts in that line. After all of which it may be said that tin and brass, defective as they are, have been settled upon as the most available, and the forms now known in the trade as the most desirable. Any horn to be good must come out of sound metal, and be perfectly joined. Ordinary joining will not do, and imperfect metal is an illusion.

The horns in the trade have names which indicate pretty clearly the character of each. First, there is the small 14-inch tin horn, whose most valuable use is for dictation and the making of talking records. It has a flaring end opening away from the line of the stem, is light, and easily slipped over the tube plate of the speaker [reproducer]. For reproduction it is one of the most unsatisfactory horns made, yet a large number of people insist upon using it for that service. Records reproduced through it are likely to squeak and rattle, and if, because of greater handiness, a small horn is desired, one of the small nickel-plated brass ones should be obtained. The test with the 14-inch tin horn is the most difficult in the record business.

The 26-inch standard tin horn is deservedly the amplifying device most used, and all things considered, gives as good results as any. It is not expensive, can be used for recording and reproducing both, and fulfills all reasonable requirements of horn service. When correctly made, block tin is used, and the joints are so fastened as to prevent rattle. If made of cheap material, it is the same abomination that all other cheap supplies for the Phonograph are. The horn is heavily japanned [painted], not for looks merely. It is held in place on a folding tripod, to the loop of which it should be attached by string, ribbon, or other non-conducting material, never by a metal hook or wire. The connection with the speaker [reproducer] of the Phonograph is effected by a short length of rubber tubing.

In the use of this, as with all other large horns, the best results are obtained many feet away from the mouth of the horn, which is so built as to project the volume of tone forward. The measurement at the bell or opening of this horn is 12 inches, and the lines from the bell to the nipple are straight. Similar in results, but different in character, is the 22-inch brass horn, preferred by some because it is thought to give a more ringing effect to the reproduction of band and orchestra music, and claimed by others to make all reproduction brighter. This horn has a flaring bell, and is 12 inches in width at its mouth. It is suspended the same as the 26-inch horn to the loop of a folding stand, and makes a striking appearance.

Larger horns of various shapes are in the market, and invariably in tin or brass. Horns four feet or more in length had a vogue at one time, but their practical value was never apparent to the writer, nor their musical superiority audible to his ear. For advertising purposes they possess merit, and possibly in heavy exhibition work, where it cannot be denied that what their enterprising owners—some of them 'Professors,' and all of them personal friends of Mr. Edison, with whom they have formerly worked, or been acquainted since boyhood—call 'putting up a great front,' is effectually [sic] accomplished by these cavernous funnels. There are some larger horns, however, which possess merit and are not to be derided—horns larger than the standard types, and quite expensive. Mr. Fox, of Philadelphia, has devised a long horn of spun brass that is really excellent, if expensive, and other experimentalists are at work in the same field, to all of whom we wish well.

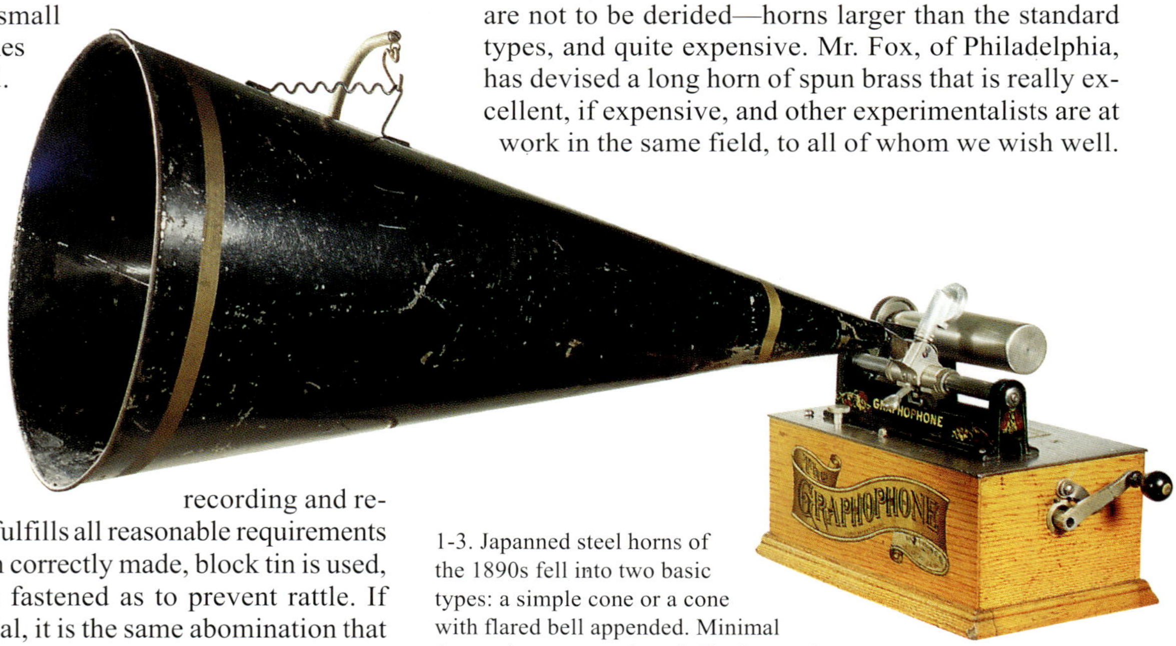


1-3. Japanned steel horns of the 1890s fell into two basic types: a simple cone or a cone with flared bell appended. Minimal decoration was employed. The base color was usually black, interrupted by one or two concentric gold stripes. Reflecting this design was this 27 1/2" x 12" horn from the 1890s (referred to in Tewksbury's text as the "26-inch standard tin horn"). These were available with slight variations of gold striping. (Value code: F)

1-4. A small flared-bell horn from the 1890s, measuring 6 3/8" x 12 7/8". Horns of this type show a wide variety of striping patterns. *Courtesy of Jean-Paul Agnard.* (Value code: D)

Notwithstanding George Tewksbury's joking assertion that all exhibitors were "personal friends of Mr. Edison," his assessment gives a rare glimpse into the contemporary development and use of talking machine horns in 1897. Significant changes in horn technology were imminent, and would relegate the horns described by Mr. Tewksbury to the realm of obsolescence, even by turn-of-the-century standards.

Flared-bell horns began to die out in late 1897 or early 1898. Berliner "Improved" Gramophones employed curved-bell horns by 1898, although the hand-driven models retained the older, flared-bell design. The Hawthorne & Sheble Company of Philadelphia pioneered the marketing of seamless (spun) brass, curved-bell horns. These horns were heavier than the tin models, and most needed supports to suspend them. Hawthorne & Sheble were among the first to offer a variety of these supports as well.

1-5. A mid-1890s black japanned horn with unusually bold stripes. 15" long. *Courtesy of Norm and Janyne Smith.* (Value code: D)

1-6. This 24" horn with 14 5/8" flared bell used comparatively elaborate embellishment, with multiple red and gold stripes and a geometric border. (Value code: C)

1-7. This 42" long horn with 15" flared bell is unusual because it was japanned *green* rather than the customary black. It used no gold accents, but the striking color aptly distinguishes it without further decoration. (Value code: D)

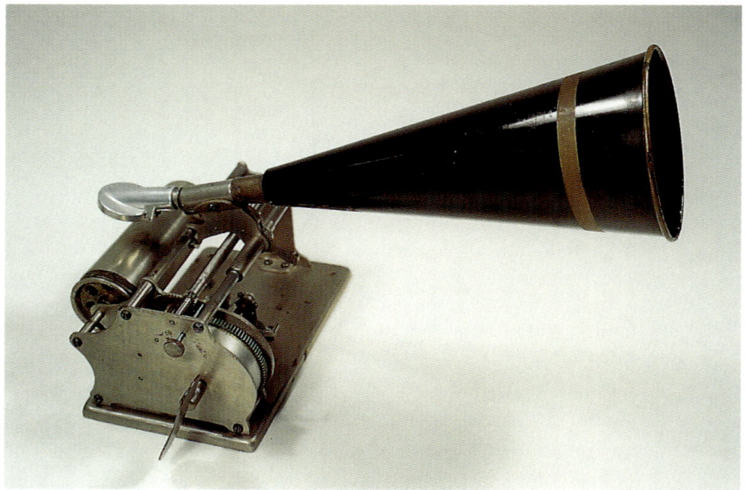

1-8. 10" conical horns, based upon the 1890s model, persisted on the smallest and least expensive cylinder talking machines throughout the first decade of the Twentieth Century. Shown here is a typical example on a Graphophone Type "Q." (Value code: F)

## Standardization

By 1900, 14" polished brass horns with curved bells were included with all Edison "Standard," "Home," "Spring-Motor," "M," and "H" (coin-operated) Phonographs. 24" brass horns with curved bells were supplied with the Edison "Concert" and all floor-cabinet coin-operated Phonographs.

Beginning in late 1900 and 1901, manufacturers were supplying horns with black painted bodies and brass bells. This was seen as an improvement, since the body would not tarnish, while the brass bell imparted some style. Hawthorne & Sheble was marketing a wide variety of horns by this time, including those of "Silveroid" (probably zinc), which were described as, "Very handsome in appearance and resemble polished silver." In addition were many sizes of hammered brass, spun brass, combination brass and silveroid, aluminum, and of course "Japanned Tin Horns." For the princely sum of $150 the company would manufacture to order its "20th Century Horn," which was 9' long (width of bell 3' 6") and was made of brass with a copper bell.

By 1901, the Columbia Phonograph Company was supplying 14" aluminum horns with several models of its cylinder Graphophones. Columbia was the only company to offer aluminum horns as standard equipment on its machines. 36" aluminum horns were available for the "AR" and "AY" Disc Graphophones for an additional $5.00.

By 1902 the "brass bell, japanned top" style horns for cylinder and disc were prominent. In addition, Hawthorne & Sheble introduced its "Silk Finish Horns":

> Something decidedly new, possessing qualities which we believe will make them the most popular horns which have ever been produced.
>
> The bodies are made of steel, Japanned on the inside, and covered on the outside with a black silky-looking cloth. The bells are made of brass.
>
> The advantages of these horns can be seen at a glance.
>
> *First.* The cloth covering on the outside of the bodies absolutely absorbs counter vibration and rattle, while the metal inside preserves the true tone of the reproduction.
>
> *Second.* The handsome appearance of these horns will insure their immediate sale. They are by far the neatest and most attractive horns which have ever been produced.
>
> *Third.* We have applied for Letters Patent on these horns so as to keep poorly constructed imitations from coming on the market.

These horns enjoyed a wide sale to owners of cylinder talking machines. They were also available for Zonophones, and later became standard equipment on "Duplex" (disc) phonographs.

The old styles sometimes died hard. As late as 1902 the Sears, Roebuck and Company catalogue offered Eagle Graphophones with black, 26" conical horns which were actually five years out of date.

The 1902–1904 period was dominated by the brass bell/black body style horn on both cylinder and disc talking machines. This was particularly true of the Edison Phonographs, which were regularly supplied with 14" black & brass horns from 1901 until October 1907. Victor talking machines were typically supplied with black-and-brass horns during this time. Other disc talking machines, particularly Talkophone, relied heavily on this style horn as well.

During this period, Victor pioneered a new configuration for supporting the horn. This was accomplished by mounting the horn directly above the playing mechanism. The utility of the idea would soon be recognized, and adapted to other disc machines and cylinder machines as well. The acoustic value of the Johnson "Rigid Arm" and the later "Tapering Arm" was probably no more attractive to buyers than the successful placement of the horn in a more convenient location.

## New Designs Emerge

By the end of 1904, the petalled or "flower" horn was enjoying huge popularity. Numerous patents were awarded to various inventors, and a bewildering range of horns from several manufacturers appeared. These "morning glory" or flower horns often appeared to be identical to one another. Methods of folding, shaping, joining and finishing were patentable features, and competitors engaged in an advertising war in an effort to establish public preference for their respective processes. Prominent among these warring factions were the Hawthorne & Sheble Company of Philadelphia, the Tea Tray Company of Newark, New Jersey, and the Standard Metal Manufacturing Company of the same city. The small, less effective horns typically supplied with Phonographs and Graphophones created a huge demand for the larger, more colorful flower horns. For several years, it would be a horn seller's market.

1905 saw several manufacturers offering compressed paper or "fibre" horns, notably the "Linenoid," the "Mega" Phono Horn, Allen's Paper Lacquered Phono Horn, and

Opposite page, bottom:
1-9. In the 1890s, brass talking machine horns were viewed within the context of existing band instruments. Cornets and trumpets had no visible seams; many sizes of talking machine horns were similarly constructed. These are usually called "seamless brass horns." By contrast, tin horns (actually tin-plated steel) of the period were crude affairs, with oblique angles and noticeable seams. It was, however, rather expensive to dovetail the brass of "seamless" horns, so brass horns followed their tin kindred into seamed construction by 1900. This 19" long "seamless" horn with 8" bell is shown suspended from a Hawthorne & Sheble support fitted to the first model Edison "Gem." (Value code: D)

the "Perfection" flower horn. So popular were these fibre horns that Hawthorne & Sheble (whose horns were fashioned from metal) felt compelled to caution the trade in 1905:

> Don't use Paper or Fibre Horns if you want clear, brilliant reproductions. They all sound woody and hollow, not natural. Nothing but metal will give a natural tone.

During 1906, the "Searchlight Horn" was introduced by the Searchlight Horn Company of Brooklyn. This bulbous, heavily ribbed horn was touted as a scientific triumph of acoustics. Models for cylinder and disc were offered in various colors and with optional floral decoration.

In July 1906, the New Jersey Sheet Metal Company introduced its "Kompakt" collapsible flower horn. 1907 brought a rash of folding horns on the market. Most were made of fabric supported on a collapsible metal frame. The Searchlight Company offered its "knockdown" version as a five-piece rendition of its existing horn; then went one better by offering it in aluminum. Thumbscrews allowed the five pieces to be assembled into a complete horn. This "Crowning Achievement of American Ingenuity" appears to have met with limited success, as the Searchlight Company soon substituted a truly collapsible horn made of flexible metal.

In August 1907, the Devineau "Ideal" horn was introduced, made by the Devineau Manufacturing Company of New York City. (Within a month or two, the firm also listed a Cleveland, Ohio, location in its advertisements.) This was the first cygnet-shaped horn offered to the public. The upper bell section was fashioned from aluminum in the familiar flower shape. The lower curved section was made of "ebonoid," a moulded material similar to gutta-percha. The horn was lightweight and convenient, perched out of the way atop a Phonograph or Graphophone, and was completely self-supporting.

## Changes in the Market

Unfortunately for the makers of the "Ideal" horn and other larger horn manufacturers as well, the Edison company began to supply its own black flower horns in October 1907. This created a panic in the horn business, and sales of aftermarket horns fell off dangerously.

The Standard Metal Manufacturing Company of Newark, New Jersey was the supplier of horns to Edison, so was spared the market repercussions brought about by the new Edison horns. However, a nationwide financial panic occurring in late 1907 adversely affected the entire talking machine business.

It was not a time conducive to the success of odd-ball merchandise. The "Orchestraphone," introduced in March 1908, was a small wooden cabinet designed to be placed upon Victor machines in place of the horn. The mouth of the back-bracket of the machine aligned with the small end of a truncated square wooden "horn." Doors mounted on the front of the "Orchestraphone" allowed for volume control. Advertised at a retail price of $20.00, the "Orchestraphone" had a short life, probably due to infringement of the Victor patent on sound-modifying doors.

In June 1908, the Standard Metal Manufacturing Company assumed control of the Searchlight Horn Company. As business worsened for the established horn manufacturers, the Shiep & Vandergrift Company of Philadelphia introduced in November 1908 its solid-wood horns called "Music Master." The company claimed these to be superior to the veneered wooden horns first offered by other manufacturers in 1907.

Another odd horn product of 1908 was the "Echo-Tone." Manufactured by the Echo-Tone Horn Company of Brooklyn, New York, it resembled a Devineau "Ideal" horn which might have been accidentally sat upon. The principle applied in the "Echo-Tone" horn was used years later in Pathé "Reflex" disc talking machines, where the sound was directed rearward into a bowl-shaped area and reverberated 180 degrees out the front of the machine. The "Echo-Tone" appears to have survived only a matter of months.

1909 was another bad year for horn manufacturers. The business climate was still arduous, although slowly improving. However, the internal-horn Victor-Victrola, introduced in August 1906, was finally making a serious impact on the talking machine industry at large. Horns were becoming old-fashioned. The $200 Victrola (along with Edison flower horns) had virtually destroyed the market for aftermarket talking machine horns.

The external talking machine horn had one last hurrah. This was the introduction in August 1909 of the Edison "Cygnet" horn. A variation of the earlier Devineau "Ideal" horn, the Edison version was made of steel—larger, heavier, and requiring a support. It was acoustically well designed, and its upright orientation kept it out of the way. Its design excellence inspired the self-supporting horn of the Edison "Opera" Phonograph and its performance was the apogee of the external horn talking machine era.

The manufacture of external horn talking machines declined drastically after 1913. The era may be said to have ended during those months prior to the First World War. The talking machine horn was a product of whimsical innocence. The horn performed an *acoustic* function, but was made into a *visual* asset. It was nurtured and grown during sun-dappled days of picnics, horseless carriages and airships. Its blossom withered and died in new era of tanks and machine guns. Those horns that survive today speak of that earlier, carefree time when inspiration was brought into the home, and music was heard from a flower.

1-11. Bettini laminated wood horn shown on a French Bettini 5" phonograph. *Courtesy of the Julien Anton collection.* (VR)

1-10. A trio of Bettini horns (l to r): painted steel body with sectional elbow and aluminum bell, 8 1/2" x 16 1/2", 1 1/8" orifice; seamless brass with brass elbow, 15 1/2" x 40", 1 1/2" orifice; pleated painted steel body with zinc elbow and aluminum bell, 10 3/4" x 20", 1 1/2" orifice. (VR)

1-12. Above all, unsupported Bettini horns needed to be lightweight. This example is made entirely of aluminum, except for a brass-reinforced connection to the reproducer. *Courtesy of John Woodward* (VR)

1-13. Glass horns were sold less commonly in the United States than in Europe. Hawthorne & Sheble listed them in catalogues from the early 1900s. This Edison "Home" Phonograph is equipped with a glass horn measuring 10 1/4" x 15". *Courtesy of Jean-Paul Agnard.* (VR)

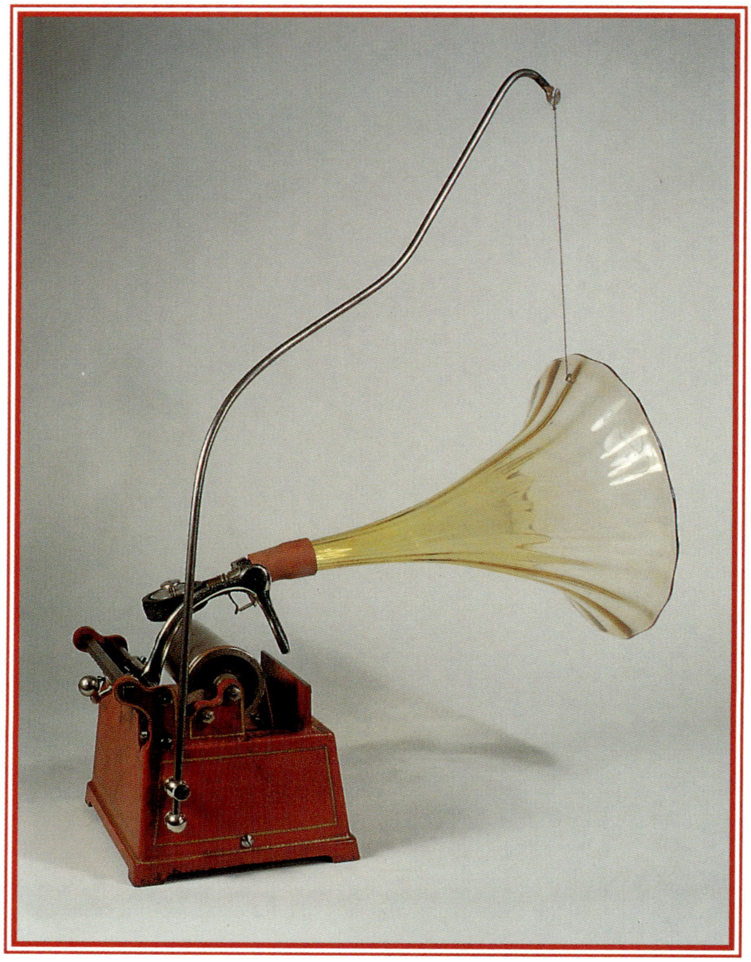

1-14. Pathé offered a fluted glass horn to fit its "Le Gaulois" cylinder machine. This horn measures 8 1/2" x 10 1/2". *Courtesy of Jean-Paul Agnard.* (VR)

1-15. Horns based on the more elegant lines of orchestral instruments were offered primarily in Europe. This "cor-de-chasse," or "hunting horn," was typical of the style, available in a variety of sizes. It is curious that these horns, which permitted greater length within a limited space, were not well represented in the American market until the introduction of Edison's cygnet horn in 1909. (Value code: C)

Opposite page top left:
1-16. Horn carriers were constructed of various materials. This one, of European origin, is made up of wooden staves. It holds a spun aluminum horn with a bell of 10 1/4" diameter. *Courtesy of Ray Phillips.* (Value code: E)

1-18. A 16" x 22" canvas-backed broadside from exhibitor A.W. Luce promoting his "Graphaphone" [sic] entertainments. Among Mr. Luce's personal papers was 1900 correspondence with the Hawthorne & Sheble Manufacturing Company of Philadelphia concerning the fabrication of the gigantic amplifying horn shown. H & S would list the identical 9' long horn in its 1901 catalogue, priced at $150.00. The machine in the poster is a Columbia "GG" Graphophone.

1-17. A large size Columbia celluloid collapsible horn with original box measuring 30" long. This was manufactured by the American Micrograph Company for Columbia. *Courtesy of Walter and Carol Myers*. (Value code: C)

1-19. A large, straight horn, nickel-plated over brass, measuring 20 1/2" x 42". *Courtesy of Jean-Paul Agnard.* (Value code: E)

1-20. Pathé phonographs rarely used horns larger than those which could be supported by the carriage. This is an unusual example of a nickel-plated brass Pathé horn measuring 11 3/8" x 26 1/4". *Courtesy of Jean-Paul Agnard.* (Value code: E)

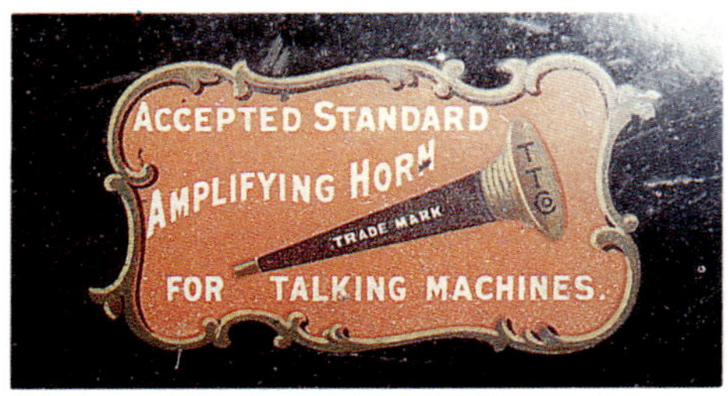


1-22. The Tea Tray Company of Newark, New Jersey, manufactured straight or trumpet-shaped horns to fit cylinder and disc talking machines, marked with this distinctive logo. The firm coined the term "Black and Gold" to refer to its brass-belled, steel-bodied horns. A 1902 catalogue also pointed to the "reamed on" bell, with its raised, crimped seam, as an improvement over the flush, soldered (and therefore weaker) joints of earlier horns.

1-21. The Standard Metal Manufacturing Company of Newark, New Jersey, made straight brass-belled cylinder horns like this one decorated with flowers on the black japanned body. 23 3/4" x 31". *Courtesy of Jean-Paul Agnard.* (Value code: D)

1-23. It is interesting to consider the purpose of this little adapter. It would convert a "front-mounted" style Victor disc talking machine horn to a cylinder machine horn. More importantly, it would allow a manufacturer to offer one horn suitable for two different purposes. (Value code: G)

1-26. This aluminum horn of identical dimensions has a neck of the right size to accept the elbow of a "front-mount" Columbia "Disc Graphophone." It might also be used in connection with the Columbia "BC" sound-amplifying cylinder model. The lack of a "locating nub" on the reduced end of this horn suggests the latter use. *Courtesy of Michael F. Khanchalian.* (Value code: D)

1-24. Another method of accomplishing the same cylinder/disc horn conversion is shown here. In fact, the manufacturer has simplified the design by incorporating Victor threads into the neck of a cylinder type horn.

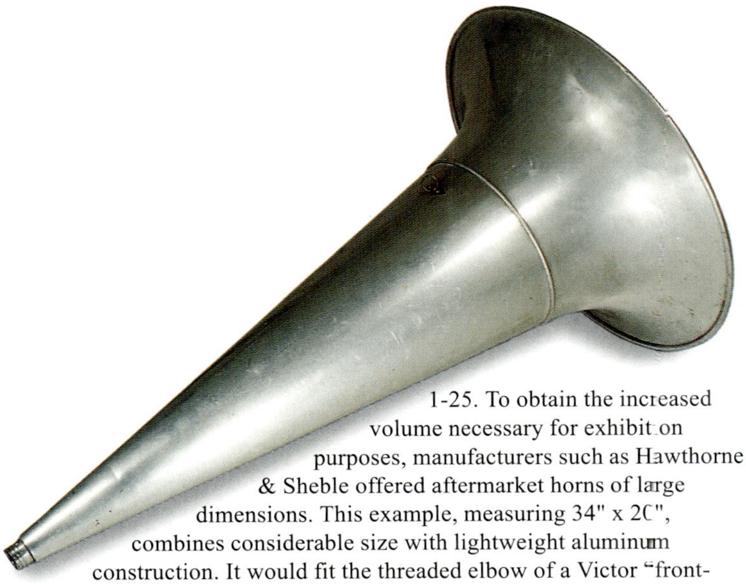

1-25. To obtain the increased volume necessary for exhibition purposes, manufacturers such as Hawthorne & Sheble offered aftermarket horns of large dimensions. This example, measuring 34" x 20", combines considerable size with lightweight aluminum construction. It would fit the threaded elbow of a Victor "front-mount" disc talking machine, and could be suspended from an ordinary floor stand. *Courtesy of Todd Emery.* (Value code: D)

1-27. This fitted canvas horn carrier features a special sleeve to accept the horn support. Encloses a 31" length horn. Described in the February 1905 *Talking Machine World* as a "Mackintosh Horn Cover," the maker was identified as the Douglas Phonograph Company of New York. "With these waterproof and wearproof covers, one can carry the phonograph or horn about in all kinds of weather without danger of any damage. Their use also preserves the tone." *Courtesy of Martin F. Bryan.* (Value code: F)

1-28. Companies such as the Douglas Phonograph Company of New York and Peter Bacigalupi of San Francisco sold horns like "Allen's Paper Lacquered Phonograph Horn" which was manufactured in Japan. Pictured is a similar Japanese-style horn of lightweight construction, decorated with oriental designs. This horn measures 18 3/4" x 29". *Courtesy of Jean-Paul Agnard.* (Value code: C)

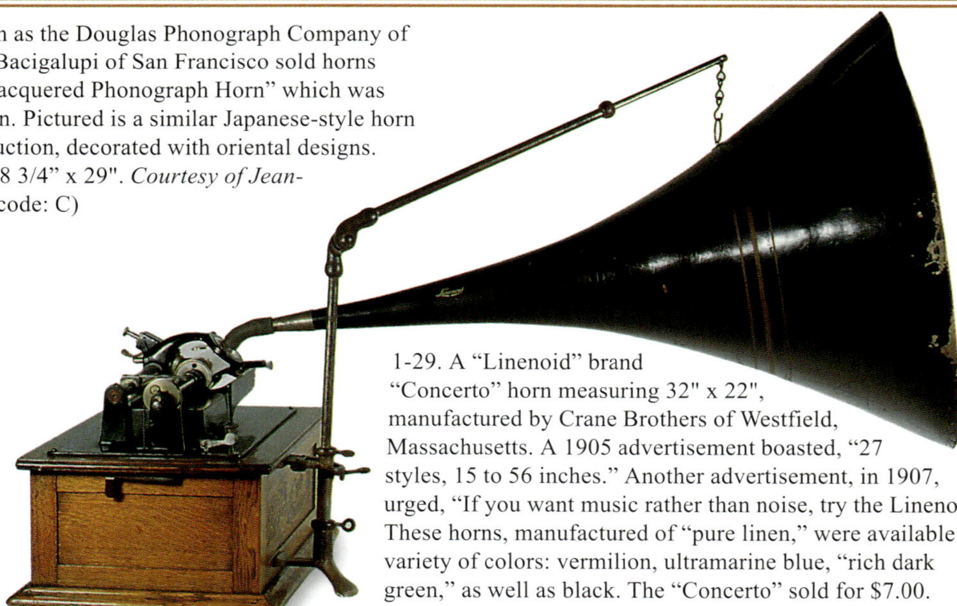

1-29. A "Linenoid" brand "Concerto" horn measuring 32" x 22", manufactured by Crane Brothers of Westfield, Massachusetts. A 1905 advertisement boasted, "27 styles, 15 to 56 inches." Another advertisement, in 1907, urged, "If you want music rather than noise, try the Linenoid." These horns, manufactured of "pure linen," were available in a variety of colors: vermilion, ultramarine blue, "rich dark green," as well as black. The "Concerto" sold for $7.00. (Value code: E)

1-30. Blue "Mega" flower horn, made of "...a special pressed fibrous material, likened to rubber for its flexibility. Not to be confused with so-called 'Fibre' horns made of strawboard, the cheapest and most fragile board made." A November 1905 advertisement in *Talking Machine World* claimed five years' experience in manufacturing this type of horn. They were available for cylinder machines and Victor machines in both flowered and "Trumpet Shape." This one measures 22 1/2" x 30 1/2". *Courtesy of Jean-Paul Agnard.* (Value code: D)

1-33. Red Hawthorne & Sheble flower horn with Silk Finish exterior. 21" x 26". (Value code: D)

1-34. Close-up of the emblem which appeared on the exterior of Hawthorne & Sheble Silk Finish Horns.

1-31. Research suggests that the correct nomenclature is "Mega Phono Horn," despite the deceptive arrangement of words on the horn decal. "Mega" horns were manufactured by E.A. and A.G. Schoettel, Maspeth, Queens County, New York. *Courtesy of Jean-Paul Agnard.*

1-32. A Hawthorne & Sheble paneled horn painted to suggest a morning glory, with patent Silk Finish exterior. 21" x 26". (Value code: D)

1-35. One of Hawthorne & Sheble's "Artistic Flower Horns" first announced in the *Talking Machine World* of September 1906. This one has variegated interior panels and a nickeled exterior. 17 1/2" x 26 1/2". *Courtesy of Norm and Janyne Smith.* (Value code: C)

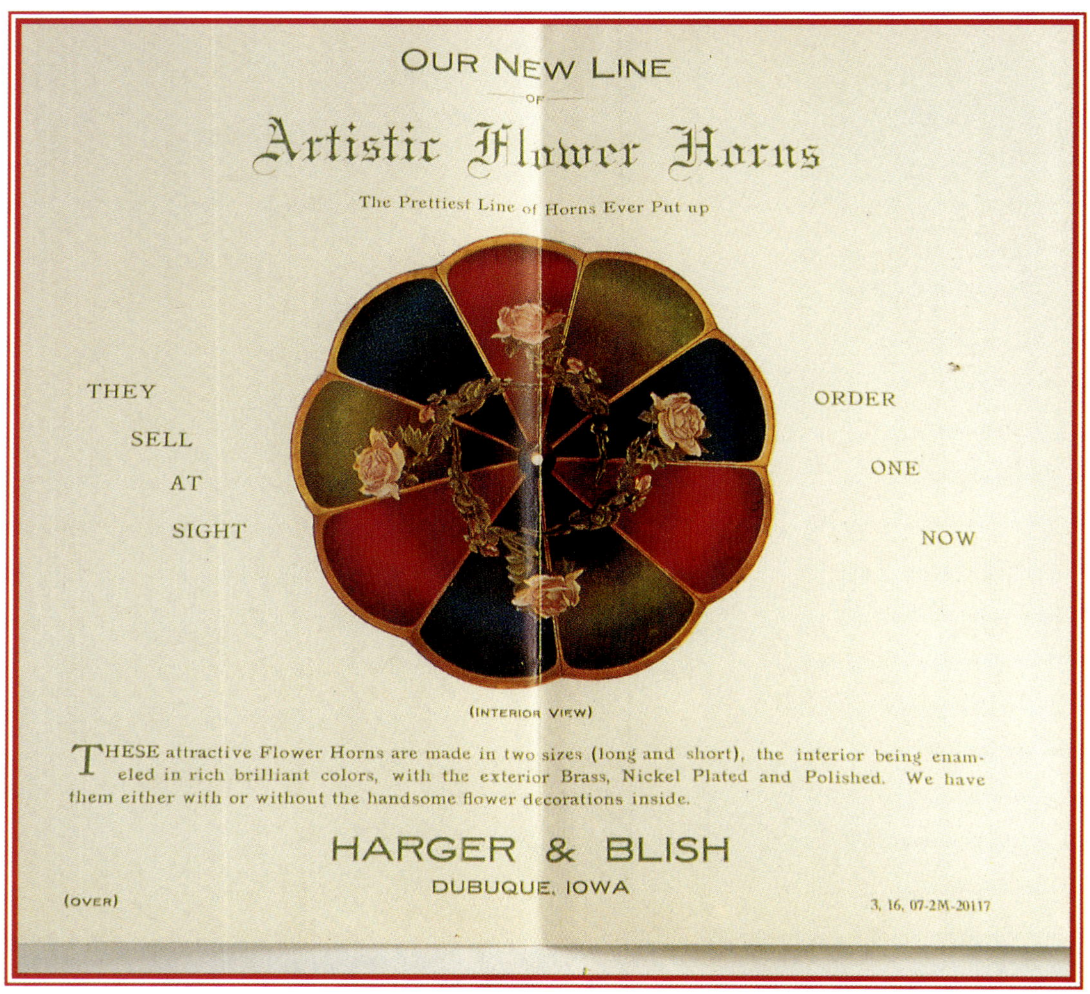


1-36. Flyer advertising Hawthorne & Sheble's "Artistic Flower Horns" distributed by Harger & Blish of Dubuque, Iowa. Dated March 16, 1907.

1-37. Hawthorne & Sheble produced a dizzying variety of ornamented horns to fit both cylinder and disc talking machines. This Victor "II" carries an optional H&S flower horn with original appliqué floral sprays (horn No.170-D). *Courtesy of Juanita Jones.* (Value code: D)

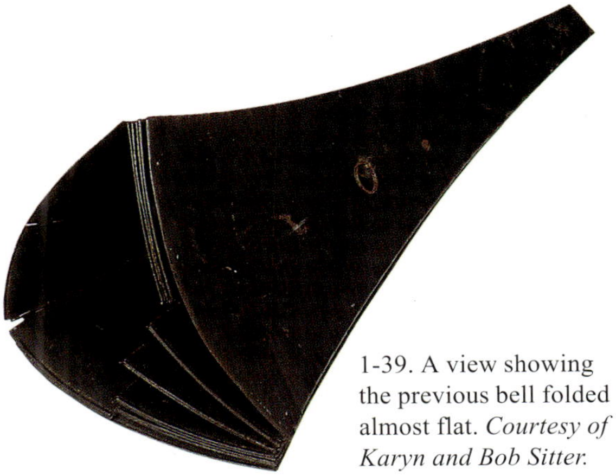

1-39. A view showing the previous bell folded almost flat. *Courtesy of Karyn and Bob Sitter.*

1-38. Collapsible metal horns enjoyed a brief vogue beginning in 1906. Firms such as the New Jersey Sheet Metal Company of Newark, New Jersey, and the Searchlight Horn Company of Brooklyn, New York, produced their own distinctive models. A partially-collapsed bell of similar manufacture is illustrated, 23" in diameter. *Courtesy of Bob and Karyn Sitter.* (Value code: E)

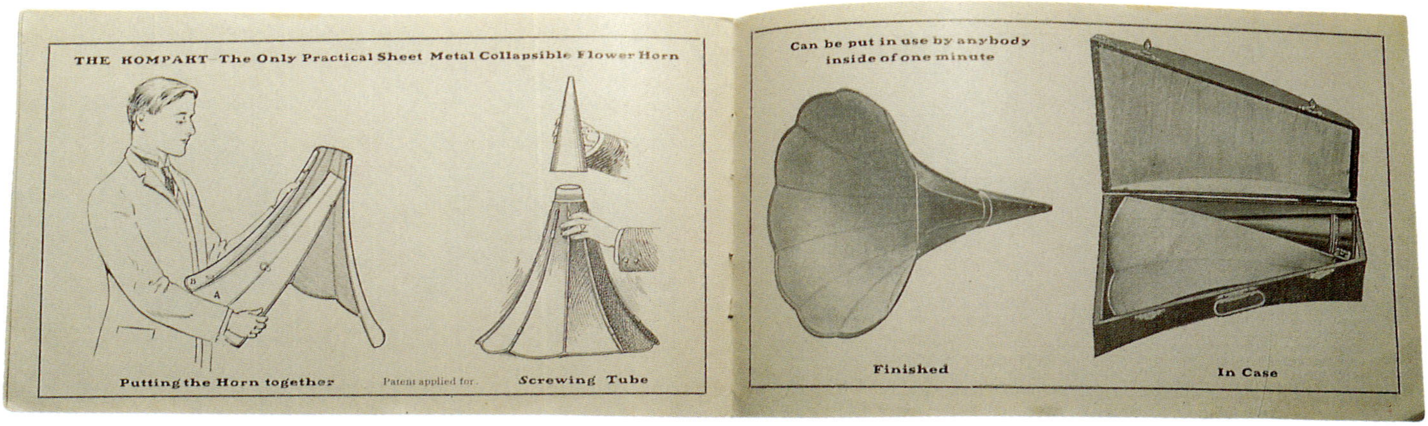


1-40. Catalogue showing the "Kompakt" collapsible horn, manufactured by the New Jersey Sheet Metal Company of Newark, New Jersey. These were made for both cylinder and disc talking machines. *Courtesy of Walter and Carol Myers.*

1-41. A "Kompakt" collapsible flower horn. It was first advertised in the September 1906 *Talking Machine World.* The company claimed that the "Kompakt" could be "...put in use inside of one minute." This horn measures 22" x 27". *Courtesy of Jean-Paul Agnard.* (Value code: C)

1-42. A view of the "Kompakt" horn disassembled. Collapsible and folding horns enjoyed brief popularity during the 1906–1909 period. The need to make cumbersome flower horns more manageable lost importance as cabinet models proliferated. *Courtesy of Jean-Paul Agnard.*

1-43. The New Jersey Horn Manufacturing Company of Newark, New Jersey, manufactured this unusually-shaped flower horn they dubbed the "Tulip." An advertisement from the July 1907 *Talking Machine World* described this design as "...the only perfect-sounding Horn in the world." Decorated with pansies, this one measures 22" x 33 1/2". *Courtesy of Jean-Paul Agnard.* (Value code: C)

1-44. Pink flower horn with red roses, measuring 22 1/4" x 31". *Courtesy of Jean-Paul Agnard.* (Value code: C)

1-45. Purple flower horn with pink pansies measuring 22 1/2" x 31". *Courtesy of Norm and Janyne Smith.* (Value code: D)

1-46. Red flower horn with "millefleur" decoration. 22 1/2" x 31". (Value code: D)

1-47. The "galvanized effect" on this Hawthorne & Sheble flower horn was described by the company as "Crystal." 22" x 31". *Courtesy of Jean-Paul Agnard.* (Value code: C)

1-48. Red flower horn manufactured by Hawthorne & Sheble, with white tulips, 22" x 31". *Courtesy of Norm and Janyne Smith.* (Value code: D)

1-49. Blue "Lily Horn" with pink roses, manufactured by the Standard Metal Manufacturing Company of Newark, New Jersey, 25 1/2" x 32 1/2". *Courtesy of Norm and Janyne Smith.* (Value code: C)

1-50. A "Searchlight" horn, manufactured by the Searchlight Horn Company of Brooklyn, New York, and introduced during the summer of 1906. The horn was so-called because it was "Designed and Constructed on the Scientific Principle of a Searchlight Reflector by a Master of Acoustics." It was available, "For all styles cylinder machines and for all Victor machines, except Victor No. 1, in Five colors. Gold Striped, Decorated and DeLuxe Decorations." Apparent lack of proper surface preparation has caused the painted finishes on these horns to fare poorly over the years. This one measures 20 1/2" x 30 1/2". During the "collapsible horn craze" of 1906–1909, the Searchlight Horn Company offered a "Knock-Down Searchlight Horn" for "all Cylinder and Disc Machines" (January 1907), a "Searchlight Folding Horn" (August 1907), and even an aluminum version of the "Knock-Down" horn (February 1907). A "Searchlight, Jr." was also sold, measuring 18 1/2" x 26". *Courtesy of Jean-Paul Agnard.* (Value code: D)

1-51. The uniquely-shaped "Searchlight" horn was sold to fit Victor talking machines "II" through "VI." Opaque or translucent colored finishes were available with or without floral decoration. The sale of these horns was taken over by the Standard Metal Manufacturing Company in May 1908. The Searchlight Company, however, continued to defend its fundamental U.S. Patent No.771,441. In 1912, it won a judgement in Federal Court against Sherman, Clay & Company of San Francisco regarding the manufacture of horns "...composed of longitudinally arranged metal strips secured together at edges by seams of such character as to produce longitudinal ribs on outer surface." The company hoped to extend this ruling to all "...horns now in general use by the talking machine trade." However, the steep decline in external-horn machine production after 1912 would have made further litigation pointless. 20 3/4" bell x 24" length. (Value code: D)

1-52. A Hawthorne & Sheble flower horn made of polished brass, measuring 21 1/2" x 26". These horns were offered in a wide variety of finishes, including polished brass outside, with interior "handsomely decorated" or "enameled and gold striped." This suggests the original interior finish of this particular horn has been removed. *Courtesy of Jean-Paul Agnard.* (Value code: D)

1-53. Purple flower horn with red roses, 22 1/2" x 31". *Courtesy of Norm and Janyne Smith.* (Value code: D)

1-54. Red flower horn with white mums, manufactured by the Standard Metal Manufacturing Company of Newark, New Jersey. 22 1/2" x 31". *Courtesy of Norm and Janyne Smith.* (Value code: D)

1-55. Flower horn, white with variegated roses, manufactured by the Standard Metal Manufacturing Company of Newark, New Jersey. 23" x 31". (Value code: C)

1-56. Red flower horn manufactured by the Tea Tray Company of Newark, New Jersey with white cabbage roses, 22" x 31". *Courtesy of Norm and Janyne Smith.* (Value code: D)

1-57. A silver flower horn with pink roses, 22 1/2" x 31". Surviving examples of this horn appear to have been initially painted blue, over-painted with silver. It is not known why this was done. With this type of horn, the striping (normally done in gold) is blue. The horn support is the No.200 Clamp Horn Crane, a product of the Tea Tray Company of Newark, New Jersey. *Courtesy of Jean-Paul Agnard.* (Value code: D, horn only)

1-58. Blue flower horn manufactured by the Tea Tray Company of Newark, New Jersey with pink dogwood blossoms. 22" x 31". *Courtesy of Norm and Janyne Smith.* (Value code: D)

1-59. Gold flower horn with pink mums, 23" x 31". *Courtesy of Norm and Janyne Smith.* (Value code: D)

1-60. Hawthorne & Sheble red flower horn with original applied roses and irises. 22 1/2" x 32". *Courtesy of Norm and Janyne Smith.* (Value code: D)

1-61. Blue horn with painted morning glory effect and pink roses, 23" x 32". *Courtesy of Norm and Janyne Smith.* (Value code: D)

1-62. Flower horn painted to resemble quarter-sawn oak, with pink roses, 23" x 31 1/2".
(Value code: C)

1-63. A red flower horn decorated with yellow pansies, measuring 21 1/4" x 29 1/2". *Courtesy of Jean-Paul Agnard.* (Value code: D)

1-64. Talking machine horns were cumbersome and difficult to transport. A number of companies attempted to overcome this problem by offering collapsible or folding horns. The "Munson" horn, made by the Folding Phonographic Horn Company, Incorporated, of New York City, was one of the most heavily advertised. An advertisement in the October 1907 *Talking Machine World* stated, "Made of selected 'LEATHERETTE' with spring steel ribs, this horn insures a sweetness of tone impossible with the sheet metal product, and when closed can be carried as conveniently as an umbrella..." *Courtesy of Todd Emery.* (Value code: C)

1-65. The "Munson" horn fully folded. They were available to fit either cylinder or disc machines. This one is for a Victor. Despite the company's claim of improved tone, the acoustic properties of "leatherette" are dubious at best. Horn measures 23" in length. *Courtesy of Todd Emery.*

1-66. Lightweight horns of laminated materials (in this example wood) were constructed for both cylinder and disc talking machines. Something of a trend began in 1907 and continued throughout the life of the external-horn talking machine. This particular model was offered through the Victor Distributing and Export Company of New York City. It is shown in its custom-made pasteboard carrier. *Courtesy of Todd Emery.* (Value code: D horn and carrier)

1-67. The "Ideal Self Supporting Aluminum Horn" was introduced in August 1907. An advertisement in the *Talking Machine World* stated: "It can be instantly attached to the reproducer of any Edison or Columbia machine without the aid of crane, support or similar device for it is *absolutely self supporting.* The balancing point of the horn being directly above the axis of the mandrel causes the friction to be reduced to a minimum." Although the "Ideal" was first advertised as "all aluminum," by 1908 the company announced that, "The elbow is made of the highest grade of ebonite, which in combination with aluminum, completely eliminates that tin sound so strongly objectionable." Ebonite was a moulded resin similar to gutta-percha (derived from tree sap). The "Ideal" sold for $7.50, and disappeared after little more than a year. (Value code: B)

1-68. In October 1907, the National Phonograph Company began equipping Edison machines with black flower horns designed for each model. This Edison "Standard" Model "D" displays the "Standard" horn, which measures 19" x 31 3/4". Supporting it is the first (non-adjustable) version of the Edison horn crane. Despite their drab appearance, the Edison flower horns (made by the Standard Metal Manufacturing Company of Newark, New Jersey) quickly depressed the "optional" horn market. *Courtesy of Jean-Paul Agnard.* (Value code: E)

1-69. Edison "Gem" black paneled horn as sold with Models "B" and "C," 19" long. *Courtesy of William G. Meyer.* (Value code: D)

1-70. The Edison "Standard" flower horn was also available with a deep indigo finish and painted mums. It was, along with the red horns on certain "Gems" and "Firesides," one of a handful of exceptions to basic black in the Edison horn line. Evidence suggests that the blue "Standard" horn was supplied to mail-order firms, most likely to catch the public eye toward the end of the external-horn era. *Courtesy of Jean-Paul Agnard.* (Value code: C)

1-71. A close-up of the decal identifying a mahogany wood-grained Edison flower horn supplied with the posh Edison "Idelia" Phonograph from October 1907 to September 1909. *Courtesy of Jean-Paul Agnard.*

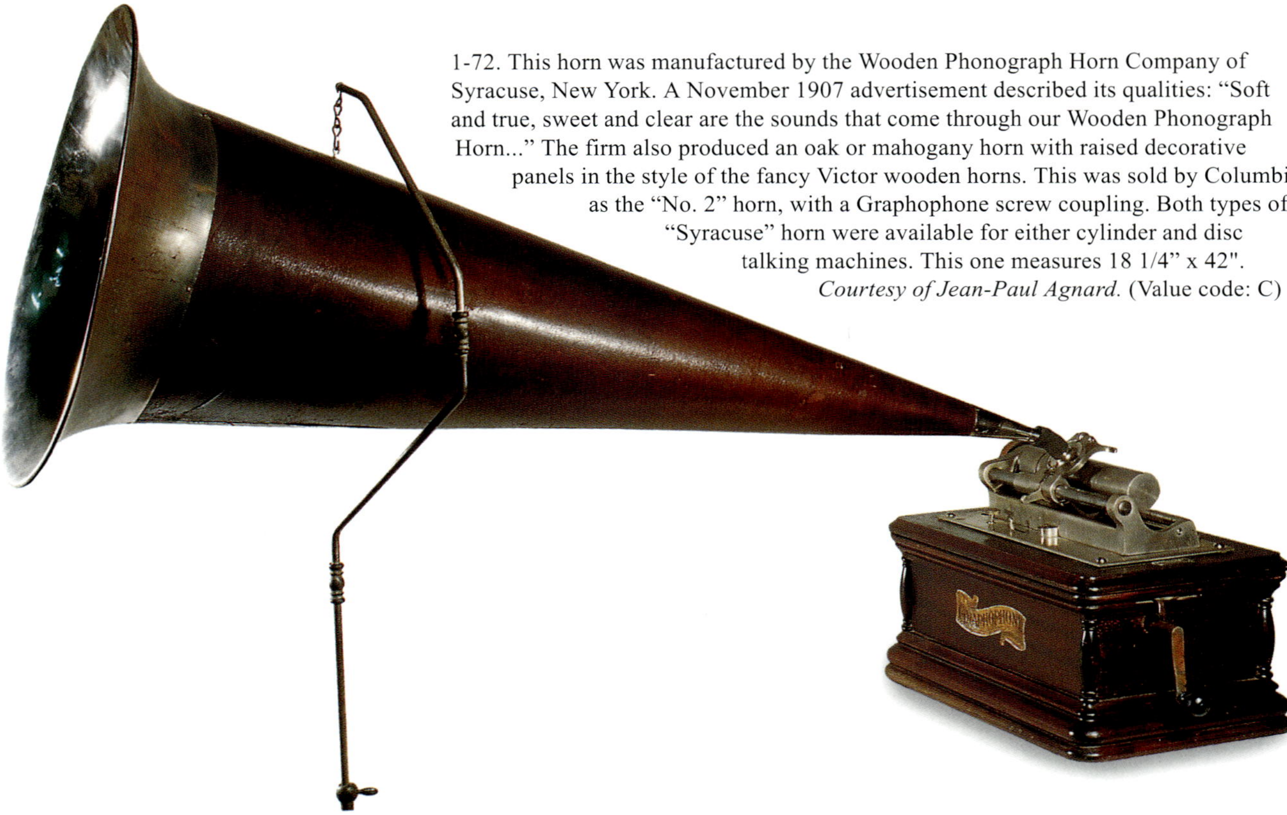

1-72. This horn was manufactured by the Wooden Phonograph Horn Company of Syracuse, New York. A November 1907 advertisement described its qualities: "Soft and true, sweet and clear are the sounds that come through our Wooden Phonograph Horn..." The firm also produced an oak or mahogany horn with raised decorative panels in the style of the fancy Victor wooden horns. This was sold by Columbia as the "No. 2" horn, with a Graphophone screw coupling. Both types of "Syracuse" horn were available for either cylinder and disc talking machines. This one measures 18 1/4" x 42". *Courtesy of Jean-Paul Agnard.* (Value code: C)

1-73. Wooden Phonograph Horn Company horns were "Made of 2-ply Veneer, highly polished in Golden Oak and Mahogany. The bell is polished brass, lacquered." Actual production models also featured nickel-plated bells, and the oak versions have mahogany-stained interiors. This example (28 3/4" x 16 3/8") has been fitted to a late Victor "MS" (1906). *Courtesy of Todd Emery.* (Value code: B)

1-74. Sheip & Vandergrift of Philadelphia introduced its solid-wood "Music Master" horns ("NOT VENEERED") in November 1908. The company sold versions to fit virtually all styles of talking machines. Available woods included oak, mahogany and spruce. Pictured is a straight horn designed for cylinder machines, 21 1/2" x 26". *Courtesy of Jean-Paul Agnard.* (Value code: A)

1-75. An extraordinary variety of horn styles was represented in this photograph. At the top, direct center, was an Edison with black cygnet horn. To the right and left were brass-belled horns on Victor talking machines. Several "flower" horns were also shown. Finally, just to the left of center, a Columbia "Disc Graphophone" sported a "No. 1" paneled wooden horn.

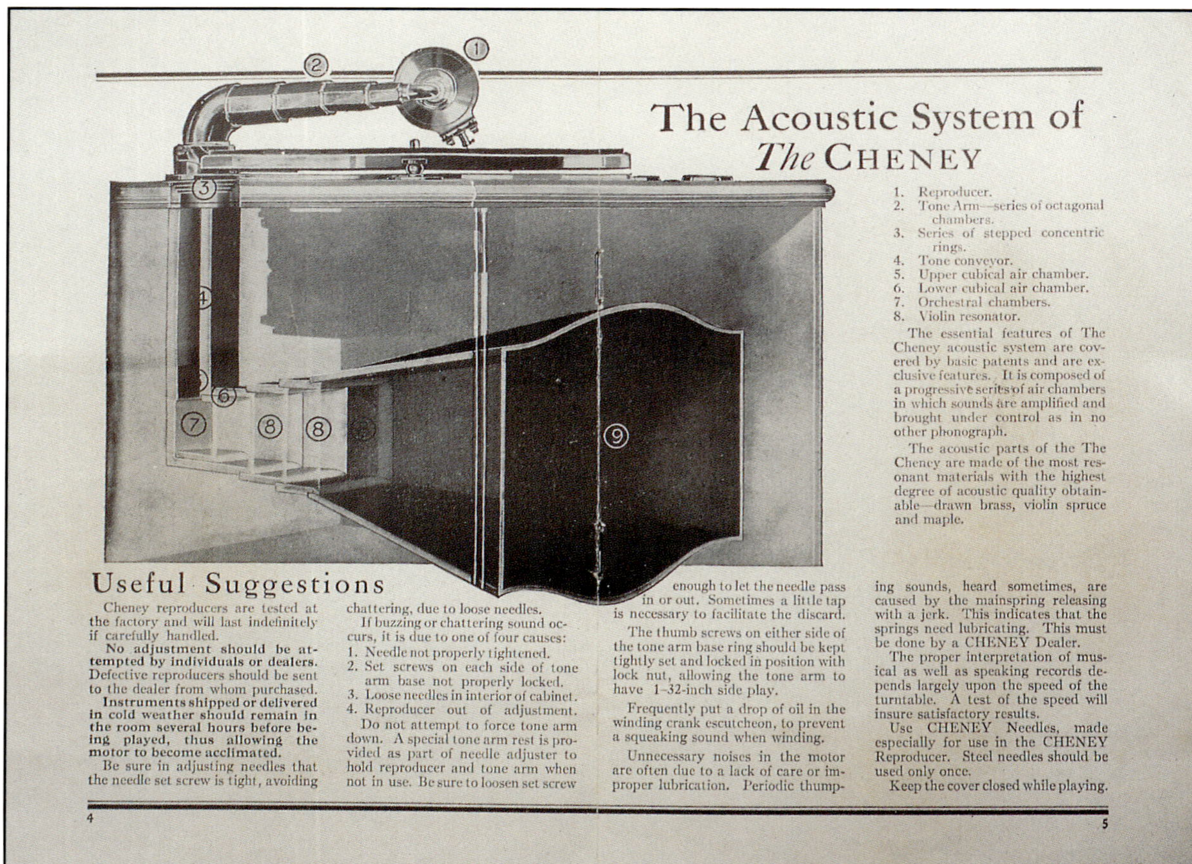

The Acoustic System of *The* CHENEY

1. Reproducer.
2. Tone Arm—series of octagonal chambers.
3. Series of stepped concentric rings.
4. Tone conveyor.
5. Upper cubical air chamber.
6. Lower cubical air chamber.
7. Orchestral chambers.
8. Violin resonator.

The essential features of The Cheney acoustic system are covered by basic patents and are exclusive features. It is composed of a progressive series of air chambers in which sounds are amplified and brought under control as in no other phonograph.

The acoustic parts of the The Cheney are made of the most resonant materials with the highest degree of acoustic quality obtainable—drawn brass, violin spruce and maple.

Useful Suggestions

Cheney reproducers are tested at the factory and will last indefinitely if carefully handled.

**No adjustment should be attempted by individuals or dealers.** Defective reproducers should be sent to the dealer from whom purchased.

**Instruments shipped or delivered in cold weather should remain in the room several hours before being played, thus allowing the motor to become acclimated.**

Be sure in adjusting needles that the needle set screw is tight, avoiding chattering, due to loose needles.

If buzzing or chattering sound occurs, it is due to one of four causes:

1. Needle not properly tightened.
2. Set screws on each side of tone arm base not properly locked.
3. Loose needles in interior of cabinet.
4. Reproducer out of adjustment.

Do not attempt to force tone arm down. A special tone arm rest is provided as part of needle adjuster to hold reproducer and tone arm when not in use. Be sure to loosen set screw enough to let the needle pass in or out. Sometimes a little tap is necessary to facilitate the discard.

The thumb screws on either side of the tone arm base ring should be kept tightly set and locked in position with lock nut, allowing the tone arm to have 1-32-inch side play.

Frequently put a drop of oil in the winding crank escutcheon, to prevent a squeaking sound when winding.

Unnecessary noises in the motor are often due to a lack of care or improper lubrication. Periodic thumping sounds, heard sometimes, are caused by the mainspring releasing with a jerk. This indicates that the springs need lubricating. This must be done by a CHENEY Dealer.

The proper interpretation of musical as well as speaking records depends largely upon the speed of the turntable. A test of the speed will insure satisfactory results.

Use CHENEY Needles, made especially for use in the CHENEY Reproducer. Steel needles should be used only once.

Keep the cover closed while playing.

4 5

1-76. We speak of the evolution from "external" horn to "internal" horn, but it is difficult to visualize this change once the "old fashioned" external-horns disappeared inside the cabinets of talking machines. It seemed as if the acoustic horn lost its identity as a separate unit, becoming a "compartment" of the cabinet itself. However, most cabinet-model talking machines retained a definable horn structure to varying degrees (with Edison's "Diamond Disc" and "Amberola" machines employing virtually unchanged external-horns, inverted and enclosed beneath the mechanism rather than exposed above it). In this 1923 Cheney Talking Machine Company catalogue, the sovereignty of the horn has remained, though hidden. In fact, the advertising copy celebrated the horn by dividing it into an impossible list of constituent parts, from "orchestral chambers" to "violin resonator," and re-naming it an "air chamber."

Chapter Two:

# Cylinder Talking Machine Gadgets

Gadgets for cylinder talking machines were less numerous and were found in somewhat less variety than those of their disc-playing brethren. There were two primary reasons for this. First, the cylinder talking machine in its earliest years was such a novelty that few attachments or improvements were yet envisioned for it. Second, once cylinder machine evolution had stabilized, disc talking machines rapidly assumed dominance, thus limiting the window of opportunity for manufacturers of cylinder gadgets.

Nevertheless, many companies (usually small and/or short-lived) manufactured and marketed various attachments for cylinder talking machines, including automatic stops, repeaters, record brushes, "tone regulators," horn cranes or supports, and at least one phonographic alarm clock. As the cylinder talking machine began to lose ground to the disc around 1908, a few attachments were offered which enabled a tone arm and horn to be mounted to the back of a cylinder machine in a manner similar to that so successfully adopted by disc machines. In addition, at least one gadget, the Devineau "Biophone" of 1907–08, converted a cylinder talking machine to a disc-playing apparatus. Such a design was indicative of the times: by 1910, cylinder attachments and gadgets had virtually disappeared from the pages of trade publications such as the *Talking Machine World* and the *Music Trades*.

From the earliest Bettini attachments of the1890s to the "disc look-alike" conversions of the cylinder talking machine's waning days, the manufacture of gadgets for cylinder apparatus represented a brief, colorful chapter in talking machine history.

2-1. Edison reproducers and recorders from the dawn of the wax cylinder era. The upper set in lacquered brass dates from 1888 and employs steel chisel points. The brass recorder (left) uses a glass diaphragm. The brass reproducer (right) has a shellacked silk diaphragm. Below, the nickel-plated pair dating from 1889 use glass diaphragms. The stylus of the nickeled reproducer (left) is steel, but now in the form of a ball. The stylus of the nickeled recorder (right) retains a more chisel-like shape for cutting the groove. *Courtesy of Ray Phillips.* (VR)

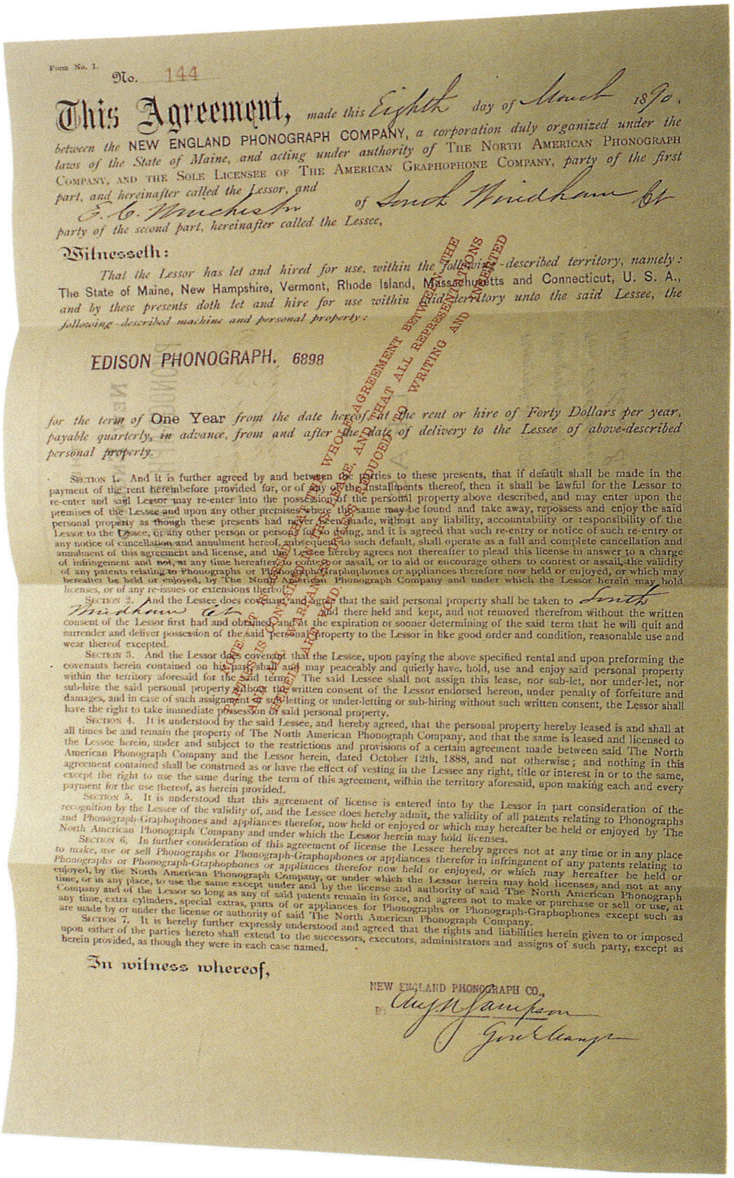

Form No. 1. No. 144

**This Agreement,** made this Eighth day of March 1890, between the NEW ENGLAND PHONOGRAPH COMPANY, a corporation duly organized under the laws of the State of Maine, and acting under authority of THE NORTH AMERICAN PHONOGRAPH COMPANY, AND THE SOLE LICENSEE OF THE AMERICAN GRAPHOPHONE COMPANY, party of the first part, and hereinafter called the Lessor, and E. C. Winchester of South Windham Ct party of the second part, hereinafter called the Lessee,

**Witnesseth:**

That the Lessor has let and hired for use, within the following-described territory, namely: The State of Maine, New Hampshire, Vermont, Rhode Island, Massachusetts and Connecticut, U. S. A., and by these presents doth let and hire for use within said territory unto the said Lessee, the following-described machine and personal property:

EDISON PHONOGRAPH. 6898

for the term of One Year from the date hereof, at the rent or hire of Forty Dollars per year, payable quarterly, in advance, from and after the date of delivery to the Lessee of above-described personal property.

SECTION 1. And it is further agreed by and between the parties to these presents, that if default shall be made in the payment of the rent hereinbefore provided for, or of any of the installments thereof, then it shall be lawful for the Lessor to re-enter and said Lessor may re-enter into the possession of the personal property above described, and may enter upon the premises of the Lessee and upon any other premises where the same may be found and take away, repossess and enjoy the said personal property as though these presents had never been made, without any liability, accountability or responsibility of the Lessor to the Lessee, or any other person or persons for so doing, and it is agreed that such re-entry or notice of such re-entry or any notice of cancellation and annulment hereof, subsequent to such default, shall operate as a full and complete cancellation and annulment of this agreement and license, and the Lessee hereby agrees not thereafter to plead this license in answer to a charge of infringement and not, at any time hereafter, to contest or assail, or to aid or encourage others to contest or assail, the validity of any patents relating to Phonographs or Phonograph-Graphophones or appliances therefore now held or enjoyed, or which may hereafter be held or enjoyed, by The North American Phonograph Company and under which the Lessor herein may hold licenses, or of any re-issues or extensions thereof.

SECTION 2. And the Lessee does covenant and agree that the said personal property shall be taken to South Windham Ct and there held and kept, and not removed therefrom without the written consent of the Lessor first had and obtained, and at the expiration or sooner determining of the said term that he will quit and surrender and deliver possession of the said personal property to the Lessor in like good order and condition, reasonable use and wear thereof excepted.

SECTION 3. And the Lessor does covenant that the Lessee, upon paying the above specified rental and upon preforming the covenants herein contained on his part, shall and may peaceably and quietly have, hold, use and enjoy said personal property within the territory aforesaid for the said term. The said Lessee shall not assign this lease, nor sub-let, nor under-let, nor sub-hire the said personal property without the written consent of the Lessor endorsed hereon, under penalty of forfeiture and damages, and in case of such assignment or sub-letting or under-letting or sub-hiring without such written consent, the Lessor shall have the right to take immediate possession of said personal property.

SECTION 4. It is understood by the said Lessee, and hereby agreed, that the personal property hereby leased is and shall at all times be and remain the property of The North American Phonograph Company, and that the same is leased and licensed to the Lessee herein, under and subject to the restrictions and provisions of a certain agreement made between said The North American Phonograph Company and the Lessor herein, dated October 12th, 1888, and not otherwise; and nothing in this agreement contained shall be construed as or have the effect of vesting in the Lessee any right, title or interest in or to the same, except the right to use the same during the term of this agreement, within the territory aforesaid, upon making each and every payment for the use thereof, as herein provided.

SECTION 5. It is understood that this agreement of license is entered into by the Lessor in part consideration of the recognition by the Lessee of the validity of, and the Lessee does hereby admit, the validity of all patents relating to Phonographs and Phonograph-Graphophones and appliances therefor, now held or enjoyed or which may hereafter be held or enjoyed by The North American Phonograph Company and under which the Lessor herein may hold licenses.

SECTION 6. In further consideration of this agreement of license the Lessee hereby agrees not at any time or in any place to make, use or sell Phonographs or Phonograph-Graphophones or appliances therefor in infringment of any patents relating to Phonographs or Phonograph-Graphophones or appliances therefor now held or enjoyed, or which may hereafter be held or enjoyed, by the North American Phonograph Company, or under which the Lessor herein may hold licenses, and not at any time, or in any place, to use the same except under and by the license and authority of said The North American Phonograph Company and of the Lessor so long as any of said patents remain in force, and agrees not to make or purchase or sell or use, at any time, extra cylinders, special extras, parts of or appliances for Phonographs or Phonograph-Graphophones except such as are made by or under the license or authority of said The North American Phonograph Company.

SECTION 7. It is hereby further expressly understood and agreed that the rights and liabilities herein given to or imposed upon either of the parties hereto shall extend to the successors, executors, administrators and assigns of such party, except as herein provided, as though they were in each case named.

**In witness whereof,**

NEW ENGLAND PHONOGRAPH CO.,
By Aug. N. Sampson
Gen'l Manager

2-2. The first Phonographs and Graphophones distributed under the umbrella of the North American Phonograph Company in the late 1880s and early '90s were leased rather than sold. This contract between a client and the New England franchisee of the North American Phonograph Company, dated March 8, 1890, pertains to the lease of an Edison Class "M" electric Phonograph. *Courtesy of Martin F. Bryan.* (VR)

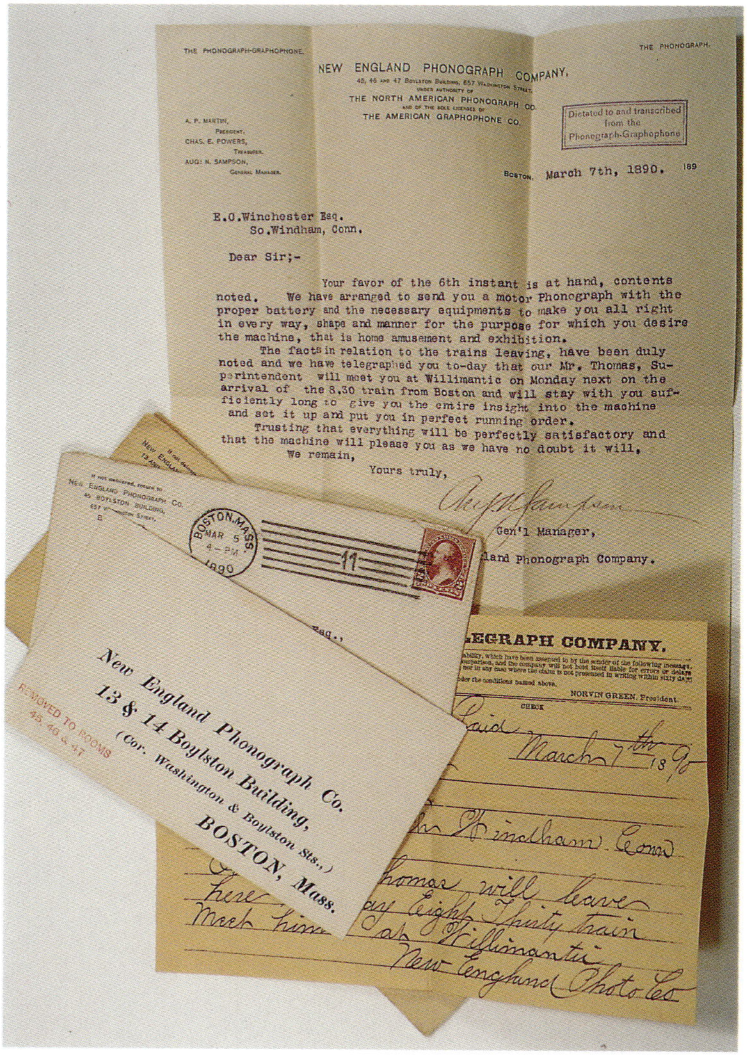

THE PHONOGRAPH-GRAPHOPHONE. THE PHONOGRAPH.

NEW ENGLAND PHONOGRAPH COMPANY,
45, 46 and 47 Boylston Building, 657 Washington Street,
under authority of
THE NORTH AMERICAN PHONOGRAPH CO.
and of the sole licensee of
THE AMERICAN GRAPHOPHONE CO.

A. P. MARTIN, President.
CHAS. E. POWERS, Treasurer.
AUG: N. SAMPSON, General Manager.

Dictated to and transcribed from the Phonograph-Graphophone

Boston, March 7th, 1890.

E.C.Winchester Esq.
So.Windham, Conn.

Dear Sir;-

Your favor of the 6th instant is at hand, contents noted. We have arranged to send you a motor Phonograph with the proper battery and the necessary equipments to make you all right in every way, shape and manner for the purpose for which you desire the machine, that is home amusement and exhibition.

The facts in relation to the trains leaving, have been duly noted and we have telegraphed you to-day that our Mr. Thomas, Superintendent will meet you at Willimantic on Monday next on the arrival of the 8.30 train from Boston and will stay with you sufficiently long to give you the entire insight into the machine and set it up and put you in perfect running order.

Trusting that everything will be perfectly satisfactory and that the machine will please you as we have no doubt it will,

We remain,

Yours truly,
Aug. N. Sampson
Gen'l Manager,
...land Phonograph Company.



2-3. Further documents accompanying the lease of the Edison Phonograph. *Courtesy of Martin F. Bryan.* (VR)

2-4. The earliest Graphophones to play in the Edison cylinder format used reproducers and recorders fashioned from gutta-percha, a kind of hardened tree sap. Pictured are a recorder (left) and a reproducer (right) in their original box. From August 1897, Columbia reproducers were made of aluminum. *Courtesy of Todd Emery.* (Value code: C, each)

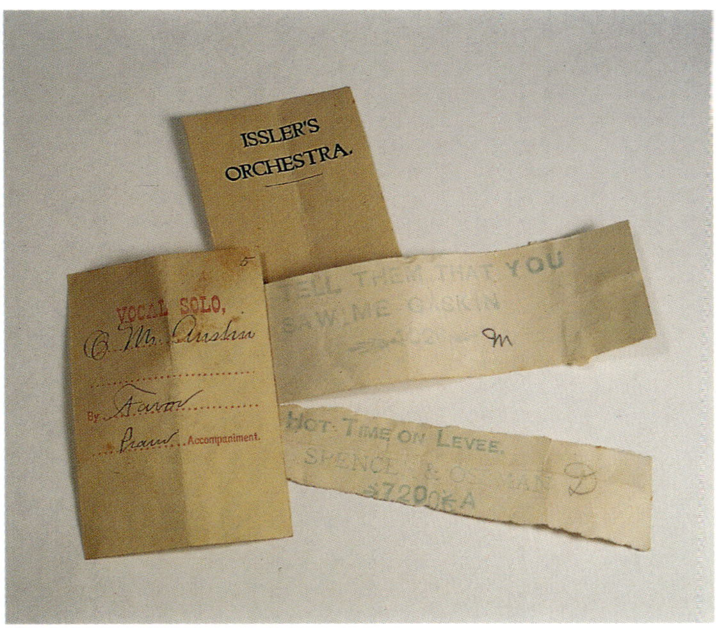


2-5. Unlike disc records, which were by design able to include title and artist information, early cylinders had to rely on separate documentation. These title slips from the 1890s show how varied this documentation could be. On the left, a slip which includes a space for indicating type of accompaniment. The irregular strips at the right were rubber-stamped and represent the title slip in its simplest form. Frequently-recorded groups like Issler's Orchestra rated their own printed headings. Issler's Orchestra, incidentally, recorded for Edison as early as 1889 and continued throughout the 1890s. (Value code: H, each)

2-6. Brown wax cylinders were usually not marked with any company or title information. Only in France did Pathé employ workers to hand-scratch titles into the rims. However, this unusual brown wax cylinder has the company name pressed into the rim. The selection is "Comic Song entitled 'I Wonder Why' presented by Russell Hunting." *Courtesy of Norm and Janyne Smith.* (VR)

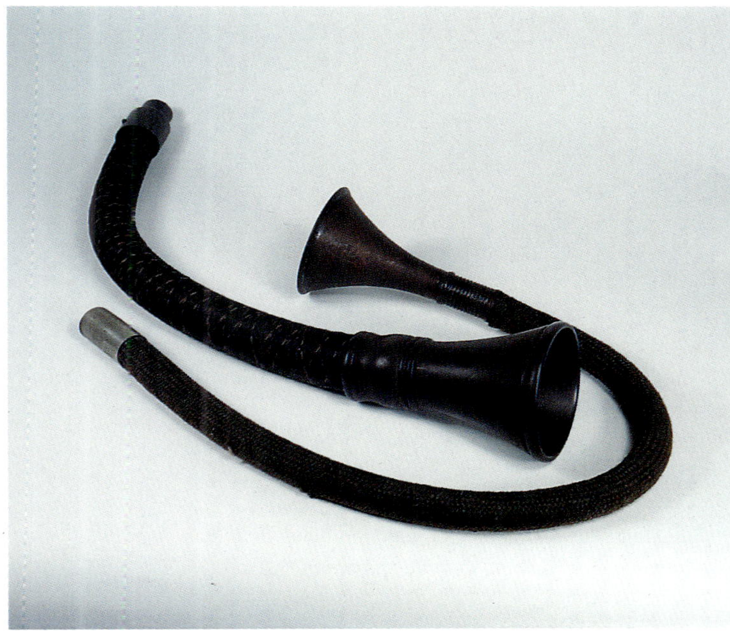

2-7. Speaking tubes were available for recording the voice from the earliest days of the wax cylinder talking machine. The tube of wider diameter is one most commonly associated with the Edison Phonograph. The thinner tube was specific to Columbia Graphophones, circa 1897, with a copper-plated metal mouthpiece. (Value code: D, each)

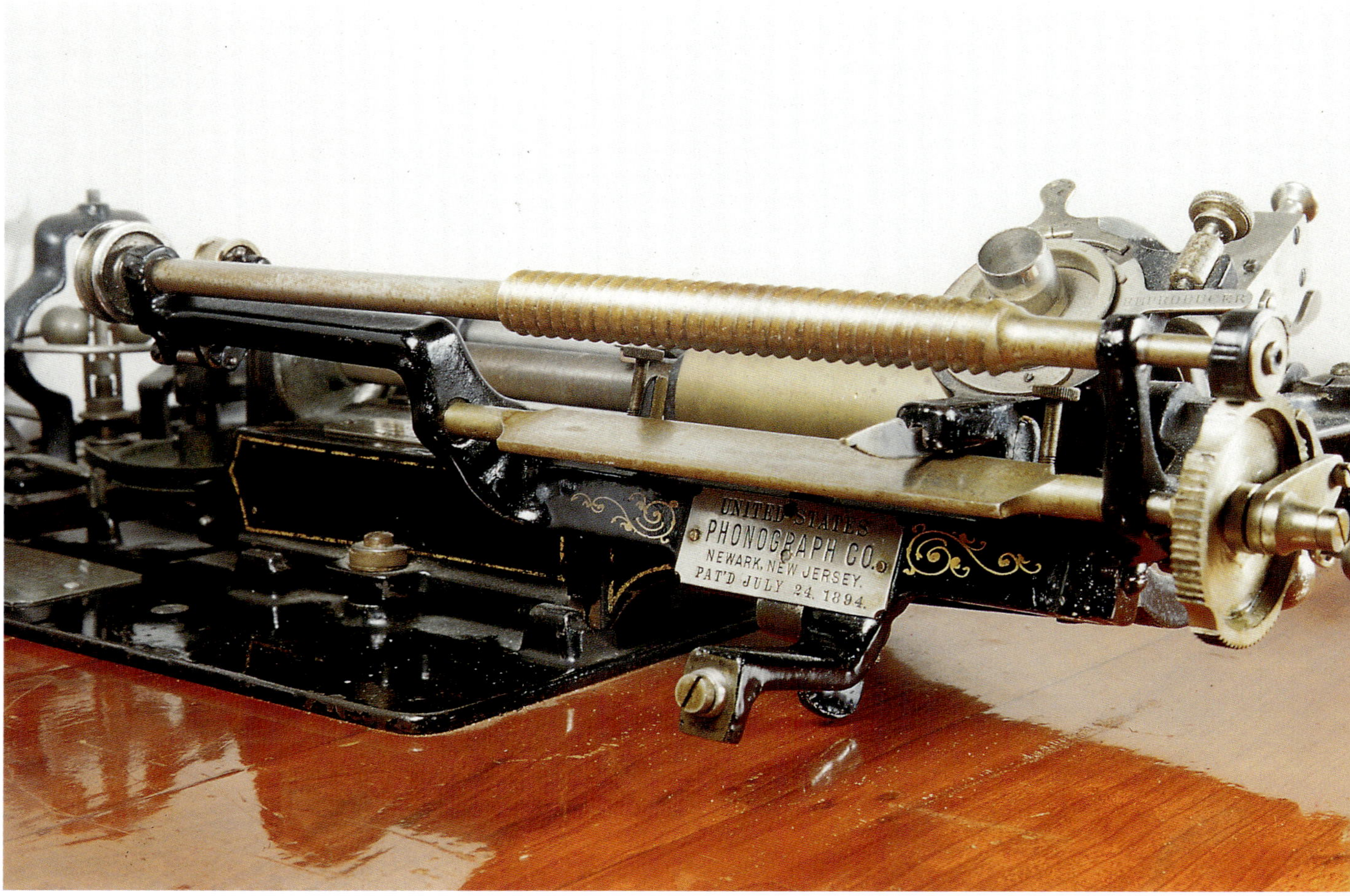
UNITED STATES
PHONOGRAPH CO.
NEWARK, NEW JERSEY.
PAT'D JULY 24, 1894.

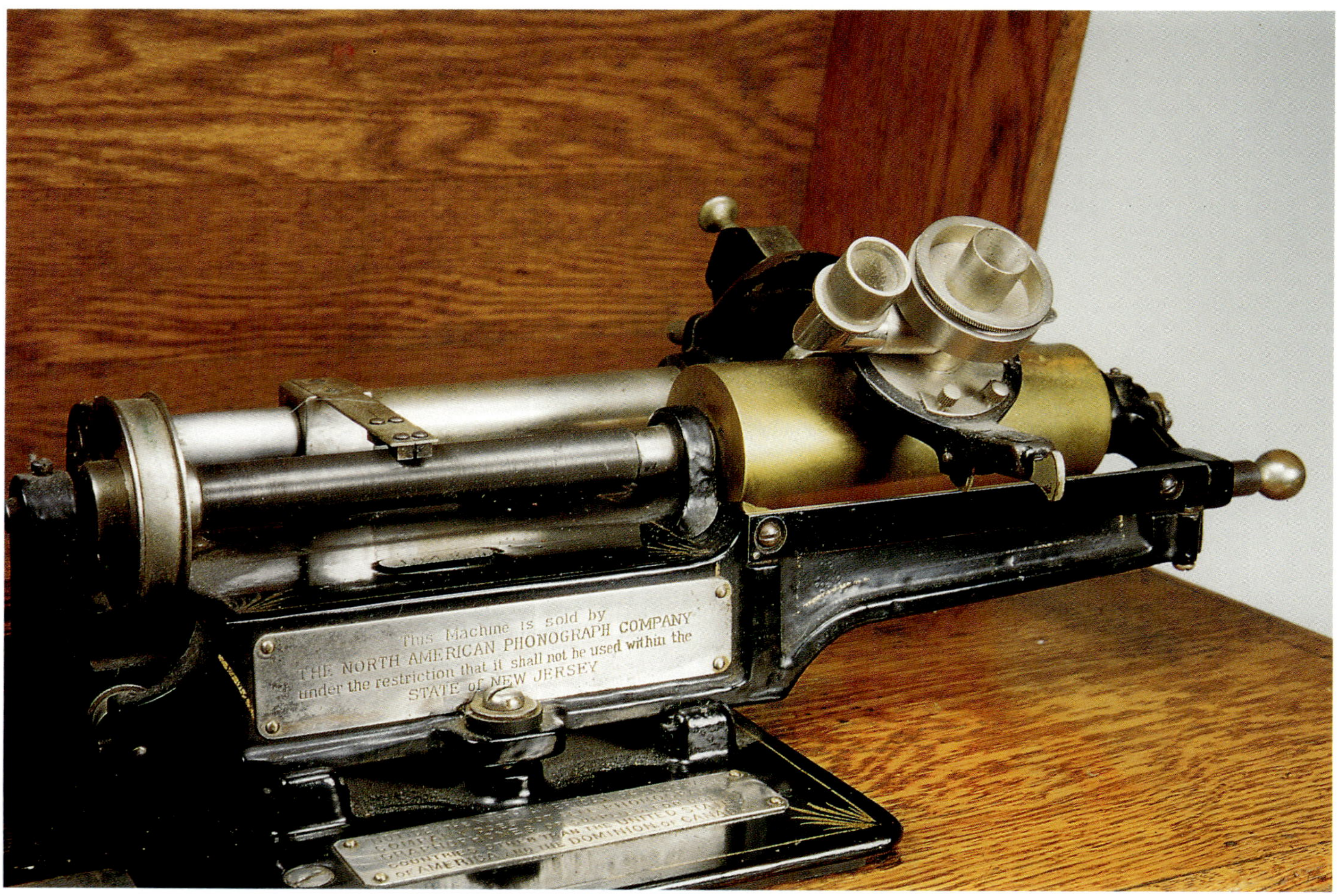
This Machine is sold by
THE NORTH AMERICAN PHONOGRAPH COMPANY
under the restriction that it shall not be used within the
STATE of NEW JERSEY

## Gianni Bettini: Crown Prince of Cylinder Gadgets

The March 3, 1892 issue of *Frank Leslie's Weekly* carried an article describing the new recording and reproducing apparatus of Lt. Gianni Bettini, formerly of the Italian cavalry. By use of these, the inventor claimed, he could create cylinder records which reproduced the human voice and music with remarkable loudness and clarity. Referring to how Bettini's reproducing diaphragm differed from a conventional Phonograph or Graphophone "speaker," the following passage was quoted:

> Instead of attaching the needle-point directly and firmly to the centre of the diaphragm, as heretofore done, M. Bettini uses what he calls a 'spider,' which is a little frame having several radial legs, the feet of which bear against the diaphragm at a number of points surrounding the centre, and at different distances from it.
>
> The object of this *spider,* with its radial bearings, is to carry out the inventor's discovery that this tensioned diaphragm does not vibrate as a whole... that it vibrates in numerous small divisions or *sectors* which may happen to be in... sympathy with the vibrating organs of the voice or of other tones directed against the diaphragm. Thus... some small sector might prove to be in exact sympathy... and would thus cause the needle, through one of the spider-legs, to respond, and in this way not only would the whole diaphragm be utilized, making the reproduced tone many times louder than by a single point of central contact, but would secure much greater variety of the *timbre...* than could occur with a single point of contact...

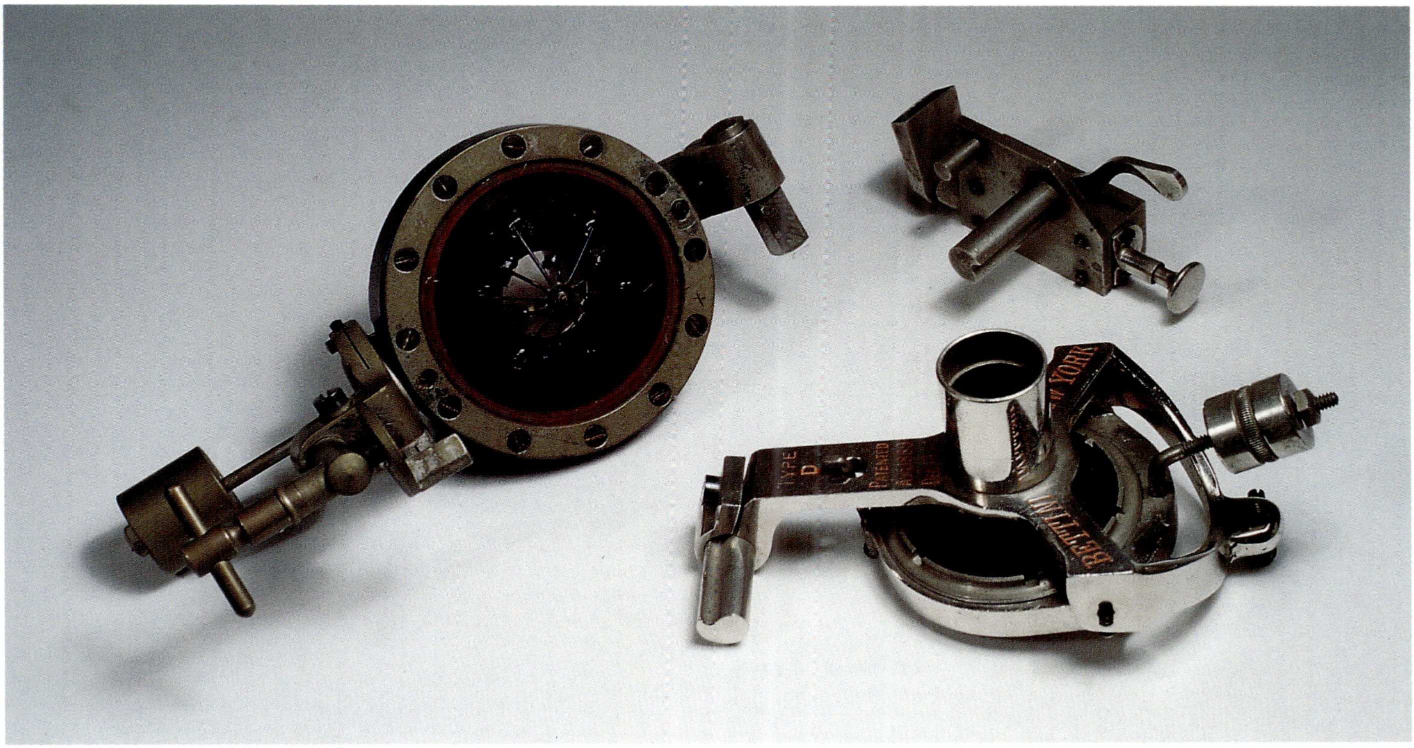


Opposite page:
Top: 2-8. The repeating attachment shown on this Edison Class "M" electric Phonograph was patented by George Tewksbury in 1894 (No.523,556). It was first used in coin-operated machines supplied by the Kansas Phonograph Company, with which Tewksbury was associated. However, in 1895 the inventor became involved with the United States Phonograph Company of Newark, New Jersey (see plate), which bought the repeater patent and began manufacturing it. *Courtesy of the Charles Hummel collections.* (VR)

Bottom: 2-9. In 1896, Edison offered the "Duplex Speaker," which was designed to capture the sound vibrations from both sides of a diaphragm. The added cost ($7.50 versus $5.00 for an ordinary reproducer), the bother of two horns and the questionable improvement in reproduction doomed the "Duplex" to a short life. *Courtesy of the Charles Hummel collections.* (VR)

2-10. Gianni Bettini marketed his "Micro-Attachments" in the United States to fit Phonographs and Graphophones throughout the last half of the 1890s and for a few years thereafter. The items shown here were meant to adapt Edison Phonographs. Clockwise from left, the early style reproducer with mica diaphragm. Next, an attachment for shaving blanks. Finally, a recorder with a reduced-diameter tube plate to concentrate the sound on the recording diaphragm. *Courtesy of John Woodward.* (Value code: A,C,A)

Gianni Bettini called his device the "Micro-Phonograph" attachment. By the time of the *Frank Leslie's* article, he had immigrated to the United States and married a young American socialite, Daisy Abbott. Bettini set up shop in the Judge Building, New York City, and began to invite denizens of the *beau monde*, as well as prominent stars of Grand Opera and the stage to visit. Using his well-publicized recording "Laboratory" to enhance his social standing, Bettini happened to capture two-minute wax cylinders of enduring historical interest. Initially, the activities of his workshop were for his own amusement and edification, as he advanced a personal archive of great performances including Nellie Melba, Yvette Guilbert, Tomaso Salvini, Frances Saville, Sigrid Arnoldsen, Emilio de Gogorza, former President Benjamin Harrison and Mark Twain. Bettini began to sell a relatively small number of copies drawn from his most historically important records, a market that never grew very large despite his increasing efforts at self-promotion.

"Sarah's robe was a most gorgeous lavender, shading on a heliotrope," gushed *Frank Leslie's* in describing a visit to the Bettini lab by French actress Sarah Bernhardt. The article continued:

> Going up in the elevator like any ordinary every-day mortal, the greatest actress on earth entered Lieutenant Bettini's room and quietly seated herself before the phonograph, which had been warranted to repeat all the tones of her wonderful voice.
>
> 'Recite something,' invited the lieutenant... When she had finished, the lieutenant set the machine going, and every shade of Sarah's voice was given perfectly...
>
> When in New York Bernhardt received ever-so-many invitations to visit various social gatherings and receptions... but Lieutenant Bettini is the only person who has had the honor of receiving the great Bernhardt in his own private sanctum.

Bettini's social aspirations and fame as an inventor both were thus given a boost—and what fabulous publicity it was. He would circulate the image of "the great Bernhardt" seated before his phonographic equipment for many years to come. By amassing an aural library of world-famous performers under the pretense of promulgating high art for art's sake, he managed to forego the fees for such services which might have pauperized him. Among members of the social hierarchy, it would have been as unseemly to ask for payment as for Mr. Bettini to suggest it.

## Record Duplicating

In 1892, another Bettini invention was patented (No.488,381) which would serve to expand his aims beyond tinkering for the rich and renowned. He had patented a *pantographic* or mechanical (as opposed to *aural* or "dubbed") method of duplicating cylinders at a time when the replication of records was an important issue. Throughout the 1890s, cylinder records were primarily produced by frequently repeated performances before banks of individual recording machines.

Emile Berliner had created a breakthrough with the easily duplicated 5" disc records which accompanied his toy Gramophones then being sold in Europe and Britain. However, this "novelty" trade was small and hardly noticed in the cylinder talking machine business. Bettini had been inspired to seek the best way to copy his archive of renowned recordings. Needless to say, one couldn't ask artists of world caliber to trot out the muse whenever the stock of cylinders ran low, especially if one wasn't paying them. Yet, as Bettini expanded his catalogue of more "ordinary" vocal and musical selections, like those the less pretentious record companies sold in abundance, his pantographic copying method was no less important.

Although it was born of his own specific requirements, Bettini's duplicating method (involving a reproducing stylus playing a "master" linked mechanically to a cutting stylus recording a duplicate) eventually would come to benefit the greater industry. He developed it further (patent No.668,154, filed July 27, 1897, granted February 19, 1901) and rights to the 1892 patent eventually came into use by Edison, who used pantographic duplicating until he finally released moulded cylinders early in 1902.

Edison and other cylinder record companies used some form of pantographic equipment all through the 1890s, sparking a lively debate about "direct" or "master" performances versus "copies." This was largely a paper tempest, with certain record companies claiming they "sold no copies." "Master record" became a cliché promoted in the advertising of firms such as Reed, Dawson and Company. Whatever their promises, it is likely that all cylinder record firms, big or small, succumbed to the physical and financial exigencies of dubbing or duplicating.

## Bettini, the Engineer

To describe Gianni Bettini as an inveterate tinkerer (he had patented a sheet music page turner in 1888) would not be doing him complete justice. He had a head for engineering as keen as his flair for self-promotion. In 1888, he had obtained or carefully copied an Edison Class "M" electric Phonograph and immediately begun a series of experiments with sound recording and reproduction which very quickly resulted in three U.S. patents (Nos. 409,003; 409,004; and 409,005; all 1889). Upon these he would base his "Micro-Phonograph" and "Micro-Graphophone" attachments.

Around 1896, Bettini decided to offer his attachments and special lightweight horns to the general public along with a catalogue of cylinder records which included copies of the priceless performances in his collection, as well as more pedestrian selections. The April 4, 1896 issue of the *Illustrated American* noted:

Just at present Lieutenant Bettini's phonograph is a somewhat expensive luxury, but if the adapter succeeds in his ambition of bringing it within the reach of even the moderately well-to-do, there is no limit to the possibilities of its future.

Like the other manufacturers of "optional" gadgets for talking machines, Bettini's object was to improve upon "standard equipment." By removing the Edison reproducer carriage or the Graphophone reproducer, the "Micro" diaphragm, with its nine-legged "spider" held in a special frame, could be appended to existing talking machines.

2-11. A Bettini "Micro-Attachment" used with an Edison "Concert" Phonograph. The wide diameter diaphragm, the patented "spider" which held the stylus, and the large orifice which accepted the special Bettini horn, produced the best quality sound of its day. *Courtesy of John Woodward.* (Value code: A)

2-12. An American Bettini 5" cylinder box. As in the case of other small firms, Bettini simply applied his own label to a conventional Columbia box. (VR)

Later, following his departure for France just after the turn-of-the-century, Bettini would offer a line of purposely designed instruments already fitted with his special reproducing head. Even this, however, was not the unifying triumph of design it should have been. For practical reasons, the lesser models were allowed to accept the "conventional" Graphophone-type floating reproducers which Bettini had worked so hard to supercede. As his European products evolved, Bettini's flamboyant signature was emblazoned ostentatiously across increasingly derivative mechanisms, until undisguised copies of the Columbia "Eagle" began to appear with nothing of special merit to commend them other than the famous autograph.

## Electrical Recording?

Gianni Bettini's eclectic imagination brought him to the edges of a number of innovations, and occasionally beyond. One area of tantalizing speculation has been created by Bettini's U.S. patent No.688,921, December 17, 1901, "Apparatus for Duplicating or Multiplying Sound-Records." It was familiar Bettini territory, but this particular method addressed copying by *electrical* impulses transmitted from a reproducing point playing a "master" record to incising points cutting several "dupes." Bettini specified that the head which reproduced the master should be a "microphone-transmitter [such as Emile Berliner had invented] ...provided with a stylus designed to follow the sound-record line of said master-cylinder." Each dupe was cut by a solenoid, "upon whose core is carried the cutting point or stylus." Low voltage from batteries would make the system operational.

Modern interpreters may extrapolate that what Bettini actually designed was a system of electrical recording, some 25 years (he filed in 1897) before it became commercially feasible. A careful reading of his patent, however, reveals that Bettini's equipment was not powerful enough nor was it intended to deeply incise a *master* record from a direct performance. Its purpose was to use an *acoustically-recorded* cylinder as the master. The Bettini system could concentrate sufficient electronic information to create acceptable dupes, not original recordings.

It would be the great achievement of the electrical recording pioneers of the early to mid-1920s to capture a live performance with sufficient intensity and fidelity to produce a great forward leap in the progress of recorded sound. Gianni Bettini, however, had been decidedly attached to acoustic recording, despite his varied and indeed visionary approach to cylinder duplication.

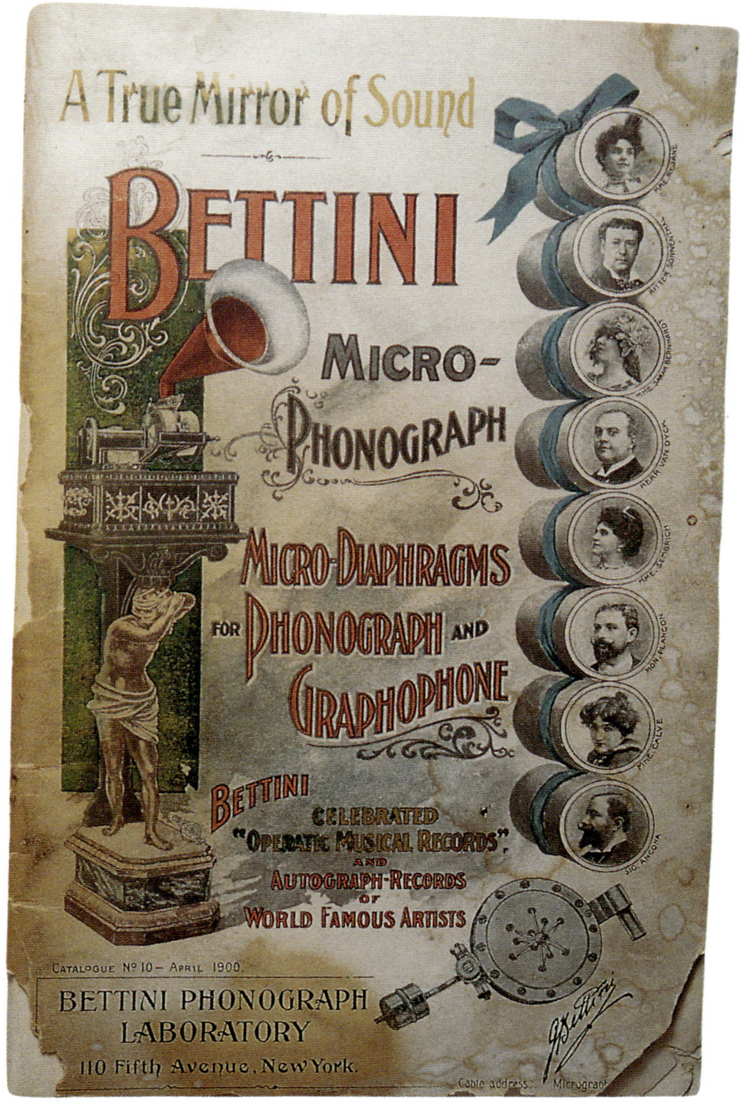


2-14. The cover of Bettini's April 1900 catalogue emphasized the luminaries whose voices he had captured. It is interesting to note that Bettini would close his American operations by the end of the year, before returning to Europe. *Courtesy of John Woodward.* (VR)

2-13. Adapability is an important factor in sales and marketing. Here, an adapter is shown which was offered by Gianni Bettini to allow conventional cylinder talking machine horns to be used with his "Micro-Attachment." Unfortunately for the purchaser, this would negate one of Bettini's most important innovations: the large horn aperture. The attachment shown was designed for Graphophones, and is clearly less complicated than those required by Edison Phonographs. (Value code: E, adapter only)

## The "Polyphone"

Another early gadget for cylinder talking machines was the "Polyphone Attachment" patented by Leon Douglass, and marketed by the Talking Machine Company of Chicago. The first known mention of the "Polyphone" appeared in the September 1898 issue of the *Phonoscope.* By the following month, Editor Russell Hunting had seen the "Polyphone" and had this to say:

> The Polyphone is perhaps the newest of devices for the practical improvement [sic], yet the Polyphone is exceedingly simple in its mechanism. It has two vibrating diaphragms or speakers. As each speaker is complete in itself and as the reproducing sapphire of each speaker travels in the same groove, on the cylinder, reproducing the same matter simultaneously, it is necessarily and as a matter of fact a double reproduction which, mechanically considered, must be twice as loud as a single one...

Notwithstanding Mr. Hunting's misunderstanding of acoustics, the pages of the *Phonoscope* fairly rang with praise for the "Polyphone." The earliest full-page ads showed attachments only for the Graphophone. In the January 1899 issue of the *Phonoscope*, it was stated that:

> The Polyphone has been perfected. The only criticism on the Polyphone has been that it was difficult to adjust the two diaphragms to always work properly together. This has now been perfected so that it is the simplest talking machine made. To say that it will work better than the ordinary automatic diaphragm is a large claim, but this is what is guaranteed... This improvement will be put on all Polyphones already sold without charge. No one has ever doubted the wonderful improvement found in the Polyphone and very few have said that it was difficult to adjust. This trouble is entirely obliterated.

The March 1899 issue of the *Phonoscope* illustrated the Edison "Gem Polyphone" and an Edison "Concert" equipped with the device, called the "Polyphone Grand," retailing at a whopping $140.00. Advertisements and editorials continued to extol the many benefits of the "Polyphone." The August 1899 issue of *Phonoscope* stated that the "sales of Polyphones and Polyphone attachments have doubled within the past month. The Polyphone attachment has been improved to such an extent that when it is adjusted it will stay in adjustment continually. Messrs. Hawthorne & Sheble have secured the Eastern United States agency for the Polyphone and Polyphone attachment. They are just issuing a new catalogue of this device and we would advise all dealers to write them for a copy." At this point, however, all mention of the "Polyphone" in the pages of the *Phonoscope* abruptly stopped.

Despite the above editorials which downplayed the skittish nature of the device, the "Polyphone" was a delicate contrivance. At least three versions of the attachment exist for Graphophones, in addition to two versions for Phonographs. This bespeaks the intense effort of the manufacturer to make the "Polyphone" a trouble-free device with broad application. Yet, after approximately 12 months, the "Polyphone" had begun to disappear from the talking machine marketplace.

2-17. Bereft of its other trappings, this "Polyphone" arm itself was surprisingly modest. This one was intended for an Edison "Standard" Phonograph. *Courtesy of the Charles Hummel collections.* (Value code: A)

Opposite page:
Bottom right: 2-15. By 1900, Gianni Bettini had added a variety of other talking machine items to his original repertoire of tony specialty recordings. On the left, catalogue No.50 of Bettini "Grand" or 5" diameter cylinders, May 1900, continued to list selections by famous artists, but also included "Concert" cylinders from the regular Edison catalogue. On the right, a January 1900 sheet included a roster of the following: Bettini Micro-Attachments and records, Edison Phonographs, Columbia Graphophones, Edison and Columbia cylinders and blanks. (VR)

2-16. In 1898, the Talking Machine Company of Chicago introduced a device known as the "Polyphone" to adapt Graphophones and, later, Phonographs. The existing reproducer carriage was replaced or modified by one housing two carefully linked reproducers. The two styli played the record groove in quick succession, thereby creating nearly simultaneous reproduction. To quote an 1899 catalogue, "WE GUARANTEE the Polyphone more than twice as loud and many times more musical than any other Talking Machine..." A "Polyphone Concert Grand" complete with horns and stand, as shown here, sold for $140. (later reduced to $130.). (Value code: A)

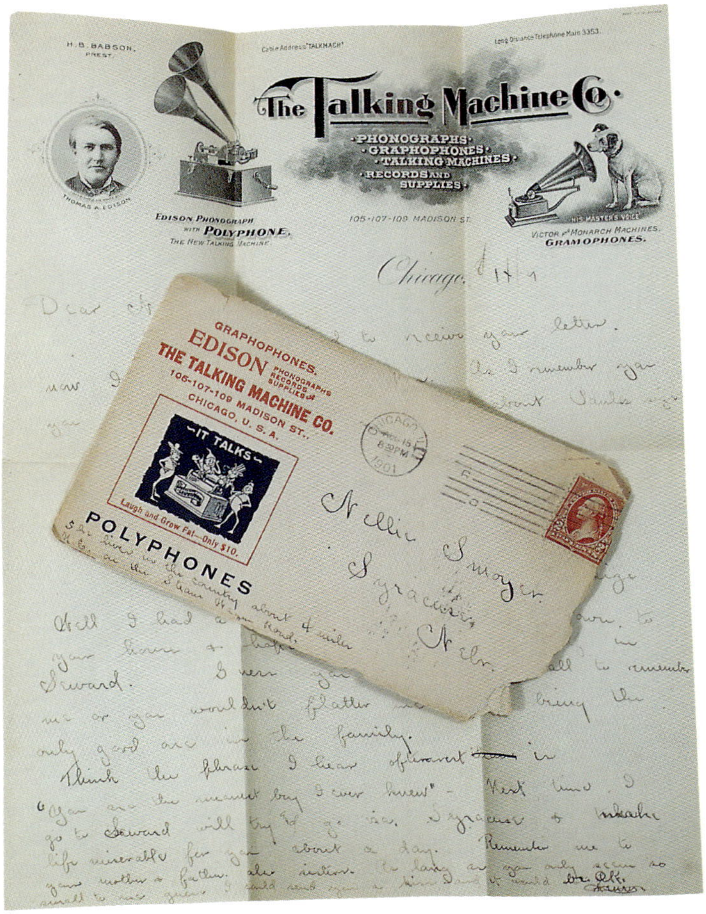


2-18. A letterhead from the Talking Machine Company of Chicago showing an Edison "Home" sporting the 14" long flared-bell horns frequently used with "Polyphone" attachments. The envelope featured Palmer Cox's "Brownie" characters, which were all the rage in the late 1890s. (Value code: G)

2-20. Eccentric adaptations of existing cylinder phonographs for exhibition use were many and varied. Here, a clever businessman has modified an Edison "Concert" Phonograph of 1899. When a coin was dropped through a slot cut in the face of the drawer (shown removed), it struck a bell, thereby alerting an otherwise occupied proprietor that a customer was ready to hear the machine play. No further adaptation of the mechanism was necessary. *Courtesy of Michael Sims.* (VR)

2-19. In its advertisements in the trade publication the *Phonoscope*, the Talking Machine Company of Chicago differentiated between "Polyphones" and "Polyphone Attachments." The floral decoration on the mechanism and the specially marked lid of this Edison "Home" Phonograph suggest that at least some complete outfits ("Polyphones") were embellished in this manner. *Courtesy of John Woodward.* (VR)

2-21. Three unusual American cylinders from the turn of the century with their containers. Left, a "Jumbo" cylinder, sold by the Talking Machine Company of Chicago was recorded at 185 rpm. A "Consolidated Record" from the Consolidated Phonograph Company Ltd., of Newark, New Jersey. Lastly an "Elite" cylinder, sold by the Shepard Company of Providence, Rhode Island. *Courtesy of Michael F. Khanchalian.* (VR)

2-22. Three unusual reproducers to be used on Edison Phonographs. On the left, an Edison "Automatic" reproducer modified by Elmer Fletcher. The unusually designed added weight was meant to produce more volume. In the center, an "Automatic" modified by Blackman. Here, the size of the floating weight has been decreased, but the tube-plate has been domed in an effort to improve the sound. The reproducer on the right is unknown. It resembles the later Edison "R" and "S" style large-diaphragm models, has a fluted Mobley-type diaphragm and a peculiar cylindrical mounting for both two and four minute styli. *Courtesy of the collection of Howard Hazelcorn.* (Value code: C, each)

2-23. Edison reproducers modified by Edwin Mobley. The Edison company sued to prevent such adaptations of its product, but not before a number of such reproducers had been sold, primarily Mobleys. The two on the left are modified "Automatics;" the two on the right are modified Model "C"s. An integral feature in all examples, but not visible here was the Mobley stamped aluminum diaphragm. *Courtesy of the collection of Howard Hazelcorn.* (Value code: C, each)

2-24. In Europe, much more use was made of additional weights to fit Pathé or Graphophone-type reproducers than in the United States. Here is a typical Pathé reproducer and the extra weight which sat in the recessed area. (Value code: G, weight)

2-25. Interesting cylinder boxes from France. On the left, four containers featuring photographs of the artists, including (far left) "Charlus & Marechal" and an "Inter" cylinder in its tan imitation leather box. Pathé's London branch issued special labels for "Inter" boxes featuring well-lithographed portraits of various artists (far right). *Courtesy of Jean-Paul Agnard.* (Value code: E)

2-26 Columbia's "Simplex" shaver could be fitted to cylinder Graphophones from 1896 forward. *Courtesy of the Scott and Denise Corbett collection.* (Value code: E)

2-27. A slightly later shaver is shown here mounted to a Columbia Graphophone Type "AF." *Courtesy of Todd Emery.* (Value code: E)

2-28. Hawthorne & Sheble offered this "hand cabinet" to enclose the first model Edison "Gem" Phonograph (1899-1901), which was not factory-equipped with a cabinet. Note also the horn socket to the right of the Edison signature trade mark. This was a H & S option to allow the use of a supported horn. *Courtesy of Michael F. Khanchalian.* (Value code: D)

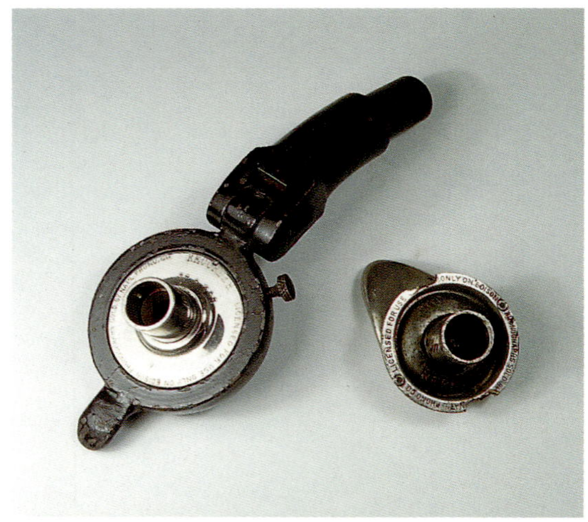

2-29. Two seldom seen Edison-related items. Left, an Edison recording attachment designed for the "Opera" Phonograph. Right, a Mobley modification of the humble "Gem" reproducer. In this instance, even the most minute improvement in sound would have been appreciated by the owner of the early "Gem!" (Value code: C)

2-30. Hawthorne & Sheble's "Dupliphone" was a short-lived effort to adapt existing Phonographs and Graphophones (shown) to play 5" diameter cylinders. Patent infringements aside, this attachment must have proven cumbersome to use, and the long extension tube for the reproducer would have negated any volume advantage offered by the 5" cylinder.

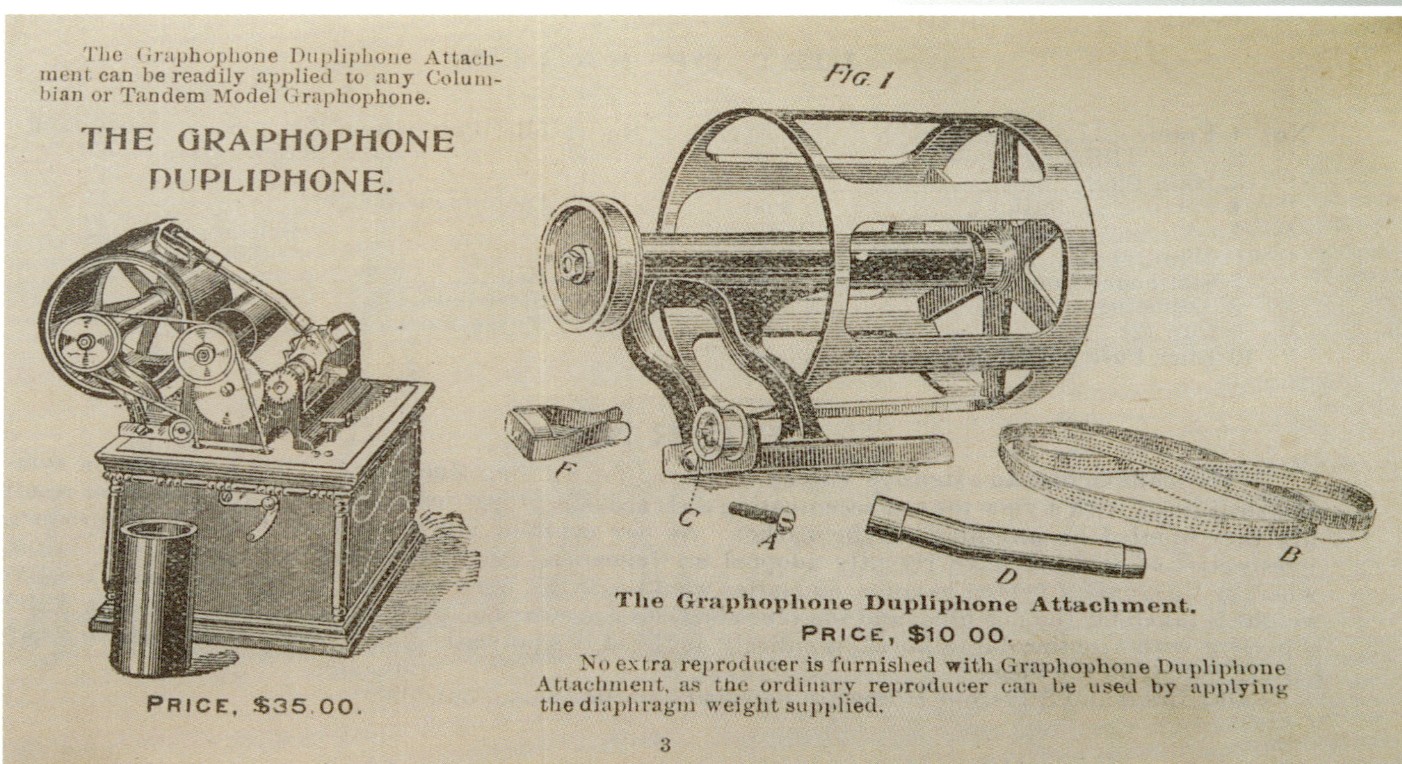

The Graphophone Dupliphone Attachment can be readily applied to any Columbian or Tandem Model Graphophone.

THE GRAPHOPHONE DUPLIPHONE.

PRICE, $35.00.

Fig. 1

F C A D B

**The Graphophone Dupliphone Attachment.**

PRICE, $10 00.

No extra reproducer is furnished with Graphophone Dupliphone Attachment, as the ordinary reproducer can be used by applying the diaphragm weight supplied.

3

2-31. Britisher Henry Seymour sold talking machines and accessories, such as this "Henry Seymour Diaphragm." His attachment, here intended for an Edison "Gem," offered the user a diaphragm substantially larger than employed by any Edison factory reproducer prior to 1909. Considering the marginal reproducers supplied with the earliest versions of the "Gem," it is easy to imagine the need for this particular example. *Courtesy of the Charles Hummel collections.* (Value code: C)

2-32. Unlike Columbia, Edison was a "belt and suspenders" man when it came to adapting his own designs. The positioning arm on which "Reproducer" was stamped was discontinued soon after the Model "C" reproducer was introduced in 1902. For a short time after this occurred, Model "C"s already drilled to accept the two screws which held this arm received tiny plugs and were stamped "REP'R." Once these pre-drilled parts were exhausted, the word "REPRODUCER" appeared around the upper periphery of the tube plate. *Courtesy of Robert Lomas.* (Value code: E)

2-33. Pathé ebonite cylinder reproducers and their original boxes. Left, the most common type. Right, the more expensive "Rex," which included a larger diaphragm. (Value code: E, D)

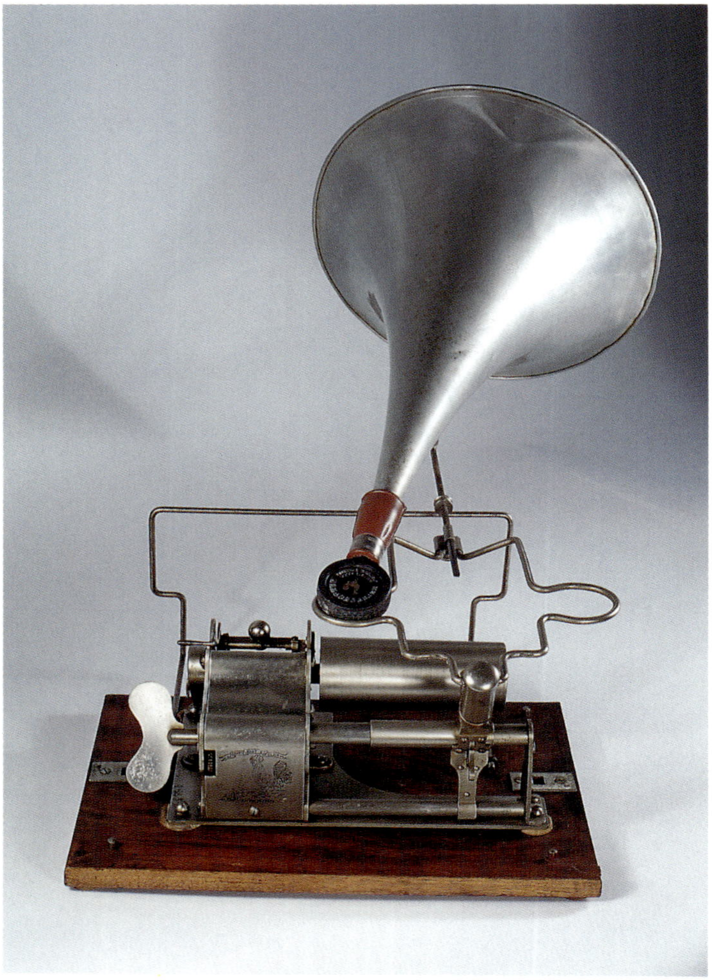

2-34. The French Girard company sold the "Systeme Verité" attachment to fit existing Pathé cylinder talking machines. The premise was to free the reproducer from its normally fixed position on the carriage. This would presumably reduce the incidence of "skipping," which was common in machines like Pathés, based on the Graphophone model. Moreover, it solved a problem which occurred after the introduction of the 3 1/2" diameter "Inter" cylinders in 1903: how to conveniently convert a machine to play both sizes of cylinder. Girard offered a mail-order version of the "Coquet" equipped with "Verité" employing a red or blue-bodied horn. However, when the attachments were fitted to other machines, such as this "Coq," a spun aluminum horn was used. (Value code: B, attachment)

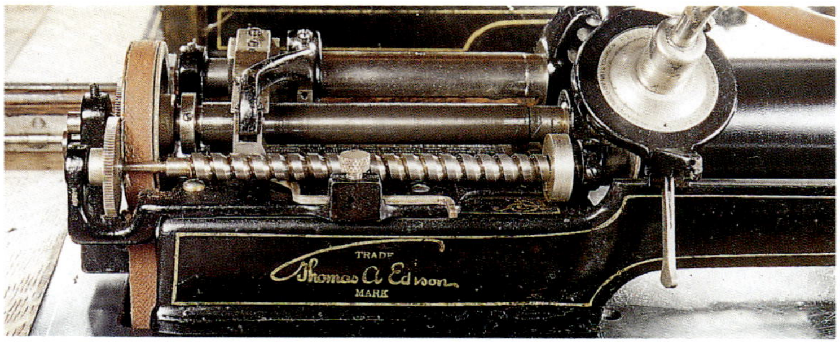


2-36. In October 1904, Edison introduced the Model "D" repeating attachment primarily to fit "Home" and "Triumph" Phonographs. It had been invented by Edward L. Aiken of the Edison staff. The device superceded a number of other more complicated and less successful repeaters on domestic and coin-operated Phonographs (shown). The Model "D" repeater sold for $7.50 and remained in the catalogue for some seven years. *Courtesy of the Charles Hummel collections.* (Value code: C, repeater)

2-35. Peter Weber invented this repeating attachment, which was available for use on the Edison "Triumph" and "Home" beginning in 1904. The sophisticated design included a chain-driven spiral screw at the rear of the top casting, which returned the reproducer carriage to the start of the record. At $15.00, however, this device was not popular, especially after Edison announced the $7.50 Model "D" repeater in October of 1904. (VR)

2-37. The Model "C" style reproducer used on certain Edison-Bell machines was labeled "NEW MODEL" (1904). Note the unusual manner in which the limit loop passes directly through the neck of the "fishtail" weight. *Courtesy of Terry Paul Baer.* (Value code: E)

2-38. A volume control contained within a hearing tube connector, and operated by a small lever. *Courtesy of the Scott and Denise Corbett collection.* (Value code: F)

2-39. Two volume controls to fit between the reproducer and horn of cylinder machines. The one on the left uses a lever to alter the size of the sound passage. The one on the right uses a "stopper" or mute which can lowered into the neck of the reproducer tube plate to reduce the level of sound. *Courtesy of Norm and Janyne Smith.* (Value code: F)

2-40. Two crazy contraptions modifying an Edison "Home" Phonograph. The "Kemmer Speed Indicator," despite its complicated appearance, merely provided a numerical scale with a pointer which could be set at the correct speed. On the other hand, the "Gilbert Repeater" (advertised by the Douglas Phonograph Company during 1905-06) is just as complex as it appears. The repeater shown here sold for $6.50. *Courtesy of the Scott and Denise Corbett collection.* (Value code: D, indicator; VR, repeater)

2-41. The Columbia "Lyric" recorder was introduced in 1905 to equip the newly-introduced "BE," "BF" and "BG" Graphophones. The popularity of home recording gradually waned throughout the first decade of the century. Consequently, recorders like this are seldom seen. (Value code: E)

2-43. The Blackman Talking Machine Company of New York City manufactured the "Place Record Brush" for both cylinder and disc talking machines. The "No.2" here shown in the original carton of one dozen, was intended to fit the Edison "Standard" or "Home" Phonographs by clipping to the narrow neck of the reproducer carriage. List price was 15 cents each. *Courtesy of the collection of Howard Hazelcorn.* (Value code: H, each)

2-42. The "Lewis Consonator" appeared as early as May 1905, selling for $3.00. It was sold by the Lewis Manufacturing Company of New York City, and was described as follows: "[It] is placed between the horn and the reproducer, and improves the tone without distorting the sound or decreasing the volume. The consonator also eliminates all rattles, harsh and metallic grating, rasping nasal sounds and blasts and produces a soft, natural tone." Contained within this device was a secondary mica diaphragm and other details intended to filter the sound. *Courtesy of Norm and Janyne Smith.* (Value code: E)

Below: 2-44. During the latter part of the century's first decade, a number of companies offered aftermarket diaphragms, meant primarily for use in Edison reproducers. Wood, vulcanite and other materials were used in order to affect the sound. Manufacturers included Pardell, Playrite, Norcross and Truetone, among others. The "Truetone Wood Diaphragm" shown here was sold by the General Phonograph Supply Company of New York City, which had evolved from the earlier Douglas Phonograph Company. *Courtesy of the Scott and Denise Corbett collection.* (Value code: H, each)

2-45. Used to concentrate the reproduction of recorded sound from the 1880s, hearing tubes (also called listening or ear-tubes) took a variety of configurations. Here, several "splitters" are shown. These permitted multiple auditions of a single recorded performance. In addition, the unit at the center contains an internal volume control valve. An article in the January 1906 issue of the *Talking Machine World* titled "Value of Hearing Tubes" stated: "Yet for obtaining the maximum of enjoyment from a record hearing tubes are absolutely unrivaled. In the first place the use of hearing tubes makes it possible to enjoy records even in the dead of night... Further, flaws and imperfections in the record are at once detected, which makes hearing tubes of value to both large and small buyers of records. The value of this hint will be understood when one remembers that in many factories records are always tested by this means." *Courtesy of the collection of Howard Hazelcorn.* (Value code: F, each)

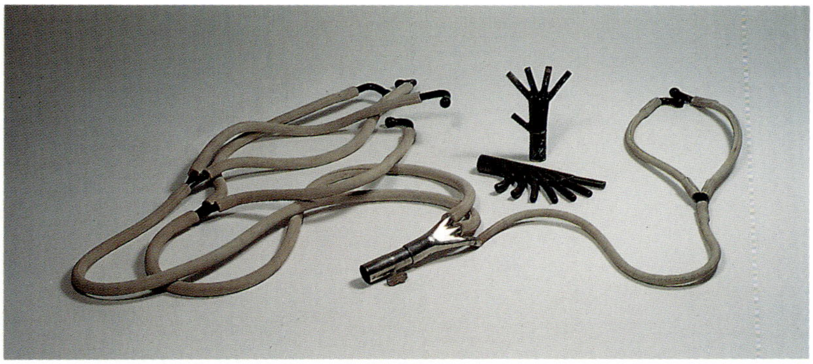

2-46. The Devineau "Biophone" was "An attachment to play disc records on any... cylinder machine." An October 1907 advertisement stated: "With the Devineau Biophone owners of the cylinder machines are enabled to add to their repertoire the magnificent selections of the greatest operatic singers of the world [an obvious reference to the success of Victor's 'Red Seal' discs]." The device is shown attached to an Edison "Standard" Phonograph of earlier vintage. The company claimed the "attachment can be connected or removed in a few seconds. It is operated by friction so that neither gear nor belt is needed in its operation. No screw, no bolt to mar the cabinet. No need of removing the attachment while playing a cylinder record. Any horn, the 'IDEAL' included [see illustration 1-67], can be instantly attached to the Biophone. Three twelve-inch disc records can be played at one winding on the Edison Standard machine... RETAILS AT 15 DOLLARS." It was manufactured by the Devineau Biophone Company of Cleveland, Ohio. *Courtesy of Pat and Jamie Jones.* (VR)

2-47. The soundbox of the "Biophone" was described as "...our patented sound box producing a full, perfectly natural sound." The concept of a talking machine which could play both cylinder and disc records was realized only sporadically. The most prominant example was one model of the "Idéal," a French machine from 1905, which incorporated both cylinder and disc capacities. *Courtesy of Pat and Jamie Jones.* (VR)

2-48. The "Tiz-It" socket connector fit between the horn and reproducer of a cylinder talking machine, and was first advertised in the *Talking Machine World* in November 1906. A January 1907 advertisement suggested the origin of the peculiar name was simple American slang. It read: "See that ball? *TIZ-IT*...-NUFFSED." Kreiling and Company of Chicago produced several versions, including one with a volume control, right. (Value code: E)

2-49. The Chicago Stand Company of Chicago introduced the "Phon-Arm Attachment for Edison Standard, Home and Triumph Phonographs" in September 1907. This device included a cast bracket which clamped to the machine, an articulated tone arm, and a horn elbow. Versions of the "Phon-Arm" to adapt Graphophones would follow. A contemporary advertisement claimed: "By using the Phon-Arm, you have no weight on Reproducer or Feed Nut." Although the following admonition would curdle the blood of a modern collector, the company advised: "You can use any disc horn or the Edison horn by cutting same off to fit the elbow of this attachment." Retail price was $7.50, reduced to $6.00 in February 1908. (VR)

2-50. The Acme Repeater Company of Indianapolis, Indiana, introduced its "J Return Attachment" late in 1907. An advertisement from January 1908 stated, "SELLS HOME machines at sight. Can be attached in five minutes. No drilling...noiseless." It sold for $6.00 and relied on a "string return" similar to the Edison "Iris" repeater (used on coin-slot Phonographs). A supplemental pulley acted like a winch to draw back the reproducer carriage at the end of the record. *Courtesy of the Charles Hummel collections.* (VR)

2-51. In August 1908, Edison announced the introduction of the "Amberol" four-minute records, which doubled the playing time of a conventional cylinder. To induce the owners of existing Edison machines to embrace the new format, the company offered "Amberol Attachments" and a group of ten introductory "Special Records." The cylinders were shipped in this wooden crate, with plenty of room for packing material. *Courtesy of the Charles Hummel collections.* (VR)

2-52. An unusual British two-minute reproducer intended to fit an Edison Phonograph. "Max Wurcker's Natural Tone Reproducer With Coomb's Patent Diaphragm" (1908). *Courtesy of Norm and Janyne Smith.* (Value code: D)

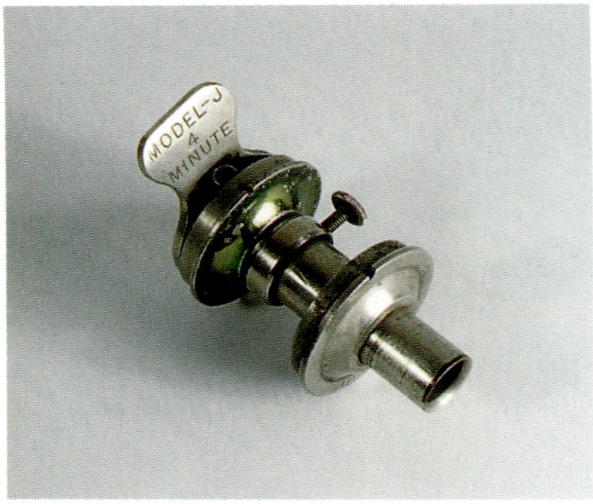


2-53. The varying diameters in which cylinder records were manufactured (2 1/8", 3 1/2", 5" and some other minor variations) caused engineering problems unknown in the field of disc records. Since adaptability was often viewed as a good selling point, the trick became to create a system in which the customer easily could play different diameter cylinders without mechanical complications. For talking machines of the "Graphophone" type, such as produced by Columbia or Pathé, the conversion between larger and smaller diameter records was accomplished either by moving the position of the mandrel or the position of the reproducer carriage. Edison Phonographs, with their fixed mandrel axis and rigid cast-iron carriage, would have presented an engineering perplexity. Fortunately, Edison cylinder machines were not designed to be "convertible"- except in England. The unusual little "reproducer extender" shown here was what was required by the Edison-Bell "Edison New Duplex" of 1902. This machine had two "telescoped" mandrels. The 5" "Concert" mandrel slipped off to allow "standard-sized" Edison or Columbia cylinders to be played. Therefore, the reproducer had to be "dropped" from its "Concert" position to the level of the smaller records. The Model "J" was a four-minute reproducer, which means this attachment would have found use after the introduction of the four-minute "Amberol" cylinders in late 1908. Of course, an ingenious American customer could have adapted his Edison "Concert" (5") Phonograph to use this same type of attachment. Many "Concerts" had their large (5" diameter) mandrels replaced with standard-sized mandrels, especially during the four-minute era. In these instances, a different (lower) reproducer carriage was usually substituted. However, if the customer changed the mandrel but not the carriage, he could have employed this "extender" to drop a Model "J" reproducer to the correct height in order to play four-minute cylinders. Courtesy of Michael F. Khanchalian. (Value code: C)

2-54. The concept of convenience became a focus of the design of many talking machine attachments. The "Wilkeslyke Automatic Start and Stop Attachment" (patent No. 860,110, July 16, 1907, by Howard Lyke and Charles H. Wilkes) unified two separate manual steps into one operation: after the cylinder was in place, locking the endgate automatically started the motor. Unlocking the endgate stopped the motor, allowing the record to be removed. An advertisement in the February 1908 issue of the *Talking Machine World* listed W.D. Andrews as sole distributor and stated: "This scientific attachment is made to fit the famous Edison Standard, Home, and Triumph Phonographs... enabling the operator to wait on customers or perform other duties. Every dealer should have one on his display machine-sells on sight." A dealer could purchase this attachment for $1.80 and retail it at $3.00. (VR)

2-55. In October 1908, the Columbia Phonograph Company purchased the Indestructible Record Company. From that point until 1912, "Indestructible" cylinders would be sold as Columbias. In November 1909, Columbia four-minute "Indestructibles" were introduced. This four-minute "Lyric" reproducer was intended to play these records. *Courtesy of Bob and Karyn Sitter.* (Value code: E)

2-56. The Morse "Clarifier" appeared in 1910 and could be used on either cylinder or disc machines (see illustration 3-80). As shown here, it has been removed from the original rubber tube which connected reproducer to horn. The "Clarifier" consisted of a small bundle of varnished fibrous tubes which, according to Morse Brothers of Minneapolis, Minnesota "...renders the sound clear, loud and distinct." *Courtesy of David P. Graber.* (Value code: E)

2-57. Edison "Standard" Model "Ds," when sold by Babson Brothers, were equipped with this simple but effective automatic stop. As the carriage reached the right side of the straight-edge, it drew the connecting rod, thereby pivoting a leather plug against the belt pulley. (Value code: F, attachment)

2-58. Babson Brothers of Chicago sold Edison "Standard" Model "D" Phonographs by mail-order in 1911. Included with the machines were these instructional papers. Note the special attention drawn to the two-and-four-minute shift button, which continues to be a problem for collectors today.

2-59. From the earliest days of the wax cylinder talking machine, optional weights had been offered to increase volume and improve tracking. Here are two later examples suitable for attachment to an Edison "Diamond B" reproducer (introduced October 1912). *Courtesy of Terry Paul Baer.* (Value code: G, each)

2-60. This Edison Amberola "30" attachment, with purposely truncated Model "H" reproducer, was offered in conjunction with the International Correspondence School's language courses. It allowed the student to use a four-minute recorder and wax blanks to audition his skills. Normally it was impossible to record one's own voice on an Amberola "30." (Value code: D)

2-61. An unusual cylinder record and the mould which created it. In 1927, Edison's dictating or "Ediphone" division produced a cylinder to commemorate the 50th anniversary of the invention of the Phonograph. The cylinder, recorded at the business standard of 150 tpi stated in part: "The Ediphone writes over a million better letters a day throughout the world. The Ediphone has been in use for years by many nearby firms who will tell you of their success. The Ediphone offers the greatest value and service, usefulness and convenience." *Courtesy of Jim Nichol.* (VR)

2-62. Interior view of cylinder mould showing title at far end. *Courtesy of Jim Nichol.* (VR)

Chapter Three:

# Disc Talking Machine Gadgets

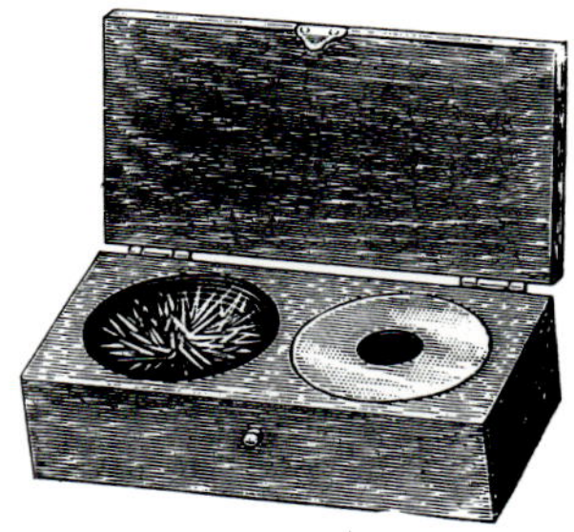

It was not until 1897, with the introduction of the Berliner "Improved Gramophone," that disc talking machines became available in substantial numbers. Over a decade would pass before the sale of disc machines would achieve parity with that of cylinder instruments. This decade might well be considered the "glory days" of the cylinder format, culminating with Edison's peak cylinder sales year: 1907.

Yet, by 1912, even Edison had introduced a "Disc Phonograph." So dynamic was the disc market during the first decade of the twentieth century, that numerous inventors and manufacturers offered a dizzying variety of disc-related products. These included variously shaped needles of steel, ivory, cactus and jewel, needle boxes and tins, needle sharpeners, "tone regulators," record brushes, special soundboxes, automatic stops, repeaters, dancing toys, supplemental lighting, automatic spring winders and many others. This cornucopia of inventive pursuit continued throughout the life of the acoustic disc talking machine, well into the radio age.

From the earliest needle boxes of the 1890s to the electric contraptions offered at the close of the acoustic era in 1929, the manufacture and marketing of disc gadgets mirrored the vitality of an infant industry growing into adulthood.

3-2. The idea of appending new and used needle receptacles directly to a talking machine was seldom exploited until the advent of internal-horn models. However, this attachment was first sold in 1908 as the "Ideal" needle box by R.R. Browne Specialty Company of Toledo, Ohio, and later, as the "Simplex" needle box by the S.B. Davega Company of New York City. Both cost 50 cents. Either box was attached to an external-horn machine by using an existing bolt in the back bracket. An advertisement for the "Simplex" from the September 1910 *Talking Machine World* says it all: "'Fills a Long-Felt Want.' The most useful, convenient, necessary attachment made." *Courtesy of the Scott and Denise Corbett collection.* (Value code: F)

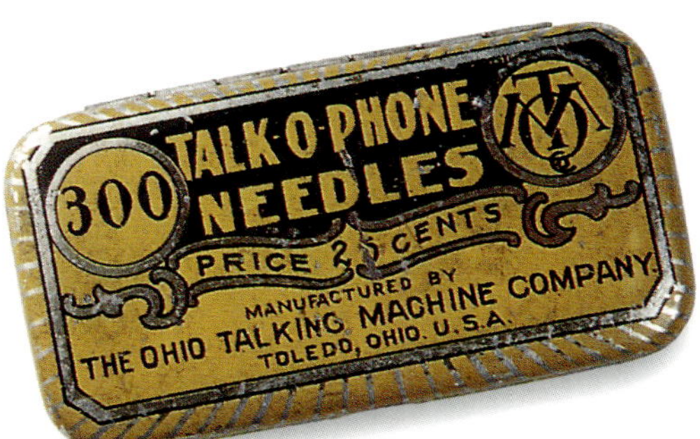


3-1. A tin of Talkophone needles circa 1904. Although Talkophone machines were popular, tins of this brand are seldom found. (Value code: F)

3-3. Needle tins clockwise from left: French "Association Phonique Des Grands Artistes" in the shape of a bound volume, circa 1905, a British tin with a realistic depiction of a panelled horn, and a German tin engagingly titled "The Boy's Delight." *Courtesy of Philippe LeRay.* (Value code: F)

3-4. European needle tins clockwise from left: British "Favorite-Record" needles, "Edelstahl" needles featuring a German-style upright talking machine, and finally, German "Casaphon." *Courtesy of Philippe LeRay.* (Value code: G)

3-5. Needle tins clockwise from left: "Pathephone" steel needles from the 1920s, "Mignonphone" needles showing the collapsible talking machine of the same name, and finally, a stylish Pathé tin from the late 1920s featuring chanteuse Ninon Valin. *Courtesy of Philippe LeRay.* (Value code: G)

3-6. European needle tins clockwise from left: "Admiral" needles with a bust suggestive of Nelson, "Winner" British needles, and two Japanese "Napoleon" tins, the red one featuring his "kabuki" pose. (Value code: F)

3-7. On the left, a long needle tin by the Herold Company of Germany featuring portraits of notable Germans. On the right, a literally designed Edison-Bell tin from England. *Courtesy of Steve and Ellie Saccente.* (Value code: F)

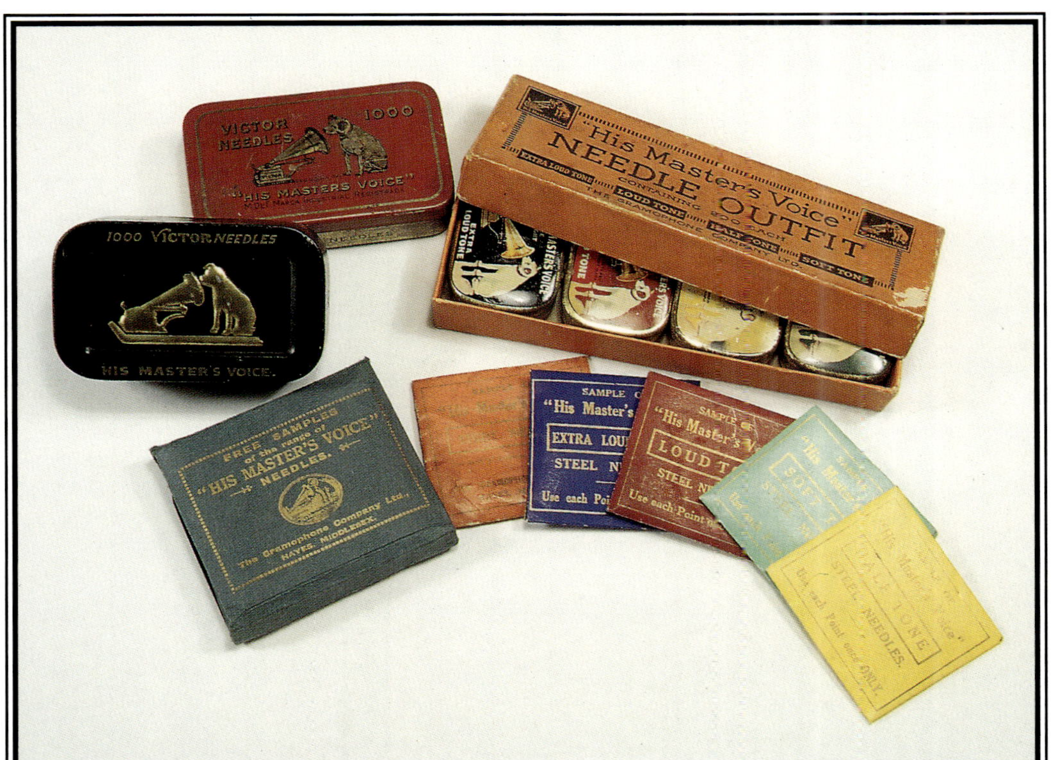


3-8. Needle tins and packages bearing the "His Master's Voice" trademark. Clockwise from top left: a red 1000 needle Victor tin circa 1910, a British set of tins from the 1920s containing all tone gradations, various packs of British needles, and finally, a black embossed Victor 1000 needle tin circa 1905. *Courtesy of Todd Emery.* (Value code: E, D set, H, E)

3-9. Canadian needle tins featuring the "His Master's Voice" trademark as used by the Berliner Gramophone Company of Montreal. (Value code: F, G, G, F)

3-12. A Columbia needle display from the late 'teens which oddly bears a resemblance to a Victor "Victrola" lid rather than a Columbia "Grafonola" lid. (12 1/4" x 15 1/4".) (Value code: C)

3-10. A display containing "Starr Needles" sold by the Starr Piano Company's Boston branch. The front of the display was enclosed in glass. *Courtesy of Martin F. Bryan.* (Value code: E)

3-11. The rear of the Starr needle display, showing how the packages were arranged. *Courtesy of Martin F. Bryan.*

3-13. This large (12 1/2" diameter) Victor needle display could hold a variety of needle types in paper envelopes and tins. These displays were surmounted by a cast effigy of "Nipper," which is sometimes *mistaken* for a free-standing statuette or paperweight when separated from the display. *Courtesy of Charles McCarn.* (Value code: B)

3-14. A close-up of the previous display, showing the small access door from which the needle packages were removed. The vertical windows allowed the dealer to check the amount of stock remaining. *Courtesy of Charles McCarn.*

3-15. A less-ambitious Victor needle display which still afforded a wide selection of needles. (17 1/2" wide.) *Courtesy of Walter and Carol Myers.* (Value code: B)

3-17. The "Winnett" needle dispenser had several clever features. The triangular window allowed the user to check the supply of needles. To its right is a slot for the disposal of used needles. Beneath the window is a hole from which a lever dispenses an individual needle. All this, and it fit in the palm of a hand! *Courtesy of Steve and Ellie Saccente.* (Value code: E)

3-16. A dealer's display of "Boye" Needles from the 1920s. 6 1/2" x 9 1/2". *Courtesy of Bob and Karyn Sitter.* (Value code: E)

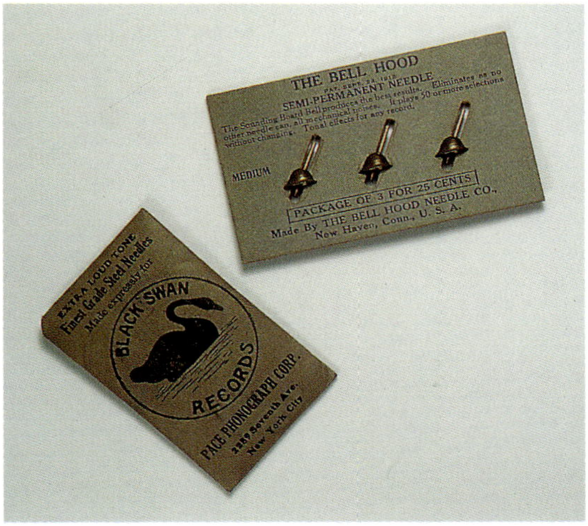


3-18. On the left, a seldom-seen packet of "Black Swan" needles from the early 1920s. On the right, a card of "Bell Hood" semi-permanent point needles from the late 'teens. One might wonder why these needles were designed in such an unusual way. According to the New England Musical Instrument Trading Company of New York City which distributed them, the answer was, "The Sounding Board Bell produces the best result." *Courtesy of the Scott and Denise Corbett collection.* (Value code: H, G)

3-20. Various needle tins, clockwise from left: "Stag" brand from England, one of two different "Parrot" (Japanese) designs, "Palladium" needles with a majestic swan, and finally, a badly-mangled interpretation of "Chantecler" (actually printed "Chaiiteciep"), made in Japan. (Value code: G)

3-19. Needle tins of interesting shapes, clockwise from the left: a Canadian dispenser tin from Eaton's department store, a triangular tin of multi-play needles, a combination tin and duster advertising Gimbel's Department Stores, and a trapeziodally-shaped "Vera" tin from Germany. (Value code: G, F, F, G)

3-21. Columbia needle tins. Clockwise from top left: three early tins specifically referring to "Disc Graphophones," and a tin from the "Vivatonal" era of the late 1920s. (Value code: G)

3-23. Clockwise from top left: a Spanish tin with characteristic "concave trapezoid" shape, "Peacock" with customary trapezoid shape, and "Meteor" with H.G. Wells-like graphics. *Courtesy of Charles McCarn.* (Value code: G)

3-22. Various European needle tins: clockwise from top left, a Herold tin with the "horseman" trademark, "Rex" with British lions, "La Gioconda" with DaVinci's famous smiler, and "Sphinx" brand Velvet Tone needles from England. (Value code: G)

3-24. An original carton of 200-needle tins sold by the Italian Gramophone company, La Voce Del Padrone. *Courtesy of Charles McCarn.* (Value code: G, each)

3-26. Two Czechoslovakian needle tins from the 1920s: on the left, a delightfully lithographed party scene. On the right, a couple undoubtedly joined in a tango. *Courtesy of Alan H. Mueller.* (Value code: F)

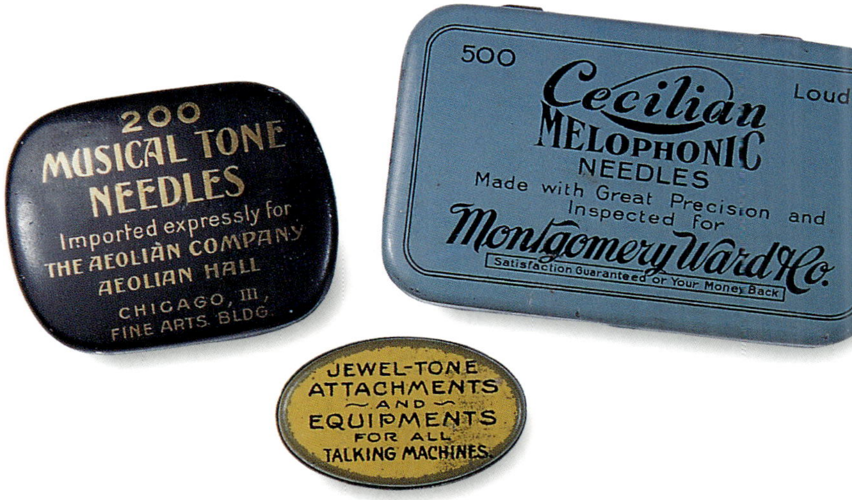


3-25. American needle tins from Chicago: top left, Aeolian Company needles, top right, Montgomery Ward & Company needles labeled to correspond with its "Cecilian" line of talking machines, below, a tiny oval tin for a sapphire stylus used in conjunction with the attachments of the Jewel Phonoparts Company. *Courtesy of Alan H. Mueller.* (Value code: G)

3-27. Clockwise from left: Sonora exhausted the limit of promotional opportunities. It even distributed elegant bookmarks. Next, a number of versions of the "long" Gramophone needle tin were marketed. They all had inner dividers to hold needles of varying gradations. This particular one was sold by the Berliner company of Canada. Finally, a Zonophone needle tin from the 1920s. Although the Zonophone passed out of existence in the United States in 1912, the brand continued to be exploited abroad, and this characteristic cruciform trademark was used during the 'teens and twenties. *Courtesy of Bob and Karyn Sitter.* (Value code: H, D, G)

3-28. The "Hughes-Stylus" was designed to allow a lateral cut talking machine to play a vertical cut disc. It was "designed especially to play the beautiful 'Pathé' records on 'talking machines' and 'Graphophones.'" The device consisted of a sapphire stylus mounted to a horizontal arm which was tightened into the needle chuck. The perpendicular arrangement of arm and diaphragm allowed the lateral soundbox to respond to vertical cut discs. Like the "Bakertone" and the "Deflex-O-Graph," the arm of the "Hughes-Stylus" could be rotated to modify the volume and quality of sound. The sole distributor was Herbert & Huesgen Company, New York City. (Value code: G)

3-29. Many attempts were made to perfect "multiple-play" needles. In the case of lateral discs, one of the most effective materials turned out to be tungsten. The Victor "Tungs-Tone" styli, which began to be manufactured during World War I were good for hundreds of plays when properly used. However, the clever idea of a renewable tungsten stylus was embodied in this tiny device, where a coil of tungsten wire is fed out at will by rotating the celluloid wheel. (Value code: G)

3-30. Edison items from the 1920s. On the left, packs of Edison steel needles for the short-lived lateral discs of 1929, and a pack of needles especially designed for the "C" model Radio-Phonographs. On the right, a ruler and a record brush promoting the Edison "Diamond Disc" Phonograph. *Courtesy of Walter and Carol Myers.* (Value code: G, G, F)

3-31. Fibre needle sharpeners were offered in a variety of configurations including those which were meant to be operated on a flat surface, and others which were hand-held. This simple model lies in the palm, and the mechanism is entirely shielded. *Courtesy of Rae Ann Rieping.* (Value code: F)

3-32. The "Ideal" fibre needle cutter was one of the more substantially constructed of these devices. The palm of the hand was used to activate the knife. *Courtesy of the Scott and Denise Corbett collection.* (Value code: F)

3-33. "The Wade" was a popular hand-held needle sharpener designed much like a set of pliers. (Value code: F)

3-35. On the left, a popular Lyon & Healy (Chicago) needle sharpener which is held in the hand and operates in a similar fashion to fingernail clippers. In the center, a needle sharpener marked "Victor" is in fact a "B&H" model sold after September 1910, when the Victor Talking Machine Company assumed control of the B&H Fibre Manufacturing Company of Chicago. A fibre needle is in position for sharpening. On the right, a genuine Victor-manufactured needle sharpener. *Courtesy of Norm and Janyne Smith.* (Value code: F)

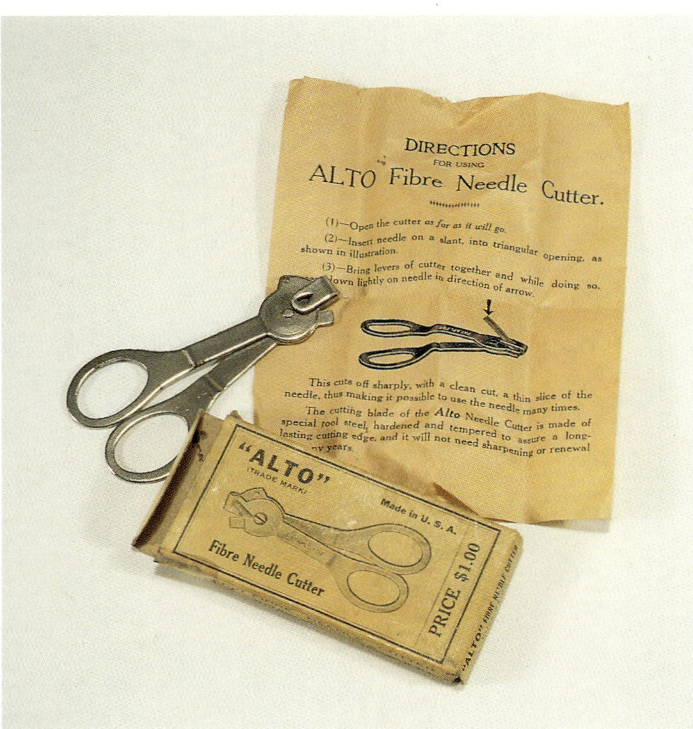


3-36. "The Alto" needle sharpener operated in the same manner as scissors. (Value code: F)

3-36. The "Red Top" and "Cactone" were identical sharpeners meant to be used with needles made of cactus spines or thorns. The following item appeared in the June 1911 issue of the *Talking Machine World*: "Residents of Arizona have discovered that cactus needles or thorns are admirable for use as talking machine reproducing points, and some of the local wiseacres look forward to a big demand for them—the discovery of a new industry, as it were." *Courtesy of Rae Ann Rieping.* (Value code: G)

3-37. The Place "No. 10" Disc Record Brush. This little accessory was sold for twenty-five cents in 1907 by the Blackman Talking Machine Company of New York City. A contemporary advertisement seemed to invest this simple device with rather complex qualities: "Automatically cleans the RECORD GROOVES and gives the needle a clean track to run in. Insures a clean Reproduction and prevents records getting scratchy. Makes the Needle wear better. SAVE THE LIFE OF YOUR RECORDS." (Value code: G, brush)

3-38. Disc record cleaning devices took a surprising variety of forms. Here are four unusual ones. Clockwise from upper left: A rectangular cleaner advertising a music store, a clever velour record pad incorporating a magnet to retrieve spilled needles, a record cleaner with a handy strap, and a bristle brush which appears capable of cleaning more than records! *Courtesy of Charles McCarn.* (Value code: G)

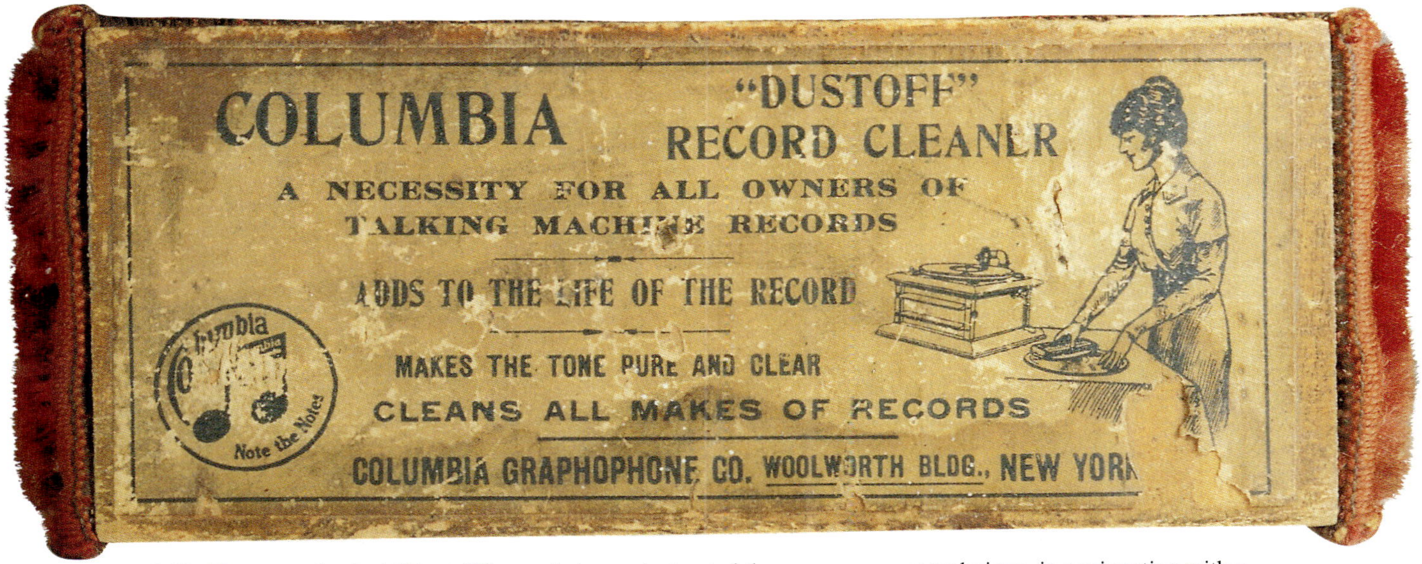


3-39. The carpet-backed "Dustoff" record cleaner instructed the user on correct technique, in conjunction with a Grafonola. *Courtesy of Walter and Carol Myers*. (Value code: G)

3-40. Round record dusters with velour pads frequently carried advertising. These three examples promoted both a record brand and the store which sold it. Left to right: Gennett; Brunswick and Vocalion. *Courtesy of Charles McCarn.* (Value code: F)

3-41. Three interesting record dusters; on the left, an advertising duster with a variegated carpet backing; in the middle, a seasonal duster; on the right, a wooden-backed duster with the "His Master's Voice" image in color. *Courtesy of Walter and Carol Myers.* (Value code: G, F, F)

3-42. The "Little Devil Self Sweeper" attached to the periphery of the soundbox. For such a simple device, the instructions seemed to be more than adequate. An advertisement in the July 4, 1917 issue of the *Phonograph*, a trade publication, splashed: "THE BIG LITTLE THING... The Real Automatic Record Cleaner. FITS EVERY DISC MACHINE... 25 cents." The "Little Devil" was made by the Herrman Self-Sweeper Company of New York City. (Value code: G)

3-43. On the left, a carpet-backed Pathé record duster. In the center, a Victrola duster with a Christmas theme. On the right, a duster suggesting the grooves of a record, and advertising "The New Edison" Phonograph. *Courtesy of Todd Emery.* (Value code: G, F, F)

3-46. Victor introduced its top of the line "No. 6" talking machine in late 1904. The company also offered a suitably ostentatious soundbox especially for the machine. The "No. 10" soundbox was based upon the "Concert" (introduced in 1901), but with multiple "His Master's Voice" trademarks embellishing the rim. *Courtesy of Michael F. Khanchalian.* (Value code: A)

3-44. Three versions of a popular Columbia record duster with hammered copper effect. *Courtesy of Todd Emery.* (Value code: F)

3-45. A light-colored brush mounted next to a soundbox with an optional handle to insure a secure grip while being raised or lowered. To quote the February 1911 issue of the *Talking Machine World*: "It is generally realized that the talking machine owner does not get the best results from his records, whether they are of the cylinder or disc type, if the sound grooves are filled with dust or other foreign matter and numerous efforts have been made to keep the records free from dirt or to clean them before playing." *Courtesy of the Scott and Denise Corbett collection.* (Value code: G)

3-47. In October 1905, Hawthorne & Sheble introduced an uniquely-designed disc talking machine soundbox. Its most important feature was its adaptability: it could be purchased to fit Victor, Zonophone, Columbia, or Talkophone machines. Edwin H. Mobley pioneered the use of stamped aluminum diaphragms, at first to adapt Edison cylinder reproducers. Later, his colorfully lacquered diaphragms were standard equipment in most of the soundboxes manufactured by Hawthorne & Sheble. To the right of the H & S soundbox and its container is a full catalogue of the company's talking machines and related products, as sold by Arthur J. O'Neill's Aretino Company of Chicago. (Value code: D, E catalogue)

3-48. The venerable Victor "Exhibition" soundbox was sold for a short time with a handy "spring-release" to facilitate changing the needle. This example, for front-mount machines, is shown with its original wooden box. (Value code: D)

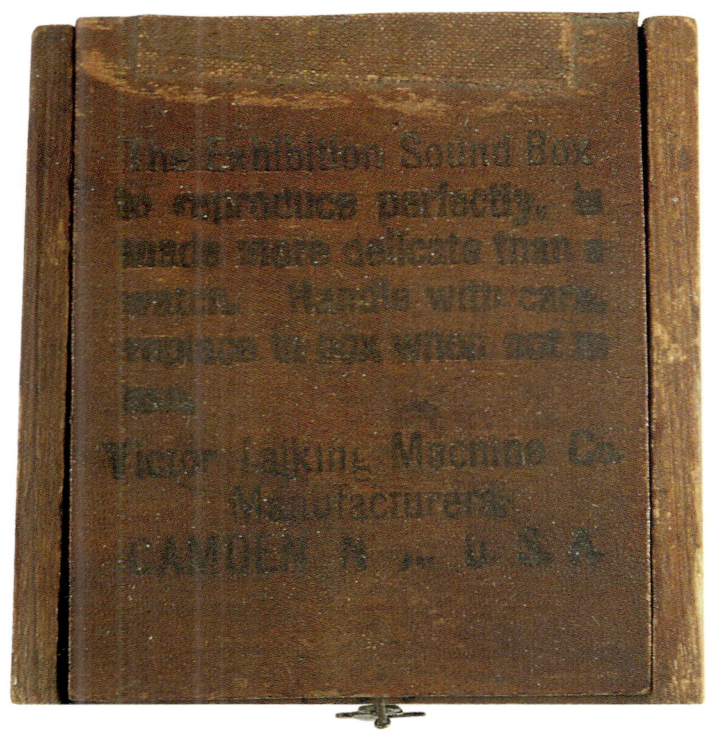


3-49. A close-up of the Victor soundbox container with its stamped admonition to "Handle with care."

3-50. The "Enterright" was a device sold by the Eureka Novelty Company of Richmond, Indiana. Attached to the U-joint of a Victrola, it afforded the user more precise needle placement on the record without having to handle the soundbox. *Courtesy of the Scott and Denise Corbett collection.* (Value code: F)

3-52. Three peculiarly designed soundboxes. Clockwise from the left, the "Ideal" with its square diaphragm defied conventional wisdom. The hexagonal design of the "Burnham" soundbox, manufactured by Fletcher, appeared innovative, but the diaphragm was the usual circular shape. This soundbox was distinguished by the unusual position of the thumbscrew in the needle chuck. The "Orotund Sound Reproducer" took from Latin the words for "mouth" and "round," meaning "clear voice." Its unusual characteristic was the placement of the needle bar *behind* the diaphragm, thus protecting it from accident. *Courtesy of Terry Paul Baer.* (Value code: G)

3-51. During the 'teens, J. H. Ellis of Milwaukee, Wisconsin produced a series of aftermarket soundboxes to fit Victor, Columbia and other talking machines. The primary design element was the "bridge" which attached the needle bar to the diaphragm. The diaphragm on the left appears to be celluloid, while others, such as the one on the right, were fibre. *Courtesy of Terry Paul Baer.* (Value code: F)

5-53. At the top, another hexagonal soundbox made by the Fletcher-Wickes Company of Chicago, this one with its original box. Below, the "Resurrectone," made by the Hoffay Talking Machine Company of New York City, had an ominous-looking structure which supported the needle bar. A 1918 advertisement asserted: "In the 'RESURRECTONE,' the diaphragm is vibrated by a 'tuning-fork' working on both sides, the resiliency of the two arms being automatically 'taken up,' accuracy of vibration and 'naturalness' of sound being therefore accomplished facts." If the customer were not already put off by the macabre name, this nonsense surely would have sent him packing! *Courtesy of the Scott and Denise Corbett collection.* (Value code: G)

3-54. During the "Orthophonic" era, a great many soundboxes employed stamped aluminum diaphragms copied more or less from Victor's model. This box of unused diaphragms to fit Victor "Orthophonic" soundboxes displays the "spider" which transferred sound vibrations from the needle bar to the diaphragm. This was a revival of a theory espoused by Gianni Bettini in the 1890s which stated that sound reproduction could be improved by accessing various sectors of a diaphragm. *Courtesy of Todd Emery.* (Value code: F, box)

3-56. Due to the support of the Pathé company, the vertical cut record was extremely popular in France a decade before it reached its American zenith in the 'teens. The American rage for "adapter" attachments which allowed customers to switch between lateral and vertical record systems found its wellspring in France. Shown are two very different adapters related to Pathé. On the left, the "Universal" slips into the tone arm of a Pathé vertical cut talking machine. It was articulated so that it could play either vertical discs with a sapphire stylus or lateral discs with an ordinary steel needle. On the right is Pathé's own attachment to replace the "Exhibition" soundbox of a Victor (lateral) talking machine. This adapter *substituted* the Pathé vertical system and, unlike the "Universal," could not play both types of disc record. (Value code: F)

3-55. The "Del Monte" Radio Phonograph Adapter was a device for amplifying a battery radio set through an existing talking machine tonearm and horn. The "Del Monte" attachment, holding a radio earphone, was substituted for the soundbox, making the radio audible to more than one person. *Courtesy of Martin F. Bryan.* (Value code: F)

3-57. The Jewel Phonoparts Company of Chicago made a wide variety of attachments to adapt talking machines of the 'teens. This particular model allows Pathé, Edison and other vertical-cut records to be played on the Victor. (Value code: E)

3-58. The first version of the "Kent Attachment" (manufactured by F.C. Kent & Company, Newark, New Jersey), which was meant to use a Victor "Exhibition" soundbox. Generations of collectors have found these articulated arms and thought them incomplete. As the box shows, no soundbox was supplied with the first of the "Kent Attachments." (Value code: F)

3-59. After Victor discouraged Kent from borrowing "Exhibition" soundboxes for use with Kent attachments, a more complete unit was introduced. Thereafter Kent utilized its own soundboxes on its devices. *Courtesy of Todd Emery.* (Value code: F)

3-60. Another "KenTone" attachment, this time employing a ball-joint. *Courtesy of Alan H. Mueller.* (Value code: F)

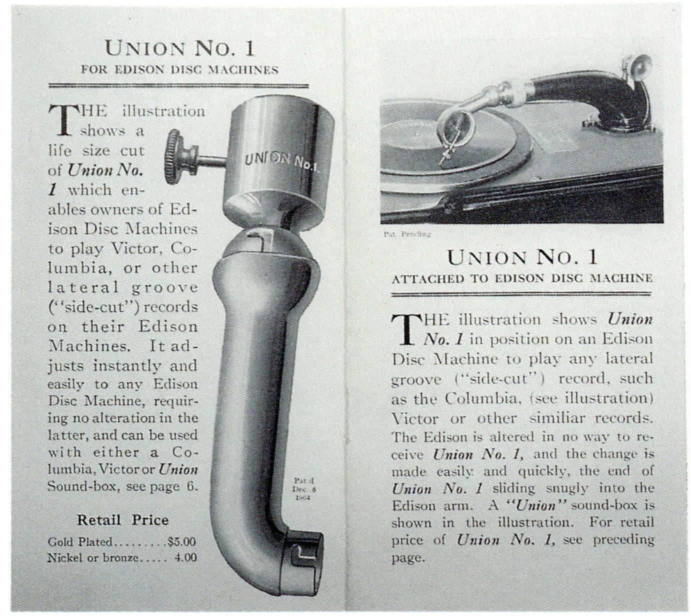

UNION NO. 1
FOR EDISON DISC MACHINES

THE illustration shows a life size cut of *Union No. 1* which enables owners of Edison Disc Machines to play Victor, Columbia, or other lateral groove ("side-cut") records on their Edison Machines. It adjusts instantly and easily to any Edison Disc Machine, requiring no alteration in the latter, and can be used with either a Columbia, Victor or *Union* Sound-box, see page 6.

Retail Price

Gold Plated.........$5.00
Nickel or bronze..... 4.00

Pat'd Dec. 8 1914

Pat. Pending

UNION NO. 1
ATTACHED TO EDISON DISC MACHINE

THE illustration shows *Union No. 1* in position on an Edison Disc Machine to play any lateral groove ("side-cut") record, such as the Columbia, (see illustration) Victor or other similiar records. The Edison is altered in no way to receive *Union No. 1*, and the change is made easily and quickly, the end of *Union No. 1* sliding snugly into the Edison arm. A *"Union"* sound-box is shown in the illustration. For retail price of *Union No. 1*, see preceding page.

3-61. The "Union No. 1" attachment for adapting Edison "Diamond Disc" Phonographs to play 78s relied upon the Victor "Exhibition" soundbox to make it functional. It was one of several such attachments which required the user to purchase an "Exhibition," a practice soon brought to an end by the Victor Talking Machine Company (which for many years maintained a policy of forbidding the use of Victor components with other talking machine devices). The thumb screw on the attachment controlled a volume shutter within the tube. Manufactured in 1913–1914 by the Union Specialty and Plating Company, Cleveland, Ohio. *Courtesy of Alan H. Mueller.*

3-63. The "Rapid Repeater," manufactured by the Rapid Repeater Company of Long Island City, New York, was one of many devices which reduced the need to attend to the talking machine. A wide variety of repeaters were offered, of which this was one of the more substantial. *Courtesy of Charles McCarn.* (Value code: F)

3-62. If the "Union" was one of the more economically-designed 78 attachments for the Edison "Diamond Disc" Phonograph, this device surely must have been one of the most flamboyant. The attachment itself was unmarked, and certainly would have evoked Victor's displeasure by employing the "Exhibition" soundbox. *Courtesy of Norm and Janyne Smith.* (Value code: E)

3-64. The "Geer Repeater" was manufactured by the Walbert Manufacturing Company of Chicago. It was a "race return" type of repeater in that the soundbox needle followed a formed groove to return it to the beginning of the selection. This one is shown inverted to display the green felt pads which allow it to noiselessly skate over the surface of the record as it played. *Courtesy of Norm and Janyne Smith.* (Value code: G)

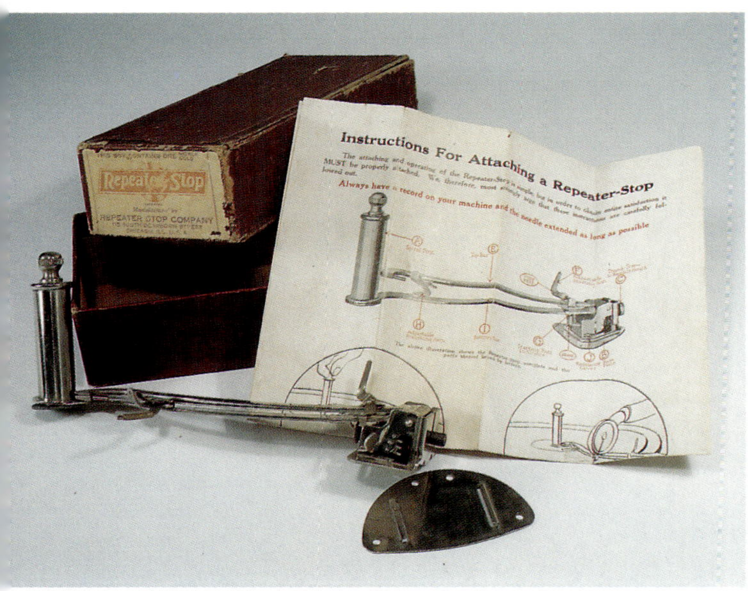


3-65. The "Repeater-Stop," manufactured in Chicago under patents awarded between 1913-1919, combined two of the era's most popular talking machine gadgets. The record repeated indefinitely or for a preset number of plays; afterward the turntable was stopped. *Courtesy of Todd Emery.* (Value code: E)

3-66. An exposed version of the vertical screw principle used in the "Repeater-Stop" was employed by the "Record Repeater," manufactured by Webster Novelty Company, Chicago, and distributed by C.H.J. Marr of the same city. *Courtesy of the Scott and Denise Corbett collection.* (Value code: E)

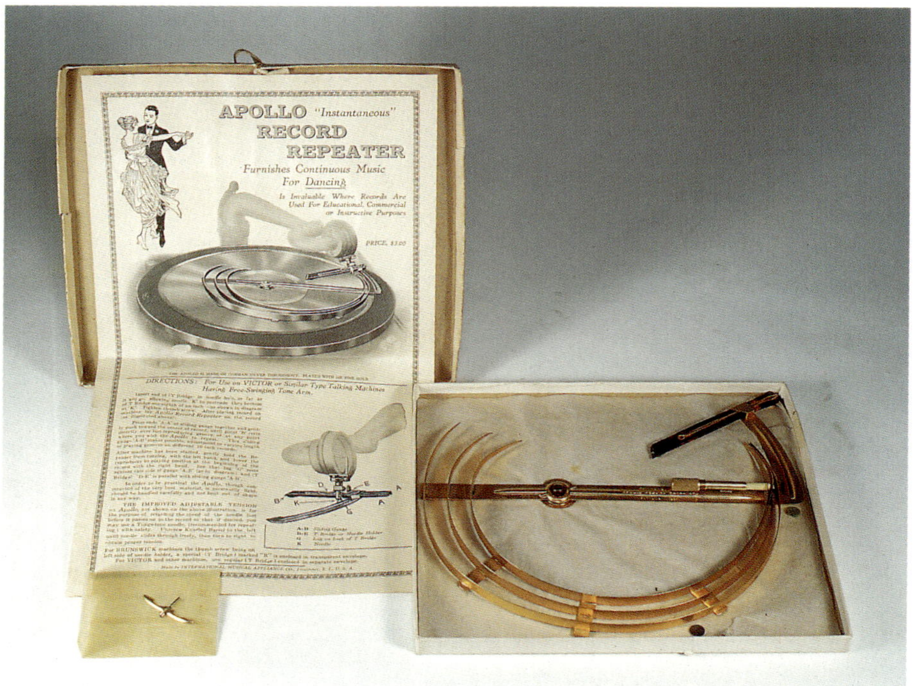


3-67. The "Apollo 'Instantaneous' Record Repeater" was a more intricately-designed mechanism than most "race-return" models. Patented in 1917 and 1920, it was manufactured by the International Musical Appliance Company of Providence, Rhode Island, and sold for $3.00. (Value code: F)

3-68. The "Phonometer," manufactured by The Phonographic Music Company of Brooklyn, New York, was a centrifugal speed indicator. It sold for $1.00. An advertisement in the June 1907 *Talking Machine World* extolled it as follows: "…By its use each and every record can be reproduced at the correct speed, and all musical records (vocal or instrumental) *reproduced in the same musical key (or pitch)* that the artists originally sang or played the selections [sic]." *Courtesy of Alan H. Mueller.* (Value code: F)

3-69. This centrifugal-type of disc speed indicator was marketed under names like "Tru-Timer" and "Lakeside Rotometer" (advertised in 1918). This device was placed over the spindle and sat on the turntable as it revolved. When the point of the indicator aligned with the "finger" on the post above the spindle, the speed was 78 rpm. *Courtesy of the Scott and Denise Corbett collection.* (Value code: G)

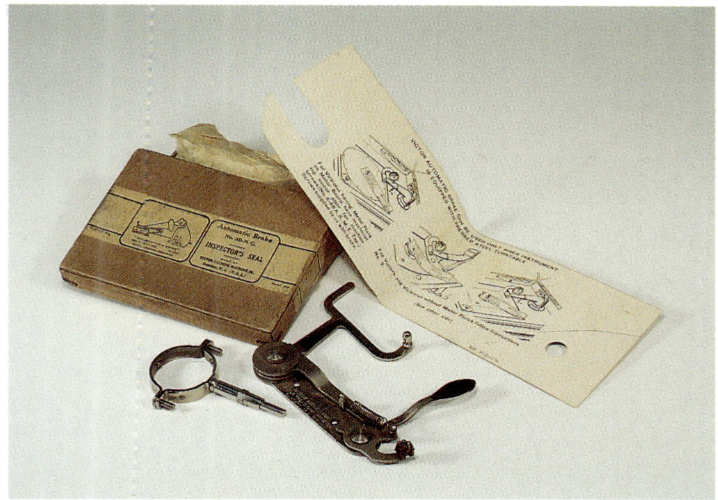

3-71. The Victor Talking Machine Company sold its own "Automatic Brake," identical to that fitted to its Victrolas of the late 'teens and twenties. This device could be appended to its earlier models, which lacked such a feature. *Courtesy of Todd Emery.* (Value code: G)

3-70. Automatic stops for disc talking machines were sold in a wide variety of styles. This one mounted to a Victor external-horn machine and was tripped by the tone arm as it reached the end of the selection. (Value code: F)

3-72. The Condon-Autostop was designed to fit Victors or Victrolas. Although it included lengthy instructions, the modification to the existing machine was not complicated.

3-73. The Condon-Autostop was available in either nickel or gold (here shown in the original carton). (Value code: E)

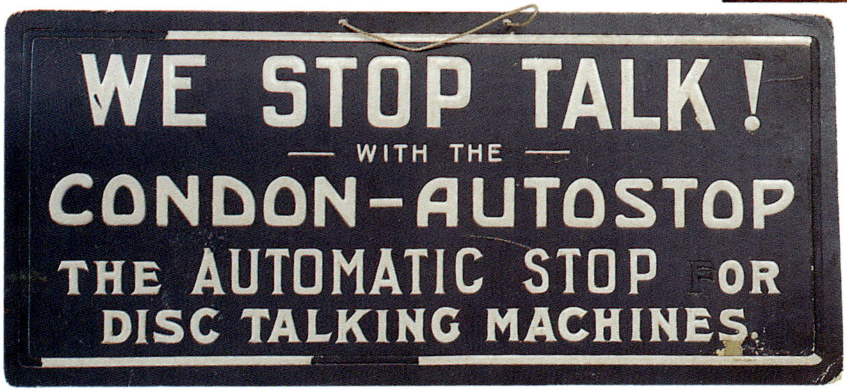


3-74. This cardboard store placard, measuring 7" x 15", advertised the Condon-Autostop. The company also offered a product called the "NOSET Automatic Start and Stop," advertised in the July 4, 1917 issue of the *Phonograph* as follows: "It starts itself. It stops itself. It sells itself—and it sells machines... $3.50." *Courtesy of the Charles Hummel collections.*

3-75. This volume control fit between the rubber backing and body of a Victor "Exhibition" soundbox. Turning the knurled knob regulated the flow of sound. (Value code: F)

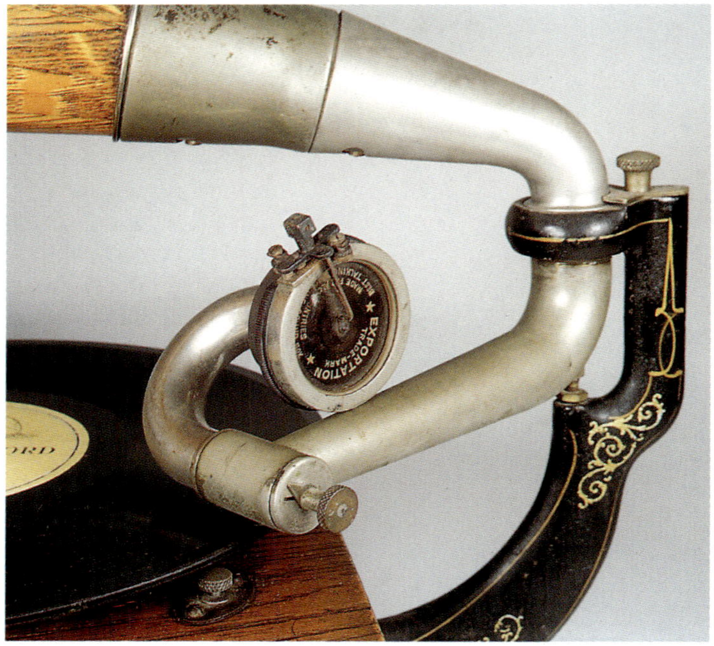


3-76. The Tone Regulator Company of Chicago, Illinois, sold a $3.00 device for disc talking machines to modify the sound. As described in the September 1905 *Talking Machine World:* "With this Tone Regulator one can change the tone of a talking machine from very loud to very soft by simply turning the thumb screw… With the Tone Regulator one can give expression to the selection, thus doing away with the *monotony* of the record." The suggestion that the operator might wish to manipulate the thumbscrew throughout the selection in order to "give expression" was a bit far-fetched. The "Tone Regulator" included a face plate (not shown) to enclose the front of the soundbox, thus reducing extraneous sound. *Courtesy of the Scott and Denise Corbett Collection.* (Value code: F)

3-77. Face-plates like this were offered by various companies to reduce sound lost from the front of the diaphragm. Later, this principle would be incorporated into the designs of certain specialty soundboxes. *Courtesy of Michael F. Khanchalian.* (Value code: G)

3-78. The "Harmony Sound Controller," here shown on a record sleeve, had adjustable vents to modify the volume of external-horn talking machines. *Courtesy of Bob and Karyn Sitter.*

3-79. "THE THOMPSON MODIFIER is entirely new and different from anything on the market. The best machine in the world is improved by its use, the poorest sounds well with its help. Made pear shape, it fits any size or shaped horn and can be used with any machine on the market." So stated an advertisement in the April 1906 *Talking Machine World.* It cost $1.00 and was manufactured by the Graphophone Modifier Company of Chicago. *Courtesy of Bob and Karyn Sitter.* (Value code: E)

3-80. This sound-modifying device, the "Morse Clarifier," which sold for $1.00, was manufactured by Morse Brothers of Minneapolis, Minnesota, to fit most types of disc talking machine, and all cylinder models. The January 1911 issue of the *Talking Machine World* stated: "A remarkable little device made to fit…between reproducer and horn of phonographs. It renders the sound loud, clear and lifelike, and eliminates that unpleasant metallic effect…" In actuality, this bundle of coated paper tubes probably did little to affect the sound other than diminish it. (See illustration 2-56) (Value code: F)

3-81. On the left: The "Bakertone." The pin at the top was inserted in the soundbox needle chuck, and the needle secured in the chuck below. Depending on where one positioned the weighted cylinder, the reproduction was variably constricted (and the record was undoubtedly the loser!). In the center, the "Junior" tone regulator. An advertisement by the Rudolph Wurlitzer Company in the October 1906 *Talking Machine World* offered this device for $1.00 and described it as follows: "The Tone Regulator does away with the soft tone needle. The volume of tone can be reduced without impairing the quality of same, thus enabling one to hear the loudest band piece in a very small room." This device was also used in conjunction with a soundbox face plate. On the right, "Attachment No. 3" by the prodigious F.C. Kent & Company of Newark, New Jersey. Kent is most remembered for its attachments to play 78s on Edison "Diamond Disc" Phonographs, however, this rarely-seen model performed the opposite service. *Courtesy of Todd Emery.* (Value code: G, F, E)

3-82. The "Deflex-O-Graph," like the "Bakertone," was a secondary needle chuck which functioned on a principle of variable interference. When positioned diagonally to the soundbox diaphragm, much of the sound from the record was lost, and reproduction affected. *Courtesy of the Scott and Denise Corbett collection.* (Value code: G)

3-83. An Edison "Diamond Disc" reproducer in its original wooden container. Edison's first Disc Phonograph models, introduced in 1912, did not employ a volume control. The company soon added a felt ball on a plunger within the horn to vary loudness, however, companies continued to make volume-controlling attachments to fit the Edison machines. In this case, the reproducer itself has been modified, using a felt "damper" within the neck. *Courtesy of Todd Emery.* (Value code: E)

3-84. The Rowland Sound Regulator was incredibly simple. The upper portion screwed into the U-joint of a Victrola. As the angled cork was rotated, it varied the size of the sound passage, acting as a volume control. The bottom piece was merely a cover to protect the fragile cork when not in use. *Courtesy of the collection of Howard Hazelcorn.* (Value code: F)

3-85. The Jones "Motrola" was a device intended to automatically maintain the tension of a spring-driven talking machine. It ran on house current and, once attached to the winding-shaft of the machine, no longer required attention. It was invented by a well-known, if not infamous, character of the early days of the talking machine. Joseph W. Jones once worked in Emile Berliner's organization, and later was granted a patent on an integral method for disc record manufacture. The "Jones Patent," as assigned to the Columbia Phonograph Company, proved the bane of many small disc producers. (Value code: E)

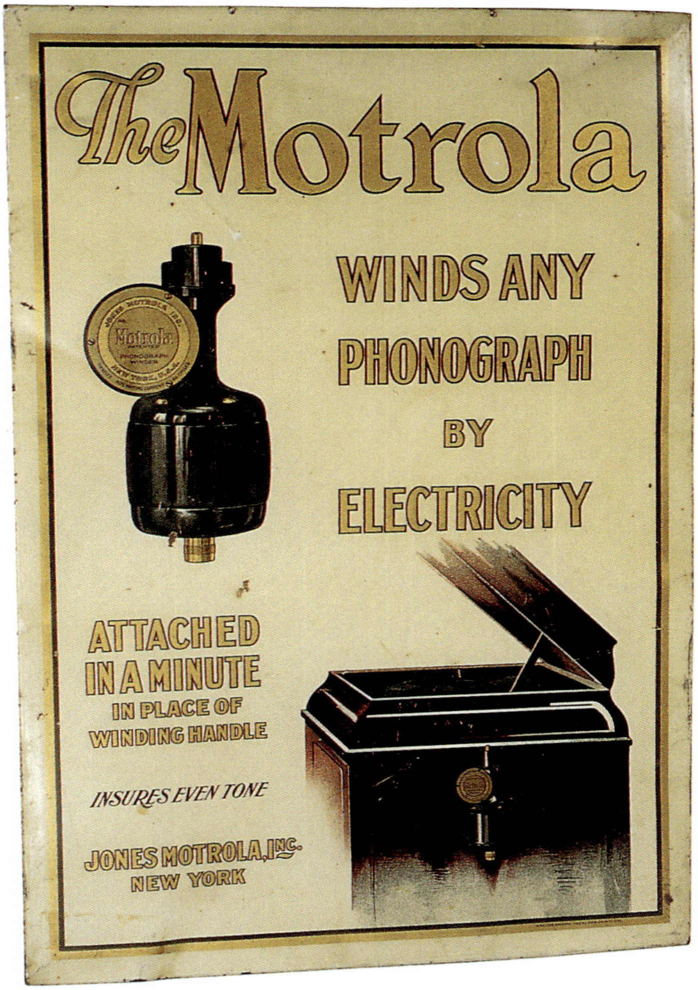


3-86. A vivid metal sign advertising the "Jones Motrola," measuring 9" x 13". An advertisement in the July 11, 1917 issue of the *Phonograph* appealed to dealers: "It makes your store pleasanter—more inviting, more up to date, with the drudgery and irritation of winding, winding, winding abolished." *Courtesy of the Charles Hummel collections.*

3-87. The Record-Lite Company of Milwaukee, Wisconsin, manufactured this battery-operated lamp to illuminate the interiors of Victrolas. It slipped on the tone arm and focused its beam on the record. (Value code: G)

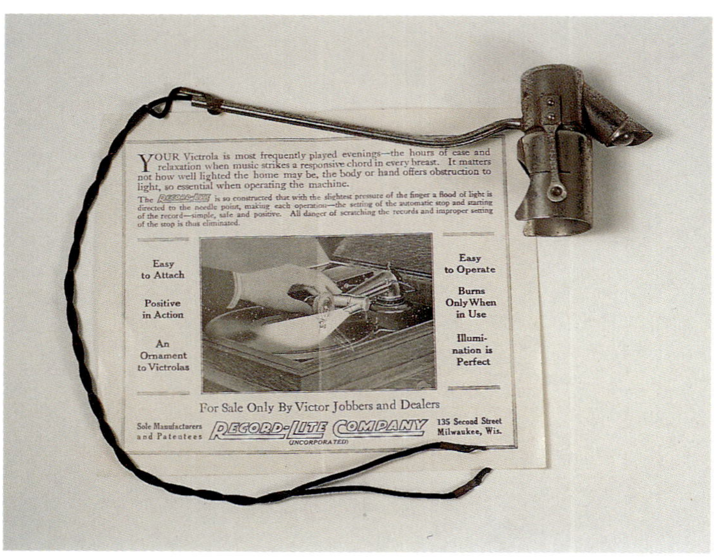

3-88. Hawthorne and Sheble manufactured a huge number of inexpensive "front-mounted" disc talking machines between 1906 and 1909. These were sold under various brands such as "Star," "True Tone," "Imperial," "Aretino," "Harmony" and "Busy Bee." These machines were designed with long, attenuated flower horns which were disproportionately large compared to their modest wooden cabinets (and lightweight motors). The original owners of these instruments very soon must have discovered what most collectors know today: the big horn tended to make the machine pitch forward and topple over! Illustrated is a little device known colloquially as the "no-tip foot." It attached by one simple screw to the horn support arm of an H & S disc talking machine (shown here on a "Busy Bee") to prevent accidents. (Value code: G)

3-89. A record spindle adapter of 1908 rather like the ones which would be used forty years later to allow 45 rpm records to play on a conventional hi-fi. This early adapter was distributed by Chicago talking machine entrepreneur Arthur J. O'Neill to make his "Aretino Record" with its 3" center hole compatible with Victor, Columbia or Zonophone talking machines. The additional rectangular hole further extended the use of this adapter to O'Neill's own "Busy Bee" machines, which boasted an additional lug on its turntable. When O'Neill designed the "Busy Bee" he had not anticipated the "Aretino," hence the need to adapt his own machine. The date stamped on the surface refers to O'Neill's patent No.874,985. (Value code: F)

3-90. An unusual Victor horn elbow from the pre-1909 period incorporating a "quick-release" feature which was not widely adopted. Most Victor elbows of this period used a "bayonet" fitting, which could occasionally prove troublesome either by allowing the horn to accidentally de-mount, or by refusing to disconnect. *Courtesy of Norm and Janyne Smith.*(Value code: E)

3-92. A box containing a Victor mainspring, featuring the famous Victor "His Master's Voice" trademark. (Value code: G)

3-91. An original counter display containing "His Master's Voice" spring lubricant. 5 1/2" square. *Courtesy of Bob and Karyn Sitter.* (Value code: D)

3-93. Brunswick items: a bottle of Brunswick "Phonograph Oil," and a Brunswick needle tin. (Value code: G)

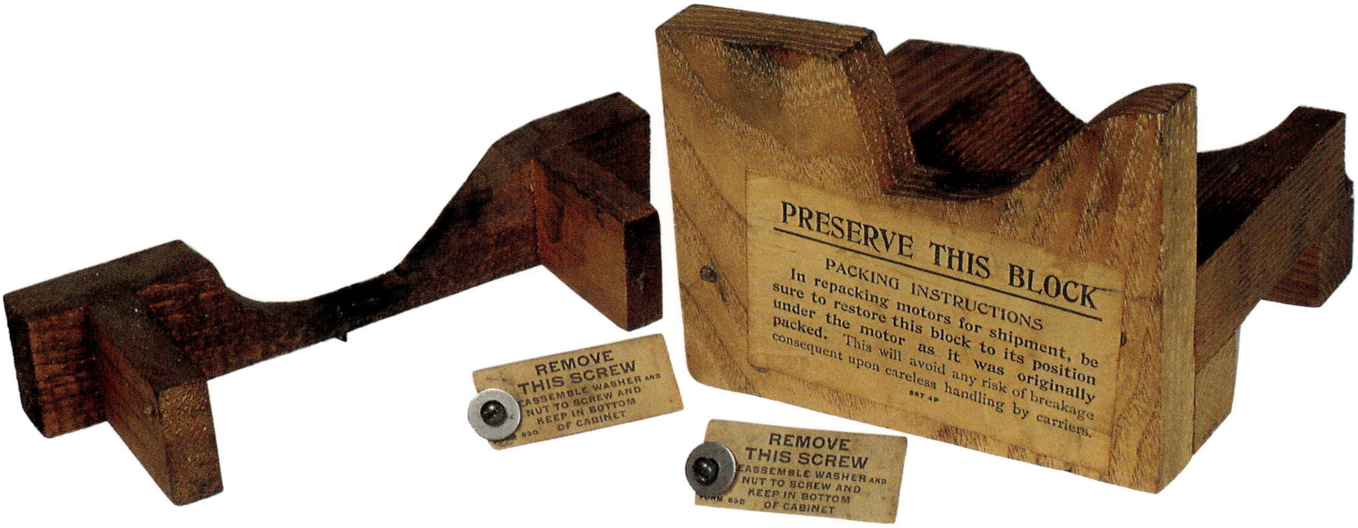


3-94. Three types of packing items which are seldom found. On the left, a support block designed to cradle the spring barrel of an "AJ" Disc Graphophone. In the center, two screws, washers and nuts with instructive tags which were meant to be removed from the top plate of an Edison Amberola "VIII" cylinder phonograph after delivery. On the right, a spring barrel support cradle from a Victor "V," which also instructed the owner to retain it for future use. (Value code: H, H, G)

3-95. Many Victor-Victrolas were sold with a boxed "Victrola Outfit" containing everything the purchaser needed to begin enjoying his talking machine. (Value code: F)

3-96. The "Echo" Disc of the late 1920s, sold by the Plaza Music Company of New York City, was one of a number of "instantaneous" recording discs. The user reversed the usual process of reproduction in his Victrola, thereby creating a home recording without a special attachment. The 6" metal disc is shown with its original sleeve. *Courtesy of Alan H. Mueller.* (Value code: H)

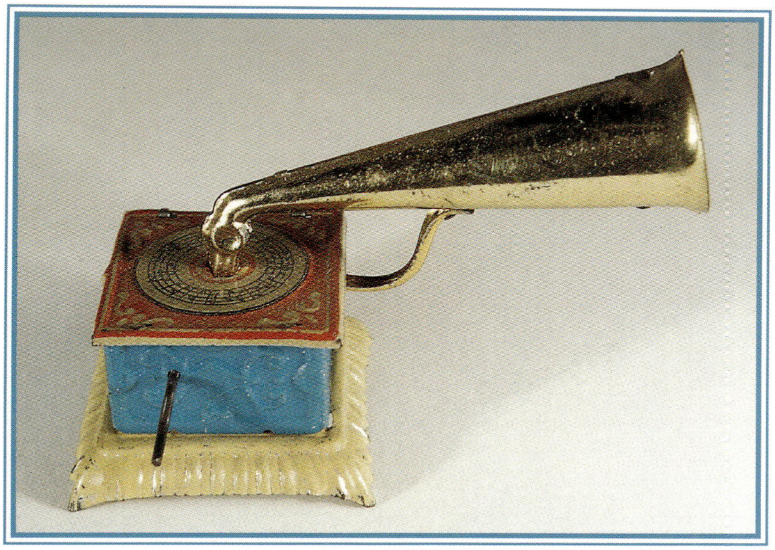

3-98. The box of the "Siam Soo" talking machine toy, manufactured by Converse. The Columbia Graphophone Company handled the marketing of these devices, and the box included plenty of promotional material for the Grafonola. *Courtesy of Norm and Janyne Smith.*

3-97. A so-called "Penny Toy" in the form of a talking machine. Advertisements of the period claimed that this 3 1/2" long lacquered tin toy played music. In actuality, turning the crank plucked a few crudely-tuned teeth inside the body. *Courtesy of Steve and Ellie Saccente.* (Value code: D)

3-99. "Siam Soo" sinuously shimmies in this time exposure. Probably the most elaborate talking machine toy in regular production, "Siam Soo" performed several simultaneous movements. Her head moved from side to side while her torso twisted horizontally and bounced vertically. "Siam Soo's" arms, hinged at the shoulders and elbows, moved up and down during her dance. Made by Morton E. Converse & Son Company of Winchendon, Massachusetts, the doll was first manufactured in 1921. The Columbia Graphophone Company arranged for exclusive distribution of "Siam Soo," and even released a record of the same title. Perhaps the lyrics said it best:

*In Siam, where strange things they do,*
*There lived a girl named Siam Soo,*
*Who shook a wicked shoulder when she danced.*
*She had the cutest jiggle,*
*And when she'd start to wiggle,*
*She'd put the men around her in a trance...*

The doll stands 11 1/2" tall. (Value code: B)

3-100. A British talking machine toy featuring a russet-haired imp, one of "Picketts Phono Figures," circa 1915. The doll is 7" tall. *Courtesy of the collection of Howard Hazelcorn.* (Value code: D)

3-101. The "Phonograph Follies" sold by the prodigious National Company of Boston in the late 'teens. Included are articulated figures representing various comic stereotypes and an undeniable caricature of Charlie Chaplin. *Courtesy of the Collection of Howard Hazelcorn.* (Value code: D)

3-102. "Dancing Sam The Famous Dancer" manufactured by the company of the same name in Cleveland, Ohio. Although it bears a strong resemblance to National's "Rastus," the mechanism was simpler and cheaper. *Courtesy of the Scott and Denise Corbett collection.* (Value code: D)

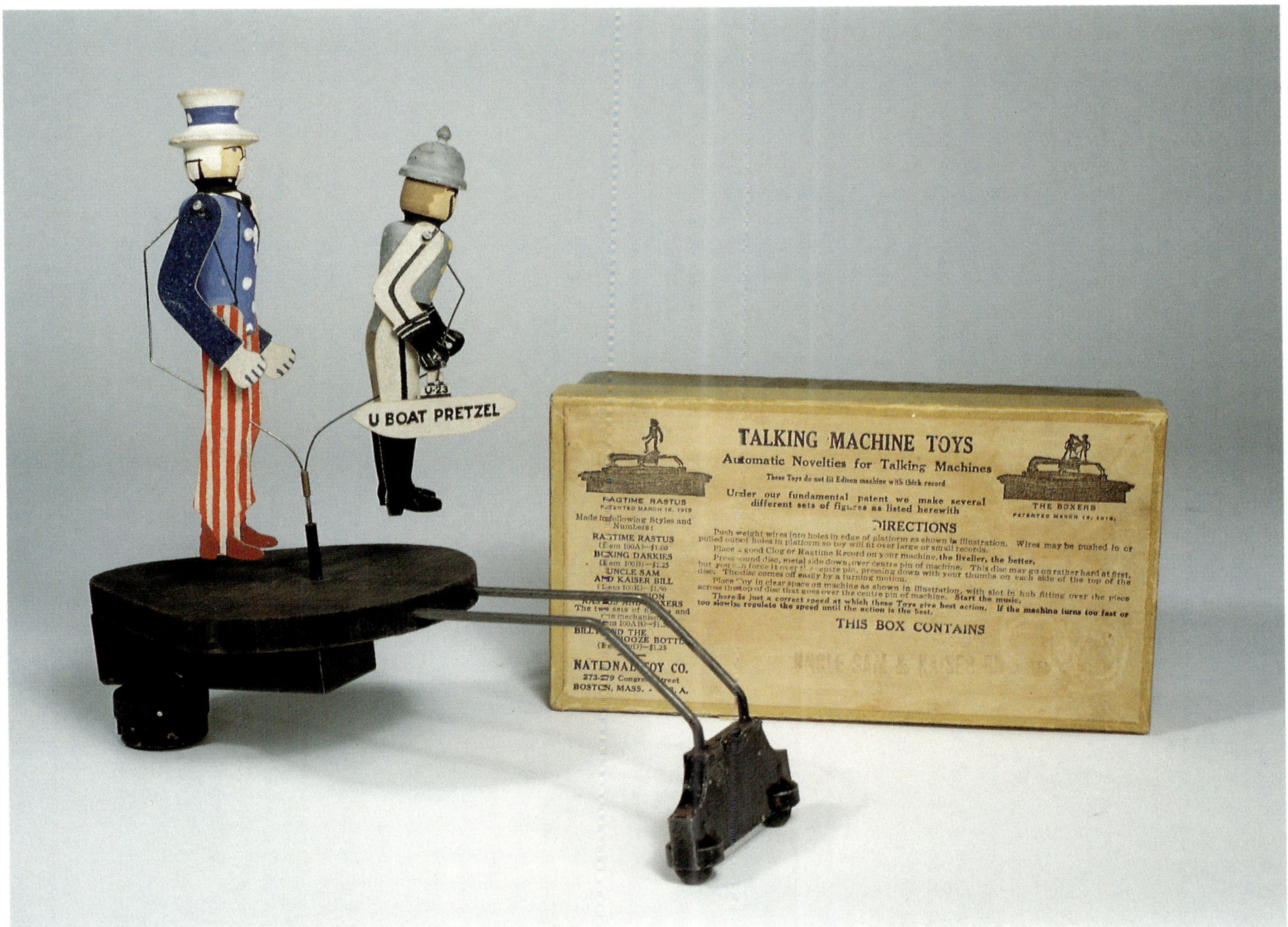


3-103. National's topical contribution to the World War I effort. Uncle Sam kicks the hapless Kaiser of Germany as the record plays. (Value code: C)

3-104. National's "Fighting Cocks" must have been one of the firm's least popular toys judging by its rarity today. (Value code: D)

## Ingenuity Sparkles in Philadelphia

Two vigorous talking machine firms sprang from the busy streets of Philadelphia in succession. As one grew strong, the other died, exhausted. It is tempting to imagine that they were in some way related by more than coincidence. An examination of their respective *oeuvres* suggests parallels in both development and design. However, beyond the notion that the recently unemployed workers of the first may have helped staff the second, there is indeed a "missing link" which united the two. This connection, largely unexplored, is the subject of this discussion.

## Hawthorne & Sheble: Entrepreneurs

First came Hawthorne & Sheble. Ellsworth A. Hawthorne (see sidebar) and Horace Sheble joined to create the Standard Typewriter Exchange in Philadelphia, which they began operating in 1895. Pioneers in the talking machine field such as Jesse Lippincott of the North American Phonograph Company (active 1888-1894) had envisioned an age in which their instruments would abet dictation and perhaps even supplant the typewriter for correspondence in business offices. It was a natural extension of selling typewriters that Hawthorne & Sheble should become the "sole dealers" of "Edison's Latest Phonograph" in Philadelphia.

Soon it was evident, however, that the talking machine as a mechanical secretary would never match the phenomenal strength of the home amusement market, and clever young fellows like Mr. H and Mr. S abandoned commercial functions in favor of popular entertainment. By 1898, the partners were occupying talking machine salesrooms at 604-606 Chestnut Street. Some blocks away, at No.1032 Chestnut, was the Columbia Phonograph Company's store. Nearby, on Filbert Street, the Berliner Gramophone was sold.

Hawthorne & Sheble's company thrived on its founders' energy and ingenuity. With highly stimulating advertising it began to offer a wide variety of inventive talking machine products. The conservative standards which the Edison company demanded of dealers in Edison Phonographs were soon eclipsed by Hawthorne & Sheble's innovative marketing and pricing policies. Edison withdrew its support and put H & S on the "black list." This little company, however, had big ideas for promoting its own gadgets and paraphernalia, as well as for supporting the efforts of other refugees from Edison's wrath such as Edwin H. Mobley (sued for offering "improved" adaptations of Edison reproducers).

Fanciful attachments such as the "Dupliphone" (illustration 2-30) and stylish talking machine cabinets with glazed lids (illustration 4-4) brightened and enhanced the home amusement market. H & S also pursued the amplifying horn business with considerable success, first with "straight" or traditionally-belled horns of all sizes and lengths; then with paneled or "flower" horns in an equally broad range of sizes (and colors). Both types of horn could be purchased with Hawthorne & Sheble's "signature" styling—"silk finish" cloth applied to the exterior.

## Success and...

By 1903, H & S had opened a factory at Oxford and Mascher in Philadelphia. In the following years, the company would support several manufacturing locations including a plant in Bridgeport, Connecticut and a related disc record factory in Springfield, Massachusetts. The peripatetic Mr. Hawthorne changed residences often, and his company juggled its principals in a similar fashion. After the firm became the Hawthorne & Sheble *Manufacturing* Company in 1903 and then incorporated, the position of corporate secretary was held first by Mr. Sheble, next by E. Manley, next by Charles W. Noyes and finally by Theo F. Bental. The Hawthorne & Sheble company was growing and evolving.

The firm was at the peak of vitality when 1908 dawned. Unfortunately, the culmination of patent litigation during the next year and a half would so crush H & S that not a trace of its products nor proprietors would be left when Boyd's (Philadelphia) Business Directory for 1910 appeared. Mr. H and Mr. S and their hard-won success would be washed away before the irresistible wave of Victor Talking Machine Company patents under which the Hawthorne and Sheble Manufacturing Company was litigated.

## Death and Transfiguration

It was at this portentous moment, as one independent stumbled, that another of equal color shot forward under the name of "Keen." The (David, Jacob and Morris) Keen family moniker had first appeared in the Philadelphia music market in the early 1890s. David Keen had been involved with the Edison Phonograph during this early period, and it had whetted his appetite for the talking machine business. In 1900, he purchased 50,000 Gramophone discs from the failing Berliner Gramophone Company. This got him into a brouhaha with the Universal Talking Machine Company (Zonophone). Universal claimed that it owned the rights to these records through a connection with Frank Seaman (Seaman's National Gramophone Company had been Berliner's distributor), and the case dragged through the courts at a snail's pace.

In 1905, Morris Keen began operating the Keen Talking Machine Company in three Philadelphia locations: 156 N. 8th, 230 N. 9th and 1114 Columbia Avenue (Morris Keen's residence). The following year, David Keen opened a similar-sounding shop, the Keen Company, in a another location on N. 8th Street. Without any mention of Morris' prior effort, David told the *Talking Machine World*, "We...have found business very satisfactory. We handle Edison, Victor and Zonophone goods [though the Zonophone suit was still pending!]."

Behind the scenes, the Keens had joined forces with members of another Philadelphia business family, the Futernicks (also spelled "Futernik"). The Keen name, split by the competing phonograph emporiums of Morris and David, would fracture further when the Futernicks broke away, taking the Keen family name with them. Benjamin and Berwick Futernick continued in the talking machine business as the Keen Company, Incorporated, though no Keens were present. Immediately, Morris launched the Keen *Phonograph* Company, Incorporated, nearly exhausting the possible variants of nomenclature!

## Too Many Keens

By 1909 the Keen situation became even more complex when Jacob Keen entered the fray at Keen's Victor and Edison Company, located not far from the Futernicks' store. One is reminded of the pizza wars of modern New York City in which Ron's Pizza might spawn Famous Ron's, World Famous Ron's, Famous Original Ron's and so on. The confusing efforts to exploit the well-recognized Keen name made an understatement of David's boast (to *Talking Machine World*) that, "I started several men in business who are now conducting successful salesrooms."

In 1909, the most influential of the diverse Keen ventures would appear under the name "Keen-O-Phone." With Morris Keen as its head, the Keen-O-Phone Company—operating concurrently with the his Keen Phonograph Company at a different location—began by selling musical instruments, and evolved into a manufacturer of unusual talking machines. Morris Keen had already tested the market for eccentric technology. In 1907, his Keen *Phonograph* Company had briefly offered a "tone arm" attachment with flower horn which clamped to the back of a conventional cylinder talking machine and redirected the sound. The claim that it "softened the reproductions" was no doubt another understatement. Keen's gadget routed the sound through such an indirect path that a great deal of volume *and quality* must have been lost along the way!

Morris' *new* firm, the Keen-O-Phone Company, would jump into the field of innovation with both feet, but only after it emerged from the competitive turmoil which occurred 1909-1910. During this period, the disparate Keen and *faux*-Keen factions reached the apex of their conflict, after which only Morris Keen would be left at the head of a music firm bearing his family name. The only survivor was the Keen-O-Phone Company, *Incorporated*, of 136 S. 4th Street. This at last was the manufacturer of fanciful disc talking machines. By 1911 a factory was operating on Orthodox Street, in an industrial area of Philadelphia along Frankford creek. As the firm evolved, the company personnel changed often, and the salesrooms eventually moved to 227 S. Broad Street, not too far from Victor's outlet.

## Missing Link

The Hawthorne & Sheble organization had already demonstrated how remarkable ingenuity could be brought before the public eye. That firm had virtually purred with novel ideas and the clever patents of Mr. Sheble, sometime corporate secretary Charles W. Noyes and a very resourceful gentleman named Thomas Kraemer.

Kraemer held a long string of patents which were assigned to H & S. Some, such as the "Yielding Pressure Feed" (a pseudo-mechanical feed device), were incorporated into products manufactured by the company. Others remained theoretical, including a couple of soundboxes adaptable to both vertical and lateral cut disc records. These soundboxes had significance even though Hawthorne & Sheble never produced machines or records for the yet undeveloped American vertical cut market (unlike France, where Pathé Frères was a major manufacturer). Thomas Kraemer's work with the vertical cut system would point directly to Keen-O-Phone, which *would* produce vertically-recorded discs. This was the first suggestion of a relationship between Hawthorne & Sheble and Keen-O-Phone.

The "Keen-O-Phone" machines of 1911 were the first manufactured in the United States to have an "adaptable" soundbox such as Kraemer had envisioned several years earlier. As the 'teens progressed, there would be a great surge of vertical cut activity in America. One might say it was initiated by Morris Keen whose "Keen-O-Phone" vertical record "laboratory" would later become the Rex Talking Machine Corporation, one of the first ripples in the vertical cut wave.

Thomas Kraemer's work at H & S had foreshadowed the developments at Keen-O-Phone in more ways than one. Kraemer's patent for a mechanical-feed talking machine was issued August 23, 1910 (No.968,483). It was nominally assigned to Hawthorne & Sheble, like Kraemer's previous patents. However, H & S was by now defunct, and here was a disc talking machine design which could truly deflect the heavy ammunition of Victor's legal department (the most dangerous of which was the so-called "Berliner patent," No.534,543, governing the passage of the soundbox across the record).

Here was an opportunity too good to waste. Indeed, a talking machine based on Thomas Kraemer's mechanical feed design soon would be introduced—by Keen-O-Phone. His mechanism appeared in "Keen-O-Phones" made during 1911 (the "Berliner patent" officially expired in early 1912). Coupled with Morris Keen's peculiar "spiral" tone arm (Patent No.907,814, December 29, 1908), Kraemer's genius invested the "Keen-O-Phone" with the same slightly bizarre brilliance which had characterized H & S products. Thomas Kraemer had found a new benefactor.

It was Kraemer, who was once again left standing when the dust settled after Keen-O-Phone's eventual demise. He would be put in charge of the Orthodox Street factory which the Rex Corporation (formed to continue production of vertical records and to introduce an inexpensive table model marketed as "The King of Entertainers") would inherit in 1914. But this is letting the story get ahead of itself.

## Keen-O-Phone, Quality in Search of a Market

"Keen-O-Phones" combined many clever contrivances, not the least of which was the Pooley automatic record filing system which was installed in a number of models. Contemporary advertising revealed it was the well-qualified Pooley Furniture Company, also of Philadelphia, which constructed the Keen-O-Phone Company's cabinets. Pooley also was doing the wood work for certain Edison models, and producing various automatic disc record cabinets under its own name.

Keen-O-Phone offered a solid line of well-constructed and technically advanced machines. It shrugged off a rather half-hearted bit of patent-rattling by Victor in September 1912. This should have left the field wide open, but despite the efforts of sales specialists E.P.H. Allen and Emil Bauer the company failed to find adequate distribution. 1913 was the make-it-or-break-it year. Keen-O-Phone, equipped with a new slate of officers (with Morris Keen merely one of the board of directors), was operating at the old S. Broad location and also at 1202 Walnut (the laboratory). The company poured everything it had into a big Christmas push. The results of this campaign did not take long to determine. By February 1914 a deal had been concluded with Rex to take over the idle Keen-O-Phone factory. The company simply ceased doing business when the Christmas season proved a bust.

## Dénouement and...

Pooley was left with literally thousands of empty Keen-O-Phone cabinets waiting to be delivered (and to be paid for). To settle this debt, Keen-O-Phone was momentarily resuscitated, and machines were completed from the stock of cabinets. Pooley was allowed to sell these (through Gimbel's department store) to recover costs. The stock was so large, however, that even though they were offered to the public at half price, some were still on hand when Pooley itself followed Keen-O-Phone into financial oblivion (Pooley's factory was sold by a receiver on October 14, 1914).

The dislodged Morris Keen moved to Atlantic City, New Jersey, and with David Keen began promoting something called the "Keen-O-Scope." Perhaps the most candid appraisal of the Keen-O-Phone affair came quite unexpectedly (and most likely unintentionally) in a June 1914 *Talking Machine World* advertisement. Emil Bauer, former field salesman, had been given the job of cleaning out (at vastly reduced prices) the last inventory of "Keen-O-Phones" on hand. His notice read, in part, "The inventor [Morris Keen], after realizing his ideal of the *world's perfect talking machine* [his emphasis], lost out because he failed to realize that 'making' is one thing and 'creating a market' another..."

Messrs. Hawthorne and Sheble are amply represented in this book by a wide variety of objects, from horns to cabinets to catalogues. The foregoing examination of their company's history, and its previously unknown connection with Morris Keen, should lend substance and humanity to their creations. Likewise, the following interview gives us a rare glimpse into the personality and accomplishments of that entrepreneurial dynamo: Ellsworth Hawthorne.

## An Interview with Davidson B. Hawthorne, Grandson of Ellsworth Hawthorne, conducted May 1986 by Timothy C. Fabrizio

*Your Grandfather's full name was?*

Ellsworth Adam Hawthorne, and he was born in Kansas City, Missouri, February 2, 1867... he married... Eliza Aldred Stewart... from the Stewart family of Philadelphia... They had five children.

*Your father was?*

Stewart Hawthorne, he was the oldest son.

*Your grandfather was living in Philadelphia when the phonograph business was taking place.*

Some of his companies [factories] were in New Jersey, some were in Philadelphia, some were in Connecticut... in Bridgeport... The factory was still standing two years ago. It had the name on the side, "Hawthorne and Sheble Company." [according to family tradition, Sheble was pronounced *SHEB-lee*.]

*Your wife said there was an unusual way that you discovered that.*

We were at an [antique] show up there and we were invited to go skeet shooting. We had a flat tire on the exit... and I looked over and I could see my grandfather's building. I had always wondered where it was in Bridgeport... The bricks had been painted over, but the overpaint had washed off.

*That's great!*

He had a lot of tough breaks in his life... His parents died in some plague and he was orphaned. My grandfather came East. He was really a self-taught person. I remember when I was a child he used to say, "I'll give you a quarter for every new word you learn."

*Do you remember him talking about phonograph business?*

He never discussed it with me because I was... a youth, very small. But I heard different things from the family... I do remember them talking about... he used to go to Europe on the steamers in the early 1900s... It seemed to me there was a lawsuit between [him and] the Victor Company. He couldn't sell... machines in the United States, but he could sell them in England. [He is referring to the aftermath of the 1909 Victor injunction.]

When I was a kid, I can remember our cellar and you know we had boxes and boxes... of the wax cylinders... hundreds of them, and we had the records [78s]. All this stuff was just thrown out eventually.

We lived on Long Island...My grandfather, he moved down there...in his later years...He went into the construction business with my father and built homes...That was the last thing he did.

*When did he die?*

He and my grandmother were killed in 1937. In the 'twenties he used to buy a lot of land in Florida, and he used to buy mortgages. In the summertime he'd go down to... St. Petersburg. There was a hot water heater in the cellar and he lit it and went up to bed, and it went out. And my father came around the next day and they were dead.

*He didn't believe in keeping the windows open?*

No...when I was a kid I used to sleep over there sometimes and I used to suffocate—mothballs!.. They thought that night air was bad for you.

*Where is your grandfather buried?*

On Long Island... West Hempstead.

*What faith was he?*

I don't think he ever went to church. We say in our family, "We didn't sin, so we don't have to go to church."

*Did he say that?*

Yes... but he wasn't an atheist.

*How do you remember him?*

To me he was a very warm man, but stern... He was always busy... He had an extensive library... He was really an active man... He always had something to keep him busy up to his last days.

3-105. The Hawthorne family after an outing circa 1898. Ellsworth slouches, his wife sits pertly, the children wiggle in their seats. Surrounding are Hawthorne-related documents and ephemera. *Materials provided by Davison B. Hawthorne.*

3-106. Keen-O-Phone produced two different external-horn models. The "IV" had a rounded mahogany cabinet of the early-'teens style, gold-plated hardware and a metal or wooden horn. Most importantly, it incorporated several peculiar features which characterized the company's unique approach. The off-set turntable betokens the mechanical-feed motor which drove the spinning record under a stationary soundbox.

3-107. The sound passage of the Keen-O-Phone "IV" included three innovative features. First, the soundbox rotated to play either lateral or vertical cut discs (Keen-O-Phone discs were vertically cut). Second, although the sound arm was not tapered, it followed a long spiral channel before reaching the horn. Morris Keen, in his patent for this device (granted December 29, 1908, No. 907,814), described the purpose as follows: "By reason of this passage through this pipe..., the sound is softened and the scratching and rasping tones which ordinarily occur...are entirely obviated, the result being a soft and melodious tone." Third, at the center of the spiral is a revolving valve designed to control volume ("...by adjusting this valve...the sound from the instrument is not nearly so great and when the opening or valve is entirely closed, the sound is still softer."). Built-in "tone regulators" were never a part of external-horn technology except in this instance. During the 'teens, they would become commonplace among cabinet models.

3-108. The Keen-O-Phone "VII," like a number of the company's cabinet models, contained the Pooley "Automatic Record Filing System." Both firms were located in Philadelphia, but more significantly, Pooley constructed the wooden cabinets for Keen-O-Phone.

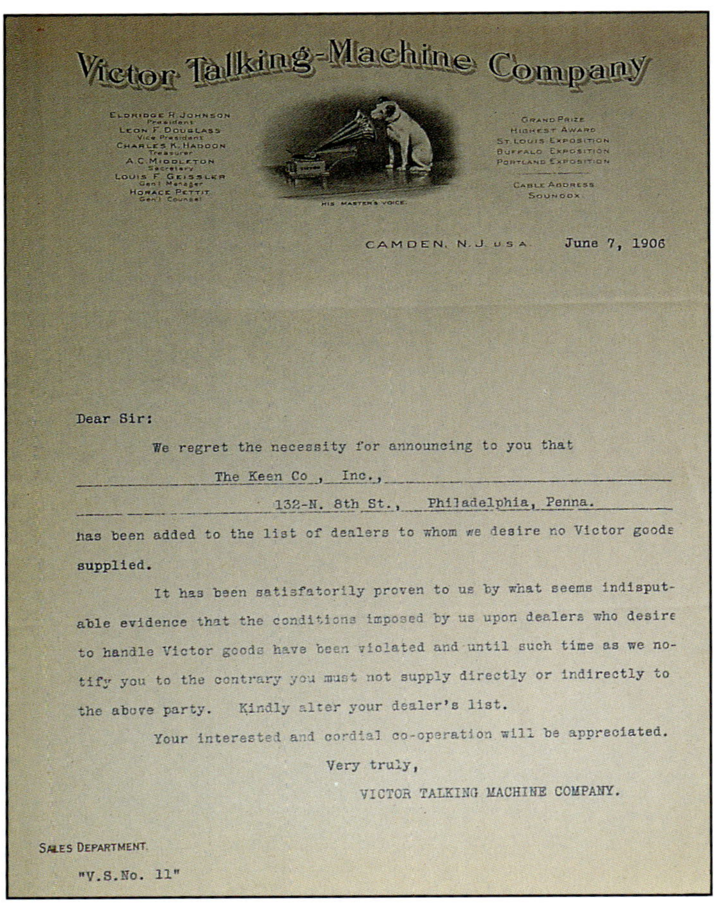

Victor Talking-Machine Company

ELDRIDGE R. JOHNSON, President
LEON F. DOUGLASS, Vice President
CHARLES K. HADDON, Treasurer
A. C. MIDDLETON, Secretary
LOUIS F. GEISSLER, Gen'l Manager
HORACE PETTIT, Gen'l Counsel

HIS MASTER'S VOICE

GRAND PRIZE
HIGHEST AWARD
ST. LOUIS EXPOSITION
BUFFALO EXPOSITION
PORTLAND EXPOSITION

CABLE ADDRESS
SOUNDBOX

CAMDEN, N. J. U.S.A. June 7, 1906

Dear Sir:

We regret the necessity for announcing to you that

The Keen Co., Inc.,

132-N. 8th St., Philadelphia, Penna.

has been added to the list of dealers to whom we desire no Victor goods supplied.

It has been satisfatorily proven to us by what seems indisputable evidence that the conditions imposed by us upon dealers who desire to handle Victor goods have been violated and until such time as we notify you to the contrary you must not supply directly or indirectly to the above party. Kindly alter your dealer's list.

Your interested and cordial co-operation will be appreciated.

Very truly,

VICTOR TALKING MACHINE COMPANY.

SALES DEPARTMENT.

"V.S.No. 11"

3-109. Evidence of the "blackballing" of the Keen Company by the Victor Talking Machine Company in 1906. Such price-fixing tactics were eventually pronounced illegal by the Supreme Court. However, Victor kept its dealers on a "short leash" until 1918. When the remaining inventory of "Keen-O-Phones" was being closed-out by Gimbel's department store in 1914, Victor went so far as to demand that no Victor records could be used to demonstrate the machines.

Chapter Four:

# Cabinets & Record Storage

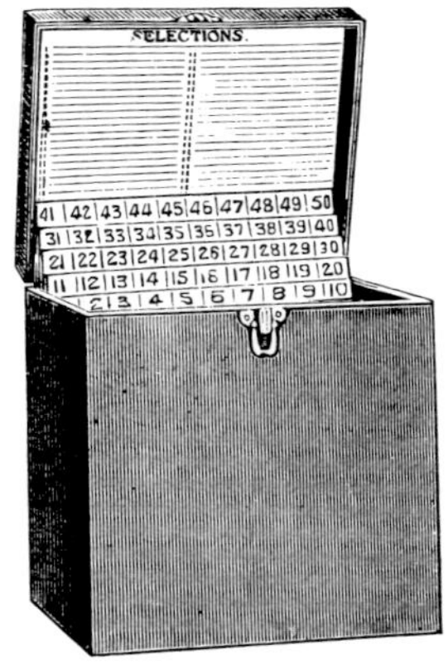


Until the advent of "floor models," talking machines were relatively portable and required a convenient flat surface on which to be played. Beginning with a custom table sold by Bergmann in 1878 to support a "Tinfoil Phonograph," furniture specially designed for the talking machine trade became increasingly popular.

In terms of storage, both cylinder and disc records provided cabinet designers with a genuine challenge. Cylinders could be arranged in conventional drawers, protected from contact with one another by their own individual pasteboard containers. In fact, some purpose-made cylinder storage cabinets were no more complicated than an average chest of drawers. Yet, devising a clever way to achieve a purpose is the essence of practical design. So, cylinder cabinets came with pegs, clips, compartments and cubbyholes to hold the records.

Discs could be stacked on top of one another, each enclosed in a paper envelope for protection. However, stacking was dangerous: it was (and remains) unwise to heap weight upon brittle 78s. Stacking also was innately disorganized: it was virtually impossible to locate a particular record without sub-dividing the stack. Lining up discs on a shelf offered little improvement over stacking: in the process of finding a selection, the whole bunch might tilt precipitously or topple over with dire results. Disc storage systems usually involved holding each record vertically between separators. In this way, a single record might be withdrawn without disturbing its neighbors. Furthermore, a number of disc cabinet designs included contraptions which retrieved the record automatically, usually with the push of a button.

Disc and cylinder record cabinets were more than an aesthetic convenience for the owner. The following article excerpted from the April 1908 *Talking Machine World* (and broken into paragraphs to aid the reader) illustrates the importance of these cabinets to the talking machine trade in general.

### *THE RECORD CABINET AS A BUSINESS DEVELOPER*

Isn't it a fact that a record cabinet doesn't go with but every fortieth machine that is sold, and why does this condition exist?.. For instance, we will say the husband has bought a machine and twenty-five records as a Christmas present for his wife. His attention is not drawn to the cabinet, and, in consequence, he does not buy it. The machine is sent to the house, is unpacked and naturally causes a great surprise and a welcome one. Of course, it is going to be set on the table in the parlor first. Oh! What joy and pleasure that machine affords the first two or three days. The recipient can barely keep away from it; in fact, is playing it every spare minute.

Whenever a friend calls he is given a little concert. When the baby doesn't want to keep quiet the machine is played for it. When "hubby" comes home at night he is entertained with a few selections on the new machine—all in all happiness is complete and nothing seems to be missing.

Saturday comes, the day when the house is cleaned, and the machine is lifted off the beautifully polished parlor table, and, to the utter dismay and astonishment of its owner, the table is found all scratched up. Of course, remarks are made, and it is decided that the machine can't be kept in the parlor, so it is removed to the table in the sitting room—the living room. This one is oak. So the lady removes the machine from the parlor into the living room and leaves it there for a week until she finds out that the library table has been as badly scratched up as the parlor table. In the meantime the baby has played with several records, pulling them off the table and breaking them. Now, she has all she can possibly do to prevent her husband from playing that machine at night for fear he might discover a broken record and get angry!

Luckily, he comes home with a package of new records, and playing them that night, he doesn't discover that some of the old ones have been broken. But she naturally says: 'What are we going to do with all these records? They are on the window-sill, they are on the tables, they are on top of the chairs, they are on the bureaus and on the chiffoniers, and wherever I look I find records, and the worst feature is when I want to play one I don't know where to find it...'

Now, we will reverse the proposition and see how this thing works when the cabinet is sold at the time the machine is sold. Once more Mr. Husband buys the outfit for his wife for Christmas. The A1 salesman realizes the situation thoroughly—has found out that the man has $75 to spend. He sells him a $40 machine, a $20 cabinet and $15 worth of records. All are sent up to the house, put in the parlor, cabinet is put in a convenient corner, the machine is put on top of the cabinet and the records placed inside and in the proper places according to the index that comes with the cabinet. 'Oh! What a beautiful outfit this is,' the recipient exclaims. 'Everything such a perfect match; everything has its place. I am so delighted with it, for it is so easy to find those records. But we have got to buy more records yet, for the cabinet is pretty nearly empty!'

Mr. Husband in due course is sent back to the store, or goes there himself, and in a feverish haste buys all the records he can possibly carry in order to fill his cabinet. All the friends coming to the house are shown the machine. It is played for them, and with a great pride their attention is drawn to the great amount of records they have got, and still there is not enough to fill the cabinet, but they will keep on buying all the new hits that come out once a month until the cabinet is filled...

Cylinder and disc record cabinets are familiar to many collectors today, usually being used just as originally intended. Yet, few collectors are knowledgeable about these well-recognized objects apart from the physical description. Cabinets, carrying cases, racks and albums seldom give a clue to their origin. This practice allowed them to be sold under a wide variety of marks, including numerous "private" music store brands. This partial list of record storage product manufacturers or primary agents is long and rather unenlightening. Yet, some may have noticed one of the following names on a particular object:

Adjustable Case Company, Minneapolis, Minnesota.
Automatic Container Company, Chicago.
Clement Beecroft, Philadelphia.
Blackman Talking Machine Company (agents), New York City.
Boston Book Company, Incorporated, New York City.
Louis Buehn and Brother (agents), Philadelphia.
Cabinet Letter File Company, New York City.
Cadillac Cabinet Company, Detroit, Michigan.
Cady cabinet Company, North Lansing, Michigan.
Chicago Case Company, Chicago.
Clement Container Company, Chicago.
Compartment Filing Cabinet Company, Chicago.
Corley Company, Richmond, Virginia.
A.E. Croft & Company, Chicago.
Douglas Phonograph Company, New York City.
Federal Equipment Company, Carlisle, Pennsylvania.
J.L. Gillespie Company (paper envelopes), Pittsburgh, Pennsylvania.
Globe-Wernicke Company, Cincinnati, Ohio.
Hawthorne and Sheble Manufacturing Company, Philadelphia.
Herzog Art Furniture Company, Saginaw, Michigan.
Humphrey Bookcase Company, Detroit, Michigan and Elkhart, Indiana.
George A. Long Cabinet Company, Hanover, Pennsylvania.
C.J. Lundstrom Manufacturing Company, Little Falls, New York.
Lyon and Healy, Chicago.
James I. Lyons (jobber), Chicago.
Lawrence McGreal, Milwaukee, Wisconsin.
Musical Echo Company, Philadelphia.
National Publishing Company, Philadelphia.
New Idea Cabinet Company, Milwaukee, Wisconsin.
New York Postcard Album Manufacturing Company, New York City.
J.B. Ogden, Lynchburg, Virginia.
Peabody Piano Company (distributor, "Eject-O-Files"), Baltimore, Maryland.
Pooley Furniture Company, Philadelphia.
Ready File Company, Incorporated, Indianapolis, Indiana.
Salter Manufacturing Company, Chicago.
Schafford Album Company, New York City.
E. Schloss and Company (agents) New York City.
G.H. Schubert, Chicago.
Benjamin Switky (sales agent), New York City.
Syracuse Cabinet Company, Syracuse, New York.
Syracuse Wire Works, Syracuse, New York.
Talking Machine Company, Chicago.
James S. Topham, Washington, D.C.
Udell Works, Indianapolis, Indiana.
Uffner Album Company, New York City.
John Wanamaker (agent), New York City.

As in all forms of competitive enterprise, record storage system manufacturers stretched the limits of human imagination to create "new," "improved" or "patented" designs. As we endeavor to understand more about this fascinating furniture, we discover a field rife with variety.

4-1. A circa 1890 pasteboard cylinder record box with a North American Phonograph Company cylinder. Boxes of this period usually incorporated positioning tubes in the lid as well as in the base. Rubber stamped information began to appear on boxes in 1895, and labels were introduced by various small companies circa 1898. *Courtesy of Ray Phillips.* (VR)

4-2. A very early (circa 1891) oak storage box for cylinders with a capacity of 20 records. *Courtesy of the Charles Hummel collections.* (VR)

4-3. In 1896, Hawthorne & Sheble first offered under their own name a line of specialized cabinets to enclose Edison cylinder Phonographs. These would later be adapted to accept Graphophones. Illustrated on these Reed, Dawson & Company cylinder record identification slips from a few years later was Hawthorne & Sheble's "Parlor Cabinet No. 4," available in light or dark quartered oak ($40.00), walnut, cherry (both $45.00) or mahogany ($55.00). Each of the three side-opening drawers held 36 cylinders. *Courtesy of the Scott and Denise Corbett collection.*

4-5. A seldom-seen identification plate, fastened to the front of the previous cabinet.

4-4. A Hawthorne & Sheble cabinet designed to house an Edison Class "M" Phonograph, accessories (top two drawers), cylinder records (bottom four drawers) and the battery necessary to power the machine (upper left door). Such a configuration is unusual, and its execution in mahogany makes it more so. Cabinet measures 36 3/4" tall x 18 1/2" deep x 35 3/4" wide. (VR)

4-6. A Hawthorne & Sheble cabinet No."1a" (36" tall x 15 5/8" deep x 20 3/8" wide). Sold by Columbia as the "Unique" for $12.00 as early as 1898 (reduced to $8.50 in July 1901), this cabinet was also available from H & S with "Special finish" (shown) for an additional $3.00. The drawer pulls on this example differ from the small circular pulls usually found on these cabinets. Each of the five drawers held 20 cylinders. *Courtesy of Todd Emery.* (Value code: B)

4-7. Another Hawthorne & Sheble cylinder cabinet (35 1/2" tall x 18" deep x 21 3/8" wide). This model was sold by Columbia in early 1901 as the "Unique No. 2," for $20.00 (reduced in July to $12.00). Each of the five drawers held 24 cylinders. Columbia's "Unique No. 3" cabinet was identical, but accommodated 30 "Grand" (5") cylinders for the same price. *Courtesy of Todd Emery.* (Value code: B)

4-8. A carrying and storage case for a Berliner "Improved" Gramophone and approximately 30 records. The soundbox may be seen atop its pasteboard container which, along with the crank and traveling arm, could be placed into fitted compartments within the case. The only part of the machine needing separate handling and storage is the seamless brass horn. (VR)

4-10. Two 7" disc record storage boxes. On the left, a circa 1899 "Gram-O-Phone Records" pasteboard box described as a "Black Canvas Case… Holds 50 records…Price, $1.00." On the right, a "Victor 7-Inch Record Case," introduced in 1901, and available in "Poplar Wood" (shown) for $1.25, or in "Polished Oak Wood" for $2.00. (Value code: D, F)

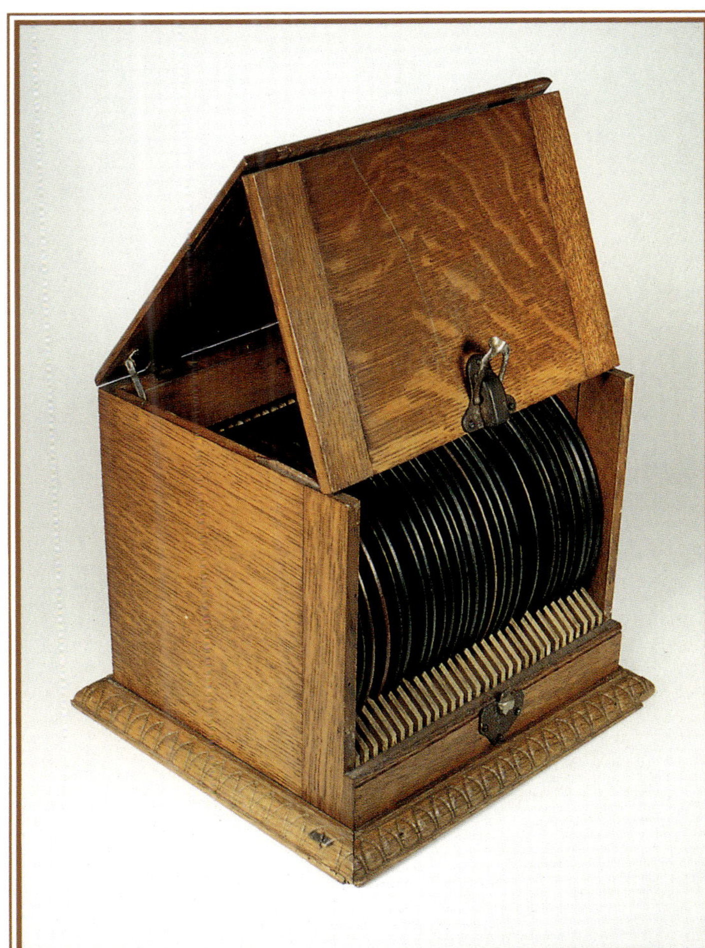

4-9. A disc record storage box, sold by the National Gramophone Company/Corporation circa 1898, was described as follows: "RECORD CABINET. Made of polished quartered oak, with quarter sawed panel door, fittings of leather and nickel. Will hold 30 records. Price, $2.50." Later, in 1900, Eldridge Johnson offered a similar box with a plainer base for $2.00. Oddly, it was claimed to hold 50 records. *Courtesy of the Charles Hummel collections.* (Value code: A)

4-13. An unmarked carrying case for 36 cylinder records (23 1/2" x 11" x 5"); typical of the 1900-1905 period. *Courtesy of Alan H. Mueller.* (Value code: G)

4-11. Two 10" disc record storage boxes. On the left, a Victor "Monarch 10-Inch Record Case," introduced in 1901, and available in Poplar wood for $1.75, or in polished Oak (shown) for $2.50. Victor Record Cases disappeared after 1906 with the advent of the Victrola. On the right is a Hawthorne & Sheble "Disc Record Carrying" case "No. 63," introduced in 1903 for $3.00. (Value code: E, G)

4-14. This "96 Peg Cabinet Case" was advertised in November 1905 by James S. Topham of Washington, D.C. as "Something Entirely New. Exclusive With Us." The advertisement included various other styles of record and machine cases. It continued: "The Pioneer Case Manufacturer. These Cases and Boxes are for the safe storage and carriage of Phonograph Records. They are the same style and quality I have been manufacturing for the past fifteen years, supplying the leading concerns in the country, such as The National Phonograph Co., and the American Graphophone and The Columbia Phonograph Cos. I have been constantly adding improvements from time to time until they are as nearly perfect for the purpose intended as can be, and at the same time the prices are lower than heretofore." *Courtesy of Alan H. Mueller.* (Value code: F)

4-12. A storage box for 7" disc records built by Hawthorne & Sheble and described in its 1901 catalogue as follows: "Gramophone Record Cabinet. Made of Quartered Oak, with 5 drawers, each drawer holding 6 records; very handsome....$15.00." Eldridge Johnson had offered this accessory in his 1900 catalogue as the "Grand Record Cabinet" for the same price. (Value code: A)

4-15. An unidentified five drawer cylinder cabinet with simplified rear legs, yet boasting fancy moulding beneath the top and an appliqué on the front apron. Each of the five drawers holds 15 cylinders. This cabinet measures 35" tall x 13" deep x 18 1/2" wide. *Courtesy of Norm and Janyne Smith.* (Value code: C)

4-16. The Udell cabinet "No. 522" was illustrated in the May 1906 issue of the *Talking Machine World*: "Don't Take Our Word For It. Write for our catalog and see for yourself why you should sell these high grade cabinets. The rich finish and artistic designs give them preference over all others… The Udell Works… Indianapolis, U.S.A." Each of the five drawers held 50 cylinders. The cabinet measures 33" tall x 23 1/2" deep x 22" wide. *Courtesy of Norm and Janyne Smith.* (Value code: B)

4-17. The Herzog Art Furniture Company of Saginaw, Michigan offered a high-quality line of cabinets for cylinder and disc records. As early as 1905, Herzog advertised itself as "the largest Record Cabinet Manufacturers in the world." However, by May 1910, Herzog's entire stock of cylinder cabinets had been sold out to the Neal, Clark & Neal Company of Buffalo, which offered them at substantial discounts. These catalogues illustrate a few of the wide variety of cabinets built by Herzog. *Courtesy of the Charles Hummel collections.*

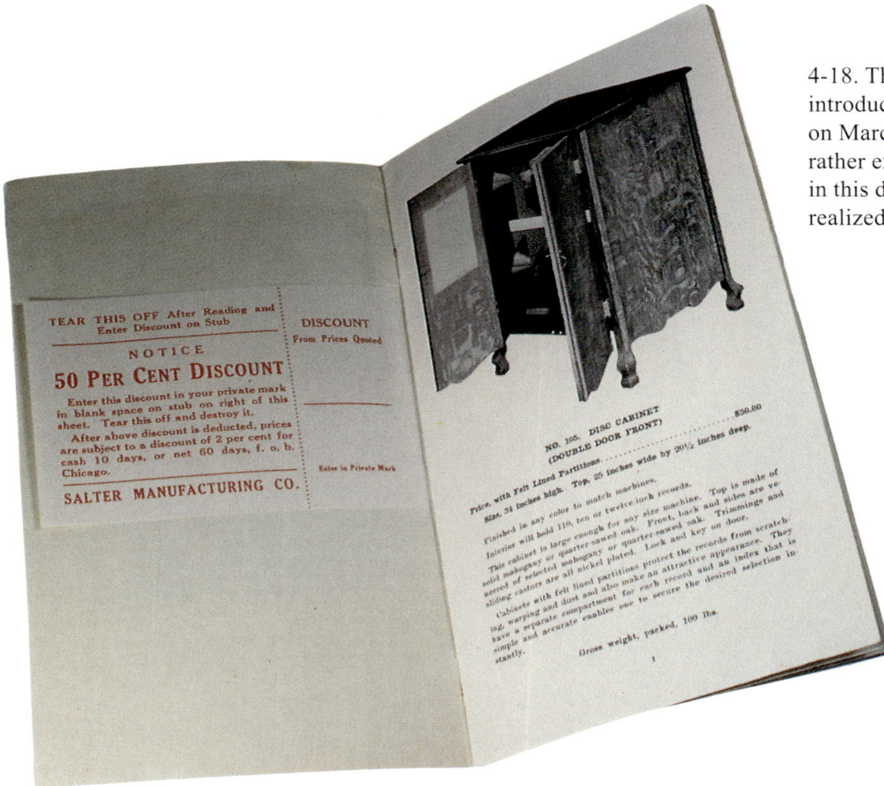


4-18. The Salter Manufacturing Company of Chicago introduced its line of talking machine record cabinets on March 1, 1905. Its products were well-made and rather expensive, and the discount slip which survives in this dealer's catalogue reveals the substantial profit realized through the sales of Salter products.

4-19. The Salter Company advertised a pivoting drawer cylinder record cabinet, similar to this one, in October 1906, but with full-depth shelves opening from one side only. This unusual oak cabinet of unknown origin was accessible from two sides, but only if free-standing, or if the foremost end were set against a wall. This example measures 36 1/2" tall x 14" deep x 22 1/2" wide. *Courtesy of Bob and Karyn Sitter.* (Value code: B)

4-20. The Herzog cabinet "No.724" in its open position. Appearing in mid-1907, this cabinet was copied by other manufacturers, but none achieved equivalent popularity. Its doors were so constructed that opening/closing either one would automatically operate the other. Manufactured for three years by the Herzog Art Furniture Company of Saginaw, Michigan, the "No. 724" was capable of storing 215 cylinders. In 1910, the Neal, Clark & Neal Company of Buffalo was wholesaling this model for $18.80, to be retailed at $23.50. *Courtesy of Michael F. Khanchalian.* (Value code: A)

4-22. One of the more stylish of the Herzog cylinder cabinets was the "No. 717," with its serpentine drawer fronts. With a capacity of 252 cylinders, the "717" was as useful as it was visually arresting. This cabinet originally sold for $20.75 and measures 36 1/2" tall x 20 1/2" deep x 24 1/2" wide. *Courtesy of Gary W. Blizzard.* (Value code: B)

4-21. Another Herzog "No. 724," but in mahogany, and in its closed position. (Value code: A)

4-23. The elegant Herzog disc record cabinet "No. 828" in mahogany (35 1/4" tall x 20" x 20"). This cabinet was illustrated in the August 1907 issue of the *Talking Machine World.* With such cabinets, the Herzog Art Furniture Company built an enviable reputation for quality. (VR)

4-24. The Herzog disc record cabinet "No.820" in oak, measuring 35" tall x 17 3/4" deep x 17 3/8" wide. First shown in the August 1907 *Talking Machine World*, this model survived for at least one year. (VR)

4-25. The Herzog Art Furniture Company offered this record cabinet as either "No. 809" for discs or as "No. 710" for cylinders. Measurements for both models were 32 1/2' tall x 20" deep x 19 1/2" wide. *Courtesy of Norm and Janyne Smith.* (Value code: A cylinder, B disc)

4-26. The Herzog Cabinet "No. 809," with a capacity of 200 12" disc records. An advertisement in the June 1908 issue of the *Talking Machine World* puffed: "We Sold Several Thousand of This Design *alone* in 1907." The "No. 809," like its twin for cylinders, the "No. 710," was available in Golden Oak (shown) or Mahogany. *Courtesy of Norm and Janyne Smith.*

4-27. The Herzog Cabinet "No. 710," with a capacity of 147 cylinders. The original numbered pegs to hold the cylinders are visible. The two shelves within the cabinet proper slide out for easier access. The casters on this particular example were added by a previous owner. *Courtesy of Jean-Paul Agnard.*

4-28. A cylinder cabinet quite similar to a Herzog "No. 704," but with six shelves rather than the usual five (the lowest shelf is missing from this example). The six shelves each accommodate 33 cylinders for a total of 196. The cabinet measures 38" tall x 16 1/2" deep x 18" wide. *Courtesy of Jean-Paul Agnard.* (Value code: C)

4-29. This cabinet appears to be a Herzog "No. 706," with characteristic slab sides and curved apron on the lower drawer. Each of the five drawers accommodates 30 cylinders. Original retail price was $10.00. Measurements are 32" tall x 19 1/2" deep x 21" wide. *Courtesy of Norm and Janyne Smith.* (Value code: C)

4-31. Another Herzog cabinet with ball-and-claw feet. This is the "No. 712" in mahogany, with a capacity of 216 cylinders. At $12.25 retail, this Herzog drawer-type cabinet was even more of a bargain than the previous example. *Courtesy of Norm and Janyne Smith.* (Value code: B)

4-30. A Herzog cabinet "No. 714" with a capacity of 216 cylinders. Retailing at $13.00, this door-type cabinet was a relatively low-cost way to store a large number of cylinders. Measurements are 34 3/4" tall x 20" deep x 21" wide. Note the ball-and-claw feet. *Courtesy of Norm and Janyne Smith.* (Value code: C)

4-32. This bizarre Herzog cabinet has an interesting history. Designed to convert an external-horn talking machine into a more "Victrola-like" instrument, this cabinet was introduced in August 1907 as the "Deluxe No. 835." As were other Herzog cabinets of the "800" series, this was for a disc machine, and included two tiers of record storage beneath the machine, all of which was concealed by a single tall door. The following month, this notice appeared in the *Talking Machine World*: "The concealed horn cabinet of the Herzog Art Furniture Co., Saginaw, Mich., known as the 'Deluxe,' has, for commercial reasons, been re-christened the 'Teddy' cabinet, by which name it will be hereafter known."

By April 1908, the cabinet had been adapted for cylinder talking machines and dubbed "The Cyclo-Phone." Available in Golden Oak or Mahogany, this cabinet appeared in two very similar versions, the "No. 740" (shown) and the "No. 742," which featured a different grille design and columns on all four corners. The "No. 740" had a capacity of 140 cylinders, whereas the "No. 742" could accommodate 196. The last illustration of this type of cabinet was in the February 1909 issue of the *Talking Machine World*, where the "No. 835" for disc machines was shown. No subsequent mention of these conversion cabinets appeared in the *TMW.* A similar cabinet manufactured by the Salter Manufacturing Company of Chicago was advertised in 1908-1909 as the "Grand," but for disc machines exclusively. Unlike the Herzog product, Salter's "Grand" cabinet made use of the machine's existing horn, and had only one tier of record storage. *Courtesy of Jean-Paul Agnard.* (Value code: A)

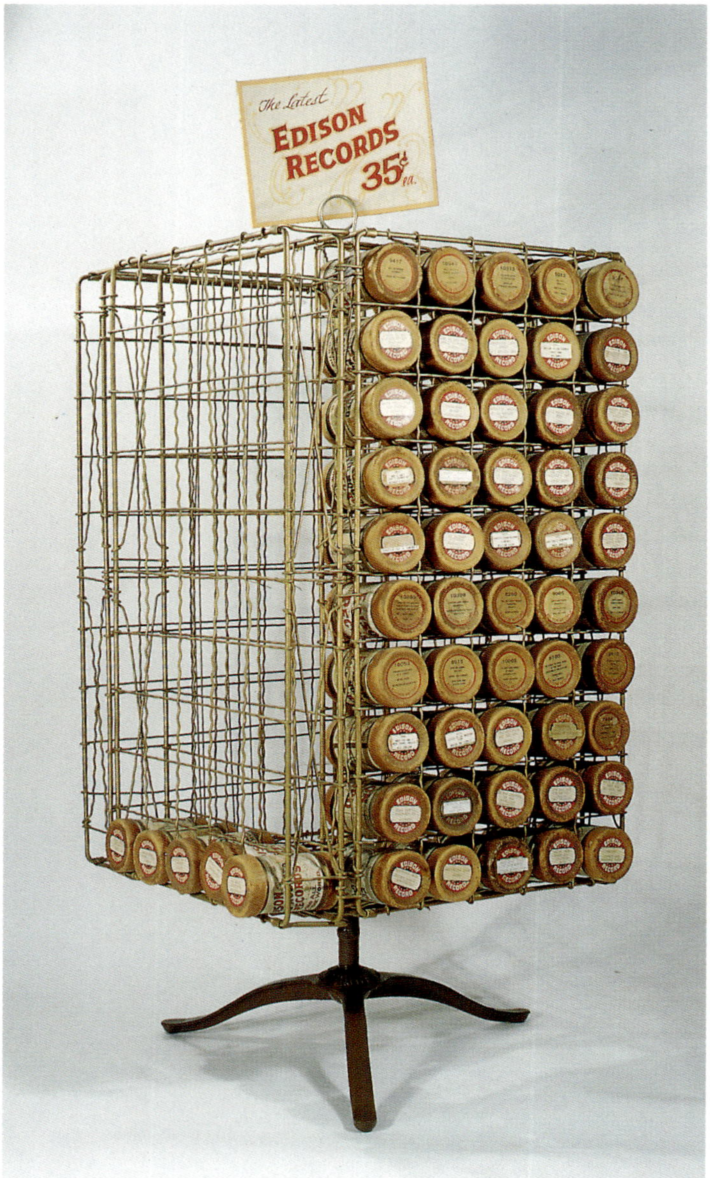


4-33. If proper record storage and access was a problem for the consumer in the early twentieth century, it could be a nightmare for record dealers. The Syracuse Wire Works of Syracuse, New York, was a consistent advertiser in the *Talking Machine World* as early as 1905. A typical ad in October 1907 advised: "BE ON YOUR GUARD. Don't let big chunks of your profit disappear through poor methods of keeping your stock. Keep your phonograph and talking machine records in the most convenient, cleanly [sic], safe and satisfactory way by purchase of... WIRE RECORD RACKS. A rack for every sort of record, cylinder or disc. Stock styles, and styles built to fit any space. Stationary rack, removable and revolving racks. GET A CATALOG." This model was illustrated in the October 1908 issue of the *Talking Machine World*. This particular example once graced the dealership of Nick Mersfelder of Fort Davis, Texas. *Courtesy of Ray Phillips.* (Value code: A)

4-34. Another model of a wire record rack probably made by the Syracuse Wire Works. This straightforward design mounted to a wall and could accommodate 100 cylinder records. *Courtesy of Ray Phillips.* (Value code: B)

4-35. The Pardee-Ellenberger Company of New Haven, Connecticut, first advertised its Pardell Folding Box in the October 1907 *Talking Machine World*: "A folding container for three, six, or twelve cylinder records. These boxes are being very generally used by phonograph dealers and are the most convenient package for delivering records to customer. Made of heavy cardboard and shipped 'knocked down'... Dealers imprint in lots of 500." Shown are the "No. 3" and "No. 6" models. *Courtesy of the collection of Howard Hazelcorn.* (Value code: G)

4-36. A fascinating response to the issue of cylinder record storage was found in this round mahogany cabinet. Inside was a rotating "tree" of 121 angled cardboard tubes for holding cylinders. For convenience and ingenuity of design, this cabinet was unbeatable. However, its more expensive-to-produce storage system must have seen limited sales, making it rare today. Measures 34 1/4" high, 23 1/4" diameter. *Courtesy of Rick Wilkins.* (Value code: A)

4-37. A stunning disc record cabinet offered by the Douglas Phonograph Company of New York City. A January 1907 advertisement in the *Talking Machine World* illustrated this cabinet, while advising to: "Ask any one who has seen our display and they will confirm our claim, that we have the Handsomest, Best Constructed and Most Practical Cabinets on the market." This example measures 35" tall x 19 3/4" deep x 21 1/2" wide. The horn on this custom cabinet Victor "V" was marketed later as the "Truetone Amplifying Horn" through the General Phonograph Supply Company of New York City. (VR)

4-38. The previous Douglas cabinet showing one of its side doors open to reveal record storage compartments. Note the cross-sectional shape of the door.

4-39. The General Phonograph Supply Company of New York City sold a line of "Eureka" products including horns ("Truetone") and cabinets, such as this double-door cylinder model with pivoting shelves. Measurements are 36" tall x 16" deep x 28 1/2" wide. *Courtesy of Norm and Janyne Smith.* (Value code: B)

4-40. The interior of the "Eureka" cylinder cabinet contains five pivoting or revolving shelves, each holding 38 cylinders. The unusual pegs feature outer sleeves for cylinder protection. The distinctive General Phonograph Supply Company decal is visible on the door. Such "overbuilt" designs lost popularity by late 1907. *Courtesy of Norm and Janyne Smith.*

4-41. One of the "Cabinet That Matches" models, offered by the Talking Machine Company of Chicago. This example is for the Victor "IV" and was described in October 1908 as follows: "Mahogany only, veneered on all four sides, double front doors. Top slide for holding records, drawer in bottom for accessories. Capacity—200 Victor Records. Cabinet $25.00. Outfit [including Victor "IV"] $85.00." This cabinet measured 35 1/2" tall x 19" deep x 19 1/8" wide. *Courtesy of Todd Emery.* (Value code: A)

4-42. Another of the "Cabinet That Matches" models, this one for the Victor "VI." The 1908 advertisement described this cabinet as: "Mahogany only, veneered on all four sides. Fourteen karat gold-plated caps on bases and tops of columns to match Victor VI Machine. Double front doors, top slide for holding records, drawer in bottom for accessories. Capacity – 220 Records. Cabinet $40.00. Outfit [including Victor "VI"] $140." This cabinet measured 37 1/2" tall x 21 1/2" deep x 21 1/2" wide. The Victor "VI" shown on the cabinet has been equipped with a spruce horn. (Value code: A)

4-43. The striking decal found inside the door of the "Cabinet That Matches" models. As can be surmised, each model cabinet was designed to accept a specific "table model" disc talking machine. Describing the introduction of "The cabinet That Matches" the Victrola "XII" in October 1909, the *Talking Machine World* stated: "A unique feature is found in the fact that the top of the cabinet is countersunk with the corners so beveled that the feet of the instrument fit snugly therein, thus making a completely harmonious outfit."

4-44. A rather massive disc record cabinet of unknown origin. Measuring 35" tall x 22" deep x 24" wide, it may have fallen short of Herzog or Salter sophistication, but was stylish and well-built. Such bold designs in mahogany enjoyed only a brief vogue in 1908-1910. (VR)

4-46. The Rockford Cabinet Company of Rockford, Illinois advertised this Record Cabinet "No. 697" in October 1908. This oak model (measuring 39" tall x 17 1/2" deep x 23 1/2" wide) held approximately 40 cylinders in each of its 5 pivoting shelves. *Courtesy of the Scott and Denise Corbett collection.* (Value code: B)

4-45. A view of the previous example in the open position, showing the needle cups (top center) for new and used steel needles, and the numbered compartments for storage of disc records.

4-47. An oak cabinet for disc records, as illustrated in the July 1909 *Talking Machine World* as "Manufactured For Louis Buehn & Bro." of Philadelphia. The company stated: "Our line is exclusive and cannot be obtained elsewhere." This example (34 3/4" tall x 16 3/8" deep x 20 7/8" wide) in oak dates from circa 1911. The styling and quality of the cabinet suggest that it was manufactured by the Pooley Furniture Company of Philadelphia. *Courtesy of Todd Emery.* (Value code: C)

4-48. With the introduction of the first "table model" Victrola in July 1909 (the VV-"XII"), several cabinet manufacturers quickly designed and offered cabinets to match this "Baby Victrola." The Victor Talking Machine Company was by now fully aware of the large sales of record cabinets for use with its external-horn machines, and with the introduction of its Victrola "XII," began supplying its own matching cabinets. Shown is the "Victrola Record cabinet No.150" intended for the VV-"XII." A tag inside lists the retail price at $55.00. This example is serial number 235, and measures 37" tall (with casters) x 20 1/2" deep x 24 3/4" wide. *Courtesy of Rae Ann Rieping.* (Value code: A)

4-49. The Salter Manufacturing Company of Chicago offered a high-quality line of cabinets for cylinder or disc records. Shown is the "No. 782" for disc records, in mahogany, which measured 37 1/2" tall x 20" deep x 17 1/4" wide. A September 1910 advertisement stated: "It is not only the outside of a cabinet that should be made and finished right, but the interior as well. Our new style of Salter Cabinets which for the past two years have been the favorite among dealers on account of their superior quality to all makes, has kept our factory working overtime." Salter introduced its first line of record cabinets in March 1905. (Value code: A)

4-50. The Salter "No. 782" in the open position. The 1910 advertisement continued: "Our patent interior arrangement stands out in a class by itself. The interiors of Salter Disc Cabinets have an individual compartment for each record. The wood shelves are lined with soft green felt to prevent records from scratching… The Disc Records lie flat on the shelves, preventing them from warping." The cups for new and used needles are visible on the interior of the door.

4-51. An unusual disc record cabinet in oak with bow front and sides. This is evidently a Salter "No. 786," which was illustrated in the September 1910 *Talking Machine World*, but the example lacks Salter's distinctive interior design. (VR)

4-52. The open position of the previous example shows a conventional arrangement for disc records: most unusual for Salter cabinets of the post-1908 period.

4-53. This beautiful Salter disc record cabinet circa 1910 featured a double bow front. Note the shape of the open door to the right. Also present in this model were Salter's distinctive horizontal felt-lined shelves. This oak cabinet measures 42" tall x 14 1/2" deep x 32 1/2"wide. (VR)

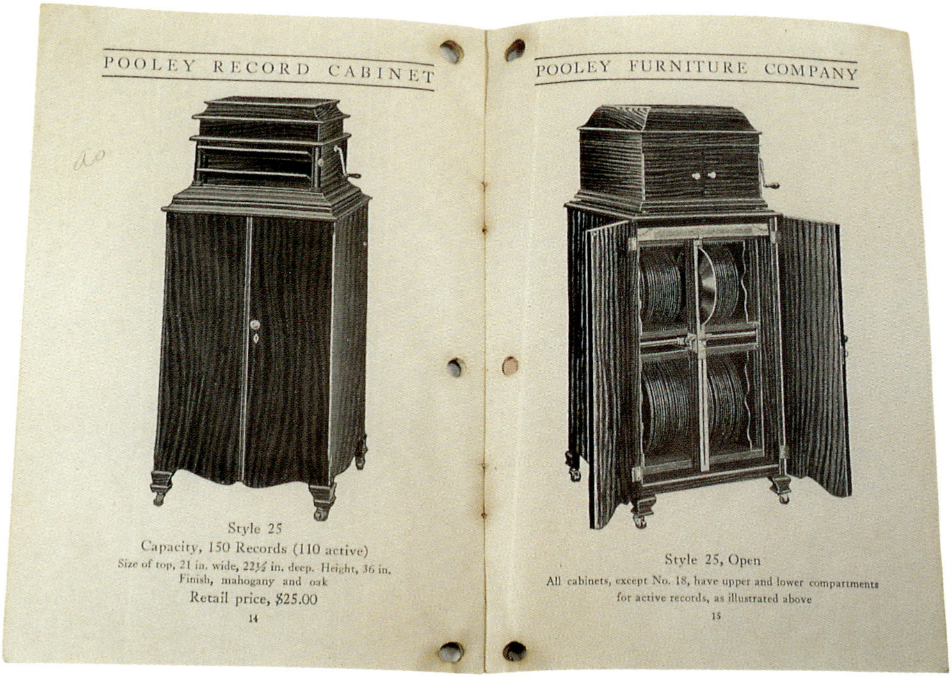


4-54. The August 1911 issue of the *Talking Machine World* announced the introduction of record cabinets by the Pooley Furniture Company of Philadelphia. "It is said of the Pooley filing system, incorporated in the cabinets, that you simply ask for the record and it rolls out to you, and that practically states the case. The cabinets are supplied with two shelves with a capacity in all of 210 disc records [in certain models] held vertically. A vertical indicator travels along a bar so notched that the indicator may be placed in front of any of the 210 records. When the indicator points to the number of the record desired a slight pressure on a lever causes the record to roll out between two parallel bars covered with felt, from whence it is easily removed for playing." The catalogue shown here illustrates the Style "25," with a capacity of 110 "active" records (in the filing system) and an additional 10 records stored on each end of both levels, for a total of 150. *Courtesy of the Charles Hummel collections.*

4-55. Edward F. Pooley was the proprietor of the Pooley Furniture Company of Philadelphia, and was awarded six different patents in 1910-1911 for various record and talking machine cabinets. The coincidentally-named Earl Pooler of Seattle, Washington was awarded his own patent (with Don C. Pooler) for a record storage and retrieval system (No.980,124, December 27, 1910). The patents of these men were combined in the Pooley Record Cabinet, "The Cabinet That Finds and Hands the Record to You." A Pooley catalogue stated: "The Pooley Way is the up-to-the-minute method of caring for talking machine records... and offers a newer, quicker and safer means of finding, caring for and preserving the valuable discs that make the talking machine a pleasure... With the Pooley System when a record is wanted for playing simply move the vertical guide bar along until the indicator is at the desired number on the scale. Then press the lever, and the record is instantly at hand. The mechanism in the back of the cabinet pushes the record just far enough forward to be easily drawn out." The customer received a record index booklet, a set of "gummed sheets of reference numbers" to be pasted on the records and labels for "indexing by kinds of selections, as operatic, popular, orchestral, etc." It is interesting to note that the cabinets were described as holding a total number of discs and an "active" number of discs. Inactive or infrequently played records were meant to be stored in the non-indexed spaces at the extreme left and right. Illustrated is Style "40" ($40.00, 150 active records) available in oak (shown) or mahogany. (Value code: B)

4-56. Earl Pooler also received a patent (No.1,030,534, June 25,1912) for a "Filling-block" to fit his record filing system. It allowed 10" discs to be stored in slots intended for 12" discs. To quote from the patent, it was "a filling-block for phonographic record cabinets being of a width [actually height] equal to the difference in diameters of different sized...records..." These were offered for sale in the Pooley company's catalogue. (Value code: F)

4-57. The Victrola "IV" was a small and unimposing table model. A number of firms offered record-storage cabinets to support or enclose this talking machine. The top edges of the cabinet shown here exactly met the bottom moulding of the Victrola (see next caption), suggesting continuity. The cabinet, though modest, reflected the curved "wing" design which had been introduced in Victor floor models in 1912, and widely imitated for over a decade, as it was here. Cabinet measures 32 1/4" high, 13 5/8" wide and 14 5/8" deep. *Courtesy of Lou Caruso.* (Value code: D, cabinet)

4-58. The top of the record cabinet designed to fit the Victrola "IV" had recessed "cups" to accept the rubber feet which normally elevated a table model Victrola by a fraction of an inch above a surface. The intent was to lower the Victrola, making a flush seam between talking machine and record cabinet. *Courtesy of Lou Caruso.*

4-59. The cabinets of Victor external-horn table models were more-or-less square in shape, but Victrolas and most other *internal-horn* talking machines were usually deeper than they were wide. When designing storage cabinets to support these rectangular models, furniture manufacturers were faced with a problem. If the front door of the base cabinet corresponded to the front of the talking machine, a storage area would result which was *deeper* than needed to contain 10" or even 12" records. "Frontal" orientation had the effect of limiting the width of the storage shelves and creating plenty of "dead" space, usually hidden behind the discs at the rear of the cabinet interior. One effort to increase the efficiency of space can be seen in this oak base cabinet supporting a Victrola "VIII." Turning the cupboard door of the cabinet by 90 degrees allowed more records to be included on the two interior shelves, transforming dead space into storage space. The side-opening door, however, might not have appealed to every customer. As in many such record cabinets, a "recessed" area was created by a raised frame of moulding around the top, into which the talking machine snugly fit. This was known in the trade as a "continuation top." Cabinet measures 32 3/4" high, 17" across the front of the machine and 21" across the side with cupboard door. *Courtesy of Lou Caruso.* (Value code: D, cabinet)

4-60. During the mid-'teens a spate of open-sided upright disc talking machine models appeared, having virtually no record storage. By 1918, a number of companies began offering supplemental record storage systems to fit these and other existing upright talking machines. Firms like the Ready File Company, Incorporated, of Indianapolis, Indiana, and the Eject-O-File Sales Company of Baltimore, Maryland, sold storage containers which (like the one shown on this triangular Davis disc machine) occupied the space between the high legs. *Courtesy of Steve and Ellie Saccente.*

4-61. The first Edison Disc records available to the public in 1912-1913 were sold in these elegant boxes. Despite the highbrow cachet which Edison lavished upon these early disc records, the expensive boxes were soon replaced by more conventional paper sleeves. (Value code: F)

4-63. Edison Diamond Disc Phonographs such as the "A-100" and "A-150" lacked record storage beyond the limited potential of a small shelf. In order to maximize this space, six self-supporting record albums (or "portfolios") were offered with each machine. If bought separately, the albums cost 75 cents apiece. *Courtesy of Jean-Paul Agnard.* (Value code: G)

4-62. This mahogany disc cabinet supported an Edison Diamond Disc "B-80," circa 1914. The upper frieze moulding suggested the lines of the talking machine's front grille, and the top edges of the cabinet were rounded to blend with the moulding and turned feet of the "B-80." Diamond Disc records were stored between two rows upright wooden dividers. Cabinet measures 35 1/2" high, 19" wide and 25" deep. *Courtesy of Lou Caruso.* (Value code: C, cabinet)

4-64. At first glance, these Edison record "portfolios" appear to be similar to the previous example except for the color. These are, however, sitting on the shelf of an Edison *Amberola* Phonograph (Model "IV"), so are designed to hold cylinder records. *Courtesy of Michael F. Khanchalian.* (VR)

4-65. An open view of the previous cylinder record "portfolios." These storage containers were available for $2.00 each, and could accommodate 30 cylinders in their original boxes, as shown. The only talking machines suitable for this accessory were the Amberolas "III" and "IV." *Courtesy of Michael F. Khanchalian.*

Opposite page:
Top left: 4-66. Following the 1915 introduction of the Edison Amberola "30," "50" and the floor-model "75," various cylinder record cabinets were offered to accommodate the table model Amberolas. Shown is a cabinet with three conventional trays of records and rather unusual moulding on the door, which imitates the grille design of the Amberola "50." (Value code: C, cabinet)

Bottom left: 4-67. The Edison Amberola "50" was available in either an oak or mahogany cabinet. These simple cabinets might match either version. Each of the three drawers held 30 cylinders. Measurements were 31 1/2" tall x 22 1/4" deep x 18" wide. *Courtesy of Jean-Paul Agnard.* (Value code: C)

Top right: 4-68. Although a talking machine was never produced by the makers of "Little Wonder" 5 1/2" discs (1914-1923), a wooden box and albums in various colors were offered for record storage. (Value code: E, H)

Bottom right: 4-69. The Brown Disc Record Cabinet was manufactured by the Globe-Wernicke Company of Cincinnati, Ohio. Operating much like a document file, this cabinet (No."4.T.") was advertised in January 1918 as appropriate "For every small talking machine given as a Christmas present...Records lie flat when drawer is closed—No warping... Records are vertical when drawer is open. Every record at your fingers' ends.... A separate compartment for every record." When a drawer was fully extended, it hinged downward so that the face of the drawer became the bottom of the record "file." Cabinet measures 32 1/2" tall x 22 1/4" deep x 18 1/4" wide. *Courtesy of Rae Ann Rieping.* (Value code: D)

Edison

Records
The Little Wonder Album of Records

Chapter Five:

# Signs, Advertising, and Ephemera

(Objects read *clockwise* and/or *left to right.*)

## Edison

5-1. This 1878 sheet music emerged from the thunderous impact on the world of Edison's invention. Sound recording and replay were the realizations of a long-held dream, such as flying. Edison's achievement created a new communication medium, and was duly celebrated in the already existing media. (Value code: D)

5-2. The North American Phonograph Company was organized in 1888 to be the sole sales agent for both the Edison Phonograph and the Graphophone (later associated with Columbia). Business affairs went quickly awry and after 1891 the Graphophone was no longer associated with North American. Edison's Phonograph continued to be sold by the firm until it bankrupted in 1894. During the early 1890s, North American was the only outlet for Edison's machines and records. A trade card showing the Masonic Temple in Chicago, home of a North American office. (Value code: F)

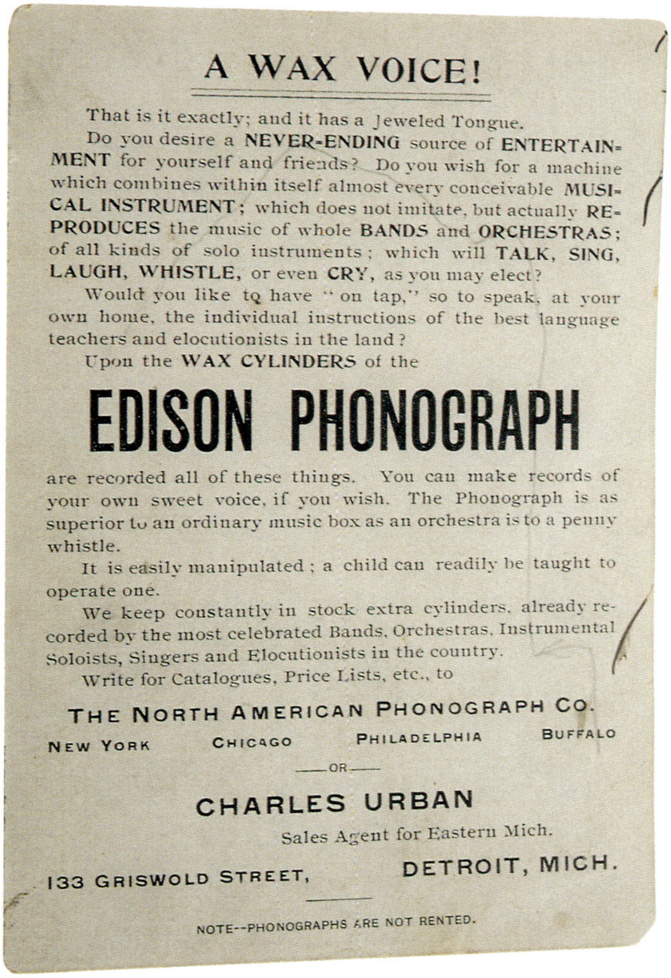

## A WAX VOICE!

That is it exactly; and it has a Jeweled Tongue.

Do you desire a **NEVER-ENDING** source of **ENTERTAINMENT** for yourself and friends? Do you wish for a machine which combines within itself almost every conceivable **MUSICAL INSTRUMENT**; which does not imitate, but actually **REPRODUCES** the music of whole **BANDS** and **ORCHESTRAS**; of all kinds of solo instruments; which will **TALK**, **SING**, **LAUGH**, **WHISTLE**, or even **CRY**, as you may elect?

Would you like to have "on tap," so to speak, at your own home, the individual instructions of the best language teachers and elocutionists in the land?

Upon the **WAX CYLINDERS** of the

# EDISON PHONOGRAPH

are recorded all of these things. You can make records of your own sweet voice, if you wish. The Phonograph is as superior to an ordinary music box as an orchestra is to a penny whistle.

It is easily manipulated; a child can readily be taught to operate one.

We keep constantly in stock extra cylinders, already recorded by the most celebrated Bands, Orchestras, Instrumental Soloists, Singers and Elocutionists in the country.

Write for Catalogues, Price Lists, etc., to

THE NORTH AMERICAN PHONOGRAPH CO.

NEW YORK CHICAGO PHILADELPHIA BUFFALO

—OR—

CHARLES URBAN

Sales Agent for Eastern Mich.

133 GRISWOLD STREET, DETROIT, MICH.

NOTE--PHONOGRAPHS ARE NOT RENTED.

5-3. The reverse of the North American card painted a glowing picture of the Phonograph's talents. Note the sentence at the very bottom, "Phonographs are not rented." North American's initial approach to distribution had been to *lease* its talking machines, a plan which had proved unpopular with the public. It soon began selling Phonographs outright, but enough people remembered the previous policy to merit a few words of clarification.

THE EDISON PHONOGRAPH

Don't let unscrupulous and irresponsible parties sell you second-hand Phonographs, etc., for new ones.

We have always on hand second-hand Phonographs, Slot Cabinets, Batteries, etc., etc., which we will sell at reduced prices.

FOR · TRAVELING · EXHIBITORS

The · Largest · Earnings · for · the · Smallest · Investment.

COMPLETE OUTFIT, $200.

INCLUDING

1 Phonograph, complete, with Electric Motor.
1 Speaking Tube.
1 20-inch Brass Horn and Stand.
1 Single Hearing Tube.
1 14-Way Hearing Attachment and Tubes (as per cut).
12 Blank Cylinders.
20 Records. Best Quality. All Originals.
1 Wooden Box, to hold 20 Records or Blanks.
1 Storage Battery, best made, designed to run Phonograph 100 Hours; or, if preferred, 1 Edison-Leland Primary Portable Battery, especially designed for the Phonograph, to run 15 Hours, and easily recharged at any time.
1 Camel's Hair Phonograph Brush for cleaning Records.
1 Phonograph Oil Can.

A full line of **extra parts, supplies,** and **novelties** always on hand, including **Record Boxes,** of Pasteboard, Stained Wood, Hardwood, or Tin, from 1 to 108 capacity; all kinds of **Horns,** and **Multiple Hearing Tubes,** for from 2 to 15 people.

We have always on hand a large assortment of **Records,** and are turning out **new selections** every day. Only the **best talent** is employed, and all records are **originals** and of the highest class.

Orders sent direct to us, or to any of our authorized dealers, will receive prompt attention.

THE NORTH AMERICAN PHONOGRAPH CO.

32 PARK PLACE, NEW YORK. 51 STATE STREET, CHICAGO.
304 CHESTNUT STREET PHILADELPHIA. 17 W. SWAN STREET, BUFFALO, N. Y.
120 EAST 14th STREET, NEW YORK.

5-4. An 8 1/2" x 14" advertising sheet with transactional jottings, circa 1893, from the North American Phonograph Company. It listed the items comprising an "Exhibition Outfit," including Class "M" Edison electric Phonograph, horn, records and accessories. It bore the dealer stamp of Morris Battery, Atlanta, Georgia. *Courtesy of the Charles Hummel collections.* (Value code: D)

5-5. An 8" x 19 5/8" broadside announcing a Phonograph exhibition which took place in 1894. In all likelihood, "Professor" Foote received his only degree from the "school of hard knocks!" *Courtesy of the Charles Hummel collections.* (Value code: E)

5-6. Artifacts of the Edison Phonograph from the early 1890s. At the top, an 1894 letter with its envelope. This local firm in Wilkes-Barre, Pennsylvania, sold Edison Phonographs supplied by the North American Phonograph Company. Below, a catalogue of Edison machines from a year or so earlier. (VR)

5-7. This restrained and refined handbill advertised a concert featuring Edison's "Improved Phonograph" in 1891. Unlike the usual side-show hoots that talking machine showmen held for a dime a head, this early exhibition had reserved seats at 35 cents! (VR)

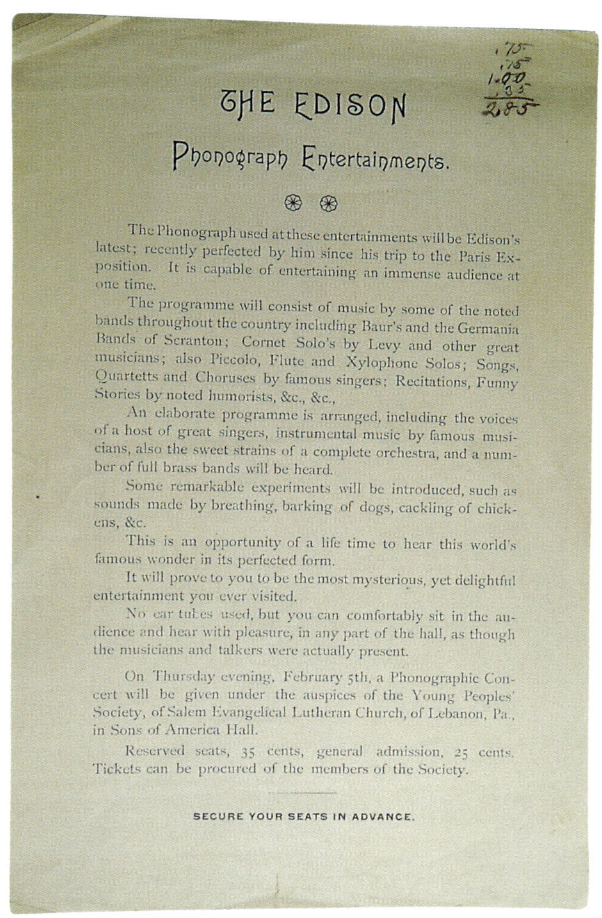

.75
.75
1.00
.35
2.85

THE EDISON

Phonograph Entertainments.

The Phonograph used at these entertainments will be Edison's latest; recently perfected by him since his trip to the Paris Exposition. It is capable of entertaining an immense audience at one time.

The programme will consist of music by some of the noted bands throughout the country including Baur's and the Germania Bands of Scranton; Cornet Solo's by Levy and other great musicians; also Piccolo, Flute and Xylophone Solos; Songs, Quartetts and Choruses by famous singers; Recitations, Funny Stories by noted humorists, &c., &c.,

An elaborate programme is arranged, including the voices of a host of great singers, instrumental music by famous musicians, also the sweet strains of a complete orchestra, and a number of full brass bands will be heard.

Some remarkable experiments will be introduced, such as sounds made by breathing, barking of dogs, cackling of chickens, &c.

This is an opportunity of a life time to hear this world's famous wonder in its perfected form.

It will prove to you to be the most mysterious, yet delightful entertainment you ever visited.

No ear tubes used, but you can comfortably sit in the audience and hear with pleasure, in any part of the hall, as though the musicians and talkers were actually present.

On Thursday evening, February 5th, a Phonographic Concert will be given under the auspices of the Young Peoples' Society, of Salem Evangelical Lutheran Church, of Lebanon, Pa., in Sons of America Hall.

Reserved seats, 35 cents, general admission, 25 cents. Tickets can be procured of the members of the Society.

SECURE YOUR SEATS IN ADVANCE.

5-8. The impact of Thomas Edison's genius was worldwide. His image appeared in books and magazines accompanied by lofty prose, and even on the lowly "trading cards" which were distributed as premiums in packages of chocolate and other food products. Counterclockwise from the left: a Chocolat Poulain card from France, with an artist's depiction of the crowds who eagerly put on ear-tubes to hear the "Improved Phonograph" at the Paris Exposition of 1889. Next, a French card which came with Abils meat extract. A fanciful representation of the nuts-and-bolts of cylinder record recording still managed to include a few accurate details amid delightful nonsense. Next, a Brunita margarine card employed a direct interpretation of a widely-published photo: Edison, exhausted after successfully completing the "Improved Phonograph." (Value code: E)

5-9. An Edison sign, circa 1903, measuring 9 3/8" x 19 3/8". On the reverse is printed, "This is a Pulveroid sign. A Pulveroid sign is the lightest and most brilliant indoor sign made and will retain its brilliance longer than any other sign. Manufactured by F. F. Pulver Company, Rochester, New York." Frank F. Pulver represented something of a one-man business blitz in the western New York city of Rochester. In the first years of the century, he was the maker of "Celluloid Novelties That Advertise. Badges, Buttons, Books, Signs, Etc..." However, he was also listed in the City Directory as president of the Pulver Chemical Manufacturing Company: the family chewing gum factory. In the days before close government regulation, it's disturbing to imagine that the same constituents might have been mixed to produce either product! *Courtesy of the Charles Hummel collections.* (Value code: B)

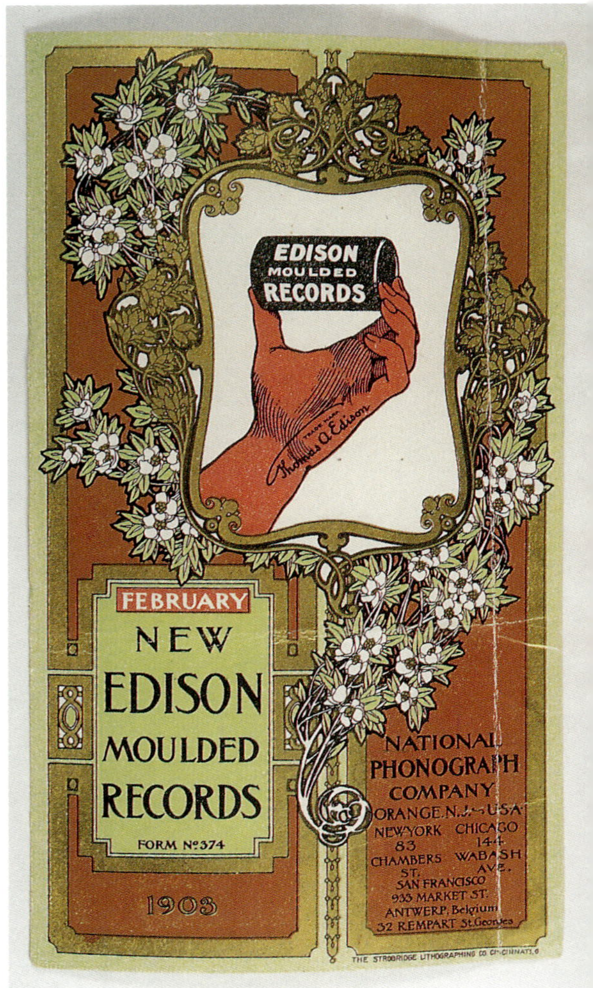


5-10. A close-up of a 1903 Edison cylinder record supplement. The selections were listed on the back. The hand/cylinder motif was used in several variations for Edison advertising. (Value code: G)

5-11. These delightfully designed Edison cylinder supplement sheets from the 1903 period listed the monthly releases on the reverse. *Courtesy of Walter and Carol Myers*. (Value code: G)

5-12. A 10" x 27 3/4" metal sign advertising Edison Phonographs, circa 1905. *Courtesy of the Charles Hummel collections.* (Value code: B)

5-13. An effort to confuse the public. "Edsonia" cigars had nothing to do with Thomas Edison. However, the colorful representation of a cylinder talking machine and the "similar-sounding" name must have attracted unwitting customers. (Label, 6 1/2" x 10".) (Value code: D)

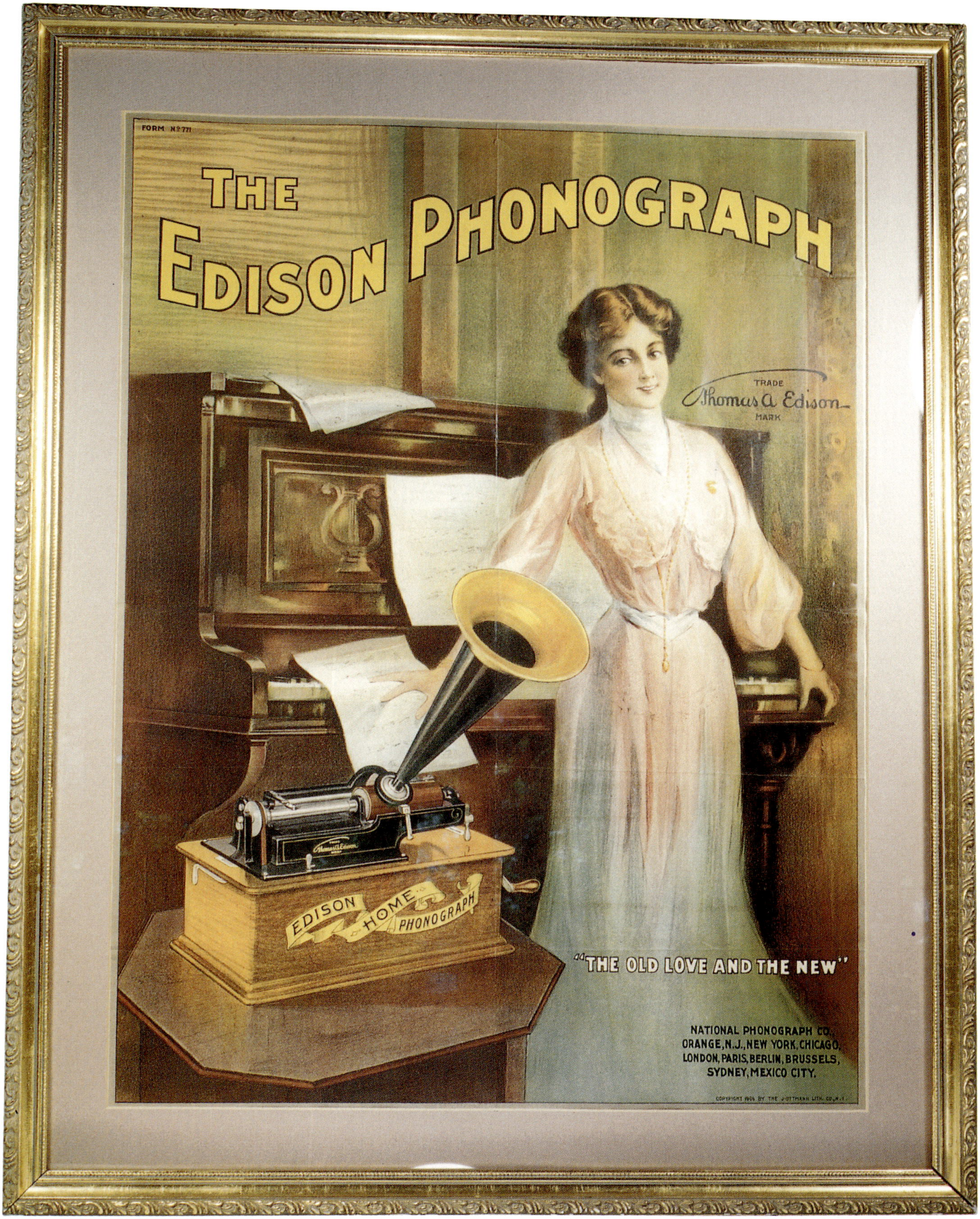


5-14. A 20" x 27" poster promoting Edison Phonographs, circa 1905. Edison advertising of the period had a decidedly domestic flavor, and particularly emphasized women. *Courtesy of the Charles Hummel collections.* (Value code: A)

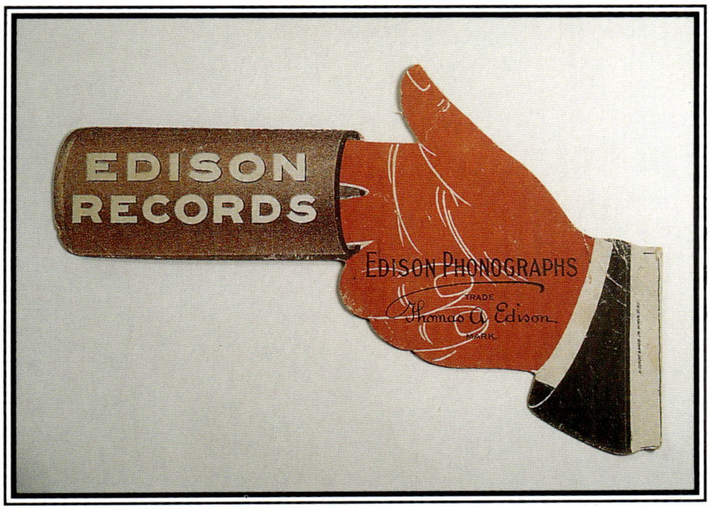


5-15. This image of a hand displaying an Edison two-minute cylinder appeared in various forms of advertising, circa 1906. The example shown here, measuring 9 1/2" long, was meant to be inserted into a larger display by the white tab at the end of the sleeve. (Value code: F)

5-16. An Edison trade card, circa 1906 implies that a Phonograph might prove an excellent distraction for babies. (Value code: G)

5-17. A metal promotional paperweight clock from the National Phonograph Company, measuring 3 1/4" diameter at the base. *Courtesy of the Charles Hummel collections.* (Value code: C)

5-18. Three souvenir badges. Left: a celluloid badge with ribbon from an excursion of Victor personnel, July 13, 1907. Center: a metal badge with "Nipper" pendant commemorating a 1918 reunion of Elks' Lodge No.293, Camden, New Jersey. Right: an elaborate 1905 badge of metal, celluloid and ribbon from Elks' Lodge No.135, Orange, New Jersey, "The Phonograph City." *Courtesy of the Charles Hummel collections.* (Value code: E)

5-19. This bucolic scene, painted by Pompeo Massani, was Edison's answer to "His Master's Voice." Acquired by the National Phonograph Company in April 1905 for $1,050, the original showed the couple listening to a european "Puck" cylinder talking machine. A copy was immediately commissioned by National, with the offending "Puck" replaced by an Edison "Standard" Phonograph. By early 1906, calendars, 17" x 25" lithographs (shown), and postcards bearing the image of an old couple (unimaginatively titled "The Phonograph") were being widely distributed. By the following year, over 400 billboards were displaying the picture throughout the United States. Within three years, however, the National Phonograph Company phased out the "old couple," reverting to the even more prosaic Edison signature trade mark. Trounced by Nipper and his Gramophone in the marketplace, Massani's painting might have proved an outright embarrassment to Edison, had Massani's original title, *"Enrico!"* been made public. (Value code: D)

5-20. A 1909 calendar which promoted Edison Phonographs and supplies. (Value code: E)

5-21. "Articulated" trade cards which unfolded to unleash a marketing salvo were popular with talking machine companies. This Edison card of 1911 showed kids rushing to enjoy a parade. (Value code: F)

5-22. Far from disappointed when they discover their mistake, the children prefer to be entertained by an Edison Phonograph.

5-23. Two bottles of Edison phonograph oil from the post-1910 period. The one on the left shows the diamond-shaped label of products related to the "Diamond Disc" machines. By the mid-1920s, however, Edison oil bottles looked like the one on the right. *Courtesy of Norm and Janyne Smith.* (Value code: G)

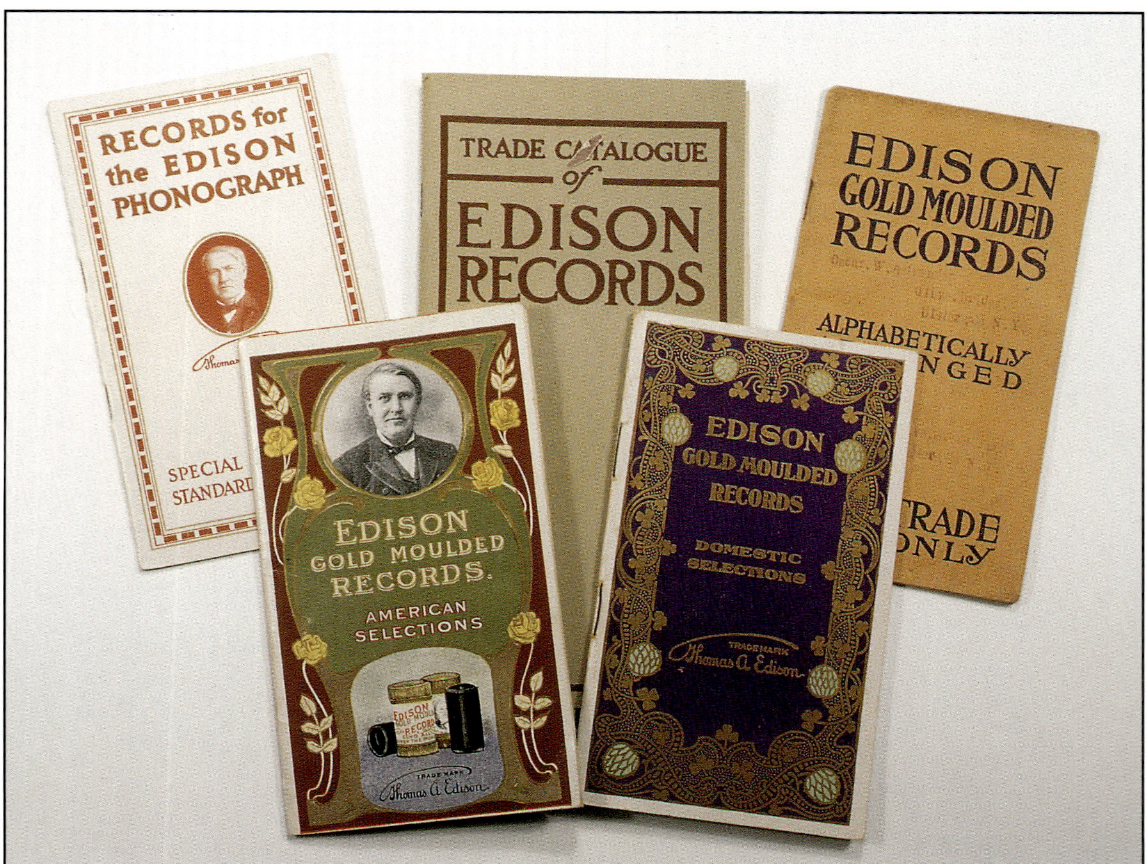


5-24. Edison cylinder record catalogues, including two at the top right intended for dealer use. *Courtesy of Martin F. Bryan*. (Value code: G)

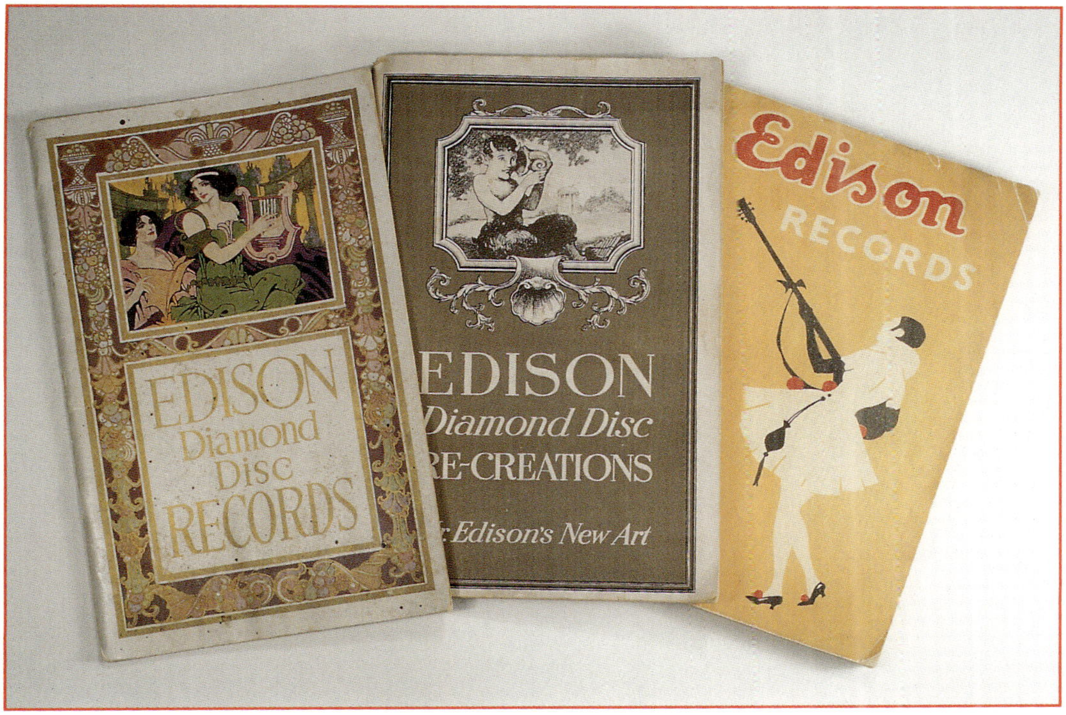


5-25. Three Edison disc record catalogues, 1914-1927. The company introduced its line of vertical cut discs in 1912 as the "Edison Disc Record," but never seemed satisfied with this title. The records came to be called "Diamond Disc Re-Creations" and finally "Edison Records," with the occasional addition of various subtexts such as, "Mr. Edison's New Art." The "New Edison Velvet Surface Record" of 1918 was another epithet, disastrously timed to coincide with a sudden rise in surface noise caused by the wartime shortage of a key record ingredient, phenol. *Courtesy of Martin F. Bryan.* (Value code: G)

5-26. An Edison cylinder phonograph catalogue from 1913, and an Edison catalogue of "Blue Amberol" cylinders (9-1-13). *Courtesy of Martin F. Bryan.* (Value code: F, G)

5-27. The Babson name was associated with the sale of Edison (cylinder) Phonographs for many years. This large (8 1/2" x 11") catalogue issued by Babson Brothers, Chicago, in 1916 featured the new line of Edison Amberolas, sold by mail-order credit terms. Babson's sales approach amounted to heaps of laudatory verbiage accented by bright colors. The machine on the right was an ordinary Amberola "30" table model enclosed in a special floor-standing cabinet sold only by Babson. (Value code: E)

5-28. Another page from the Babson catalogue pictorially follows the ordering of an Edison Amberola "30" from the pen of the *paterfamilias* to the pleasures of the parlor. Babson graphics were a little clumsy, but undeniably effective.

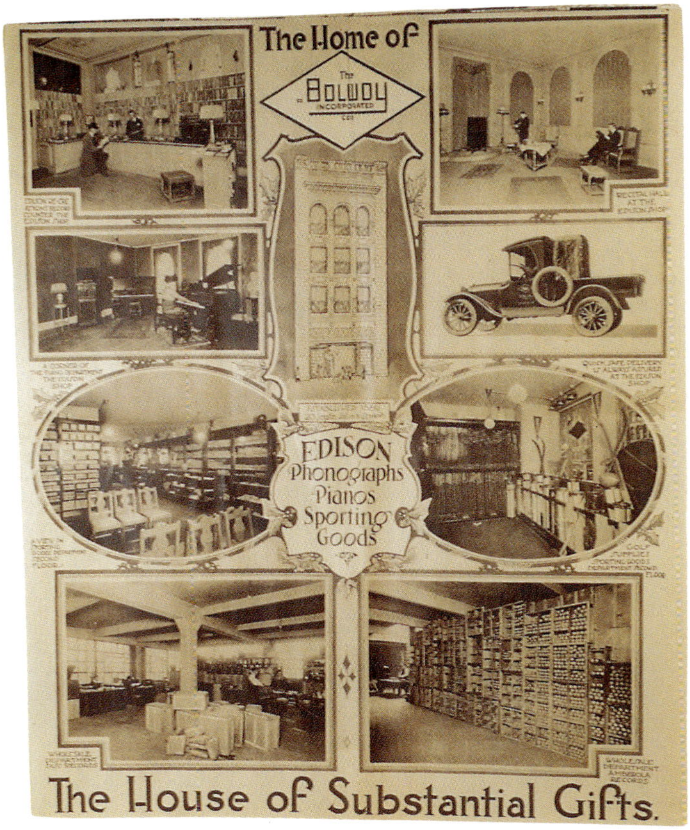


5-29. An advertising page from the December 15, 1918 issue of the *Syracuse Post-Standard* shows the extensive facilities of the Bolway store in Syracuse, New York. Bolway clearly believed that elegant surroundings would induce customers to purchase Edison phonographs. Note the "Blue Amberol" cylinder records stacked at the bottom right corner. *Courtesy of William G. Meyer.* (Value code: H)

5-30. "Edison Diamond Points" was the dealer magazine produced by Edison to support its "Diamond Disc" Phonograph line. Here are three issues, the one on top from 1919. *Courtesy of Charles McCarn.* (Value code: H)

5-31. *Along Broadway* was the periodical used to promote Edison "Diamond Disc" records to the public. Issues, like these from 1919-20, contained information designed to publicize specific selections and artists. *Courtesy of Martin F. Bryan.* (Value code: H)

5-32. Various Edison Phonograph lubricants. Left to right: a tube of gear grease from the mid-'teens; Edison grease in a milk glass jar from the 1920s; Edison "Diamond" (disc) grease from the World War I period; spring lubricant from the mid-'teens. *Courtesy of Norm and Janyne Smith.* (Value code: H)

5-33. An Edison "Diamond Disc" dealer used this "Cabinet Retouching Outfit" to correct minor nicks and scratches. The wooden box measures 6" x 6" x 13". *Courtesy of the Charles Hummel collections.* (Value code: D)

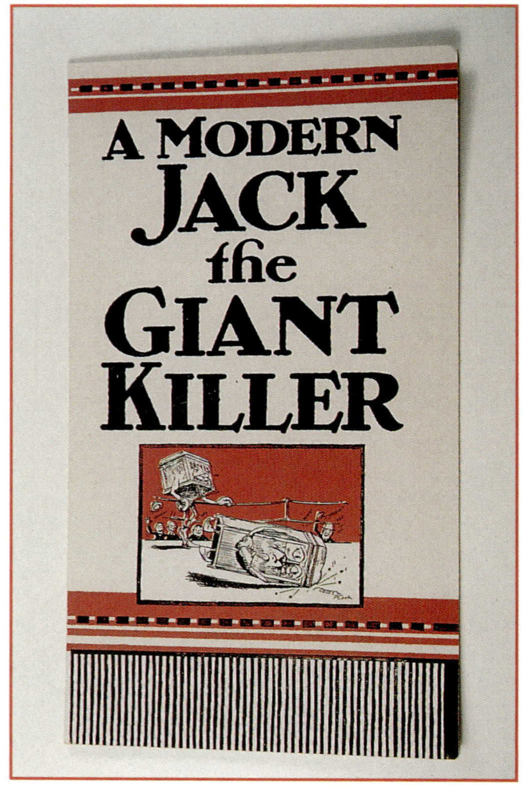


5-34. In the late 'teens, the Edison company launched an advertising campaign claiming that its modestly-constructed Amberola "50" cylinder phonograph had beaten certain big, substantially-made disc talking machines (read: "Victrolas") in consumer preference tests. Long before the days when cigarette packs with long, shapely legs would dance on TV, Edison entertained its dealers at the 1918 Convention with an apparition dubbed the "Knock-Out Kid." A muscular gentleman attired in boxing trunks and gloves came out wearing the cabinet of an Amberola "50" over his head! This brochure, despite the endearing graphics, gives a misleading impression. In actuality, the deficiencies of the Amberolas of this period (cheap cabinets, inadequate internal-horns, poorly dubbed cylinders) discouraged many customers from the cylinder format. (Value code: G)

5-35. This "textured" lithograph of an Edison portrait was offered to Phonograph dealers in the 1920s. It measures 25 1/2" x 31 1/2". *Courtesy of Walter and Carol Myers.* (Value code: D)

5-36. "Pin-back" buttons were handy communication tools long before they became icons of popular culture and social ferment in the 1960s. The Edison company used them extensively, and distributed "birthday" buttons to honor the Great Man himself. On the left, a button commemorates Edison's seventy-fifth birthday. The "pin-back" on the right carries the Edison logo from the late 1920s: a variation of his own handwriting. (Value code: F)

5-38. The last comprehensive catalogue of Edison "Blue Amberol" cylinders was issued in 1927 and oddly titled *The Golden Treasury, first edition* (left). Diminishing sales and declining press runs meant that only monthly supplements would be offered thereafter. Right, a brochure announcing the Edison "Long Playing" discs of 1926. Far ahead of their time, these microgroove records were impugned by the unsatisfactory mechanical method of reproduction used by Edison. The repertoire, too, was perfectly lifeless, insuring a rapid discontinuation of the project. *Courtesy of Martin F. Bryan.* (Value code: F, G)

5-37. The Ediphone was Thomas A. Edison Incorporated's office dictating machine. In this cutaway display model from the 1920s, the complex design of the recorder/reproducer is shown in relation to the cylinder surface. *Courtesy of Christopher J. Stephens.* (Value code: F)

5-39. The phonograph and record division of Thomas A. Edison, Incorporated, the oldest name in talking machines, fizzled slowly into oblivion by the fall of 1929—but not before it kicked a couple of times. Late in 1927, the venerable vertical cut "Diamond Disc" record finally began to be electrically recorded. Then, in August of 1929, an excellent line of lateral cut "electric" discs was introduced. Unfortunately, both projects were doomed by the "too-little-too-late" mentality which affected the Edison company during this period. Additionally, the last 300 or so "Blue Amberol" cylinder records were dubbed from electric discs, though the market for cylinders had all but disappeared. On the left, a list of electric "Diamond Discs" (marked January 1929). In the middle, the *next to the last* "Blue Amberol" monthly supplement, April 1929. To the right, a packet of steel needles intended for Edison lateral records. *Courtesy of Martin F. Bryan.* (Value code: H)

5-40. These up-to-date advertising materials, complete with die-cut paper record, were sent to an Edison dealer to introduce the electrically-recorded "needle-cut" disc of 1929. Within months, however, Edison would withdraw from the record and phonograph market altogether. Measures 16 3/4" x 22 1/2". *Courtesy of Charles McCarn.* (Value code: D, lot)

5-41. Along with the lateral cut discs of 1929, Edison offered two plainly-designed portables intended to play only the "needle" records. It's difficult to imagine which "heiress" would choose such nondescript luggage, contrary to the suggestion of the advertising copy. Measures 19" x 24". *Courtesy of Charles McCarn.* (Value code: E)

5-42. Not much remains of Edison's ill-fated foray into lateral cut discs. A counter display for Edison steel needles is therefore a special treat. Body of display measures 13" high, cardboard pieces at top substituted for a missing header. *Courtesy of the Charles Hummel collections.* (VR)

5-43. Edison disc record supplements from the mid to late 1920s. The one on the left is a seldom-seen "Needle Record" supplement. *Courtesy of Martin F. Bryan.* (Value code: H)

5-44. This 11" x 14" Columbia store placard from 1899 succinctly expresses the appeal of the "BS" coin-slot Graphophone: inexpensive and profitable. (VR)

5-45. A placard advertising the "Toy Graphophone." By 1899, the astounding success of Emile Berliner's Gramophone inspired Columbia to attempt to break into the disc talking machine market. Due to legalities and logistics, a substantial disc machine under the Columbia brand was years away. In the meantime, the company offered this hand-driven novelty in 1899 for only $3.00 (quickly reduced to $1.50). The records were wax, vertically recorded and reproduced in much the same way as the cylinder Graphophones of the period. Compared to the hand-driven Gramophone, the barely functional "Toy" was no competition. (VR)

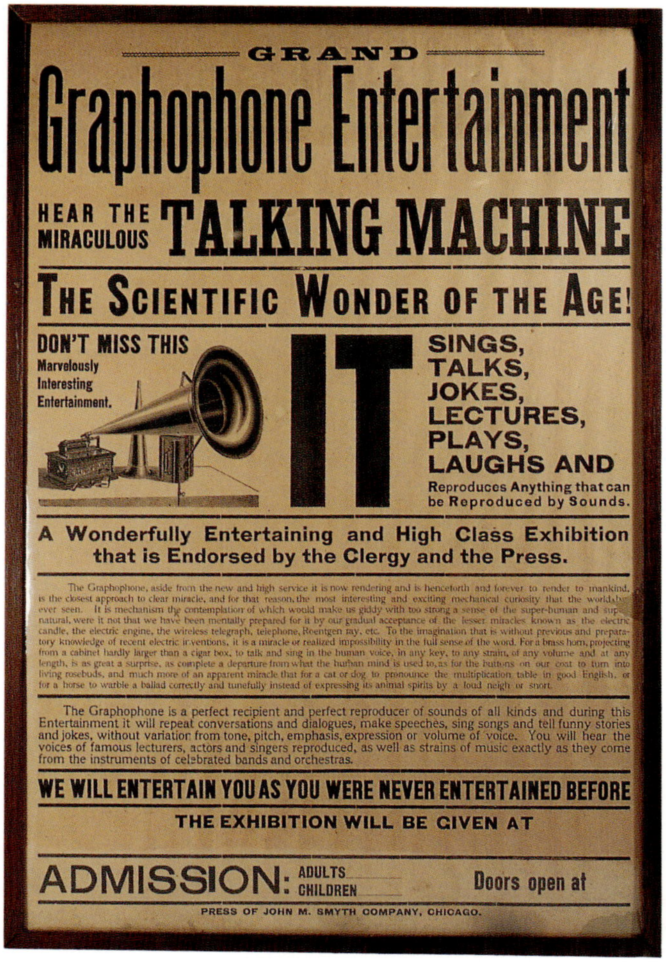


5-46. Various mail order firms like Sears, Roebuck & Company of Chicago made ample use of the talking machine's novelty in the "Exhibition Outfits" it began offering by mail-order in the late 1890s. The customer received everything he needed to present talking machine "entertainments." Included were necessities such as tickets and eye-catching posters (shown). This one measures 14" x 21". *Courtesy of the collection of Howard Hazelcorn.* (Value code: E)

5-47. After Columbia introduced its "Columbia Grand" Type "AG" 5" cylinder Graphophone in 1900, Sears prepared an exhibition outfit which included the new model. Posters such as this one (14" x 21") ardently proclaimed the merits of the "Graphophone Grand." *Courtesy of the collection of Howard Hazelcorn.* (Value code: E)

5-48. Three admission tickets from early talking machine "entertainments," including a Sears, Roebuck & Company example at the upper right. (Value code: H)

5-49. Two Columbia cylinder record catalogues. On the left: an exclusive listing of 6" long "Twentieth Century" or "Half Foot" records, which were introduced with much fanfare in 1905. On the right: the back cover of a complete catalogue of cylinders, which featured a panoramic view of the American Graphophone factory at Bridgeport, Connecticut. Columbia, unlike Edison, exploited the image of its vigorous plant for promotional purposes. It even appeared on a label affixed to the reverse of certain single-faced discs. (Value code: G)

5-50. Various Columbia ephemera. Clockwise from top left, a flyer advertising a rarely documented type of Disc Graphophone from 1908: Type "B.N.I." or "New Ideal." Next, a complete 1906 catalogue of Columbia cylinder and disc machines. Next, A 1913 sheet promoting the latest Tin Pan Alley hit. Finally, a 1906 record supplement which repeats the often-quoted, "music hath charms..." (Value code: H, E, H, H)

5-51. Issues of *The Columbia Record*, a monthly dealer magazine. Shown are examples from 1907 and 1908. *Courtesy of Michael F. Khanchalian.* (Value code: G)

5-52. Various Columbia ephemera, with record supplements displayed over a copy of the company's house organ *The Columbia Record*. The charming advertisement on the right appeared in magazines in 1909 promoting the durability of the "Indestructible" celluloid cylinders. *Courtesy of Martin F. Bryan*. (Value code: G)

5-53. This wooden whistle was given away circa 1909 by a store selling sporting goods as well as Columbia Graphophones. (Value code: F)

5-54. Columbia offered its dealers 10" (shown) and 12" lithographed metal "Imitation Records" for display purposes. These ersatz discs could not be broken, would not warp in a sunny store window and protected the turntable material on a display machine from damage or fading. (Value code: D)

5-55. After Columbia discontinued its cylinder record line in 1912, its disc record supplements evolved into a larger (5" x 6 3/4") format. As the covers of these examples suggest, Columbia's was a busy and aggressive art department. *Courtesy of Martin F. Bryan.* (Value code: H)

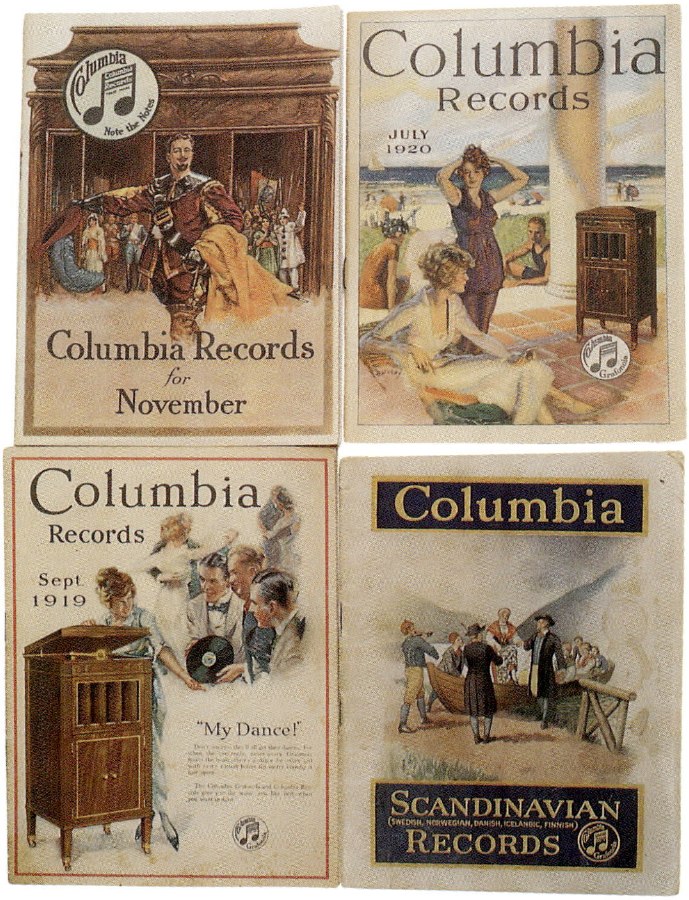


5-56. More Columbia disc supplements, which made the concurrent offerings of other record companies look drab by comparison. *Courtesy of Martin F. Bryan.* (Value code: H)

5-57. A sheet metal sign measuring 11 7/8" x 23 5/8", from the period 1909-1915 when a dealer might sell both the external-horn Graphophone and the internal-horn Grafonola.
*Courtesy of Walter and Carol Myers*. (Value code: C)

5-58. A trolley sign measuring 10" x 19 3/4", promoting the Columbia Grafonola. *Courtesy of Walter and Carol Myers*. (Value code: C)

5-59. A 14 1/2" x 21" metal sign advertising Columbia products, circa 1920. *Courtesy of the Charles Hummel collections.* (Value code: B)

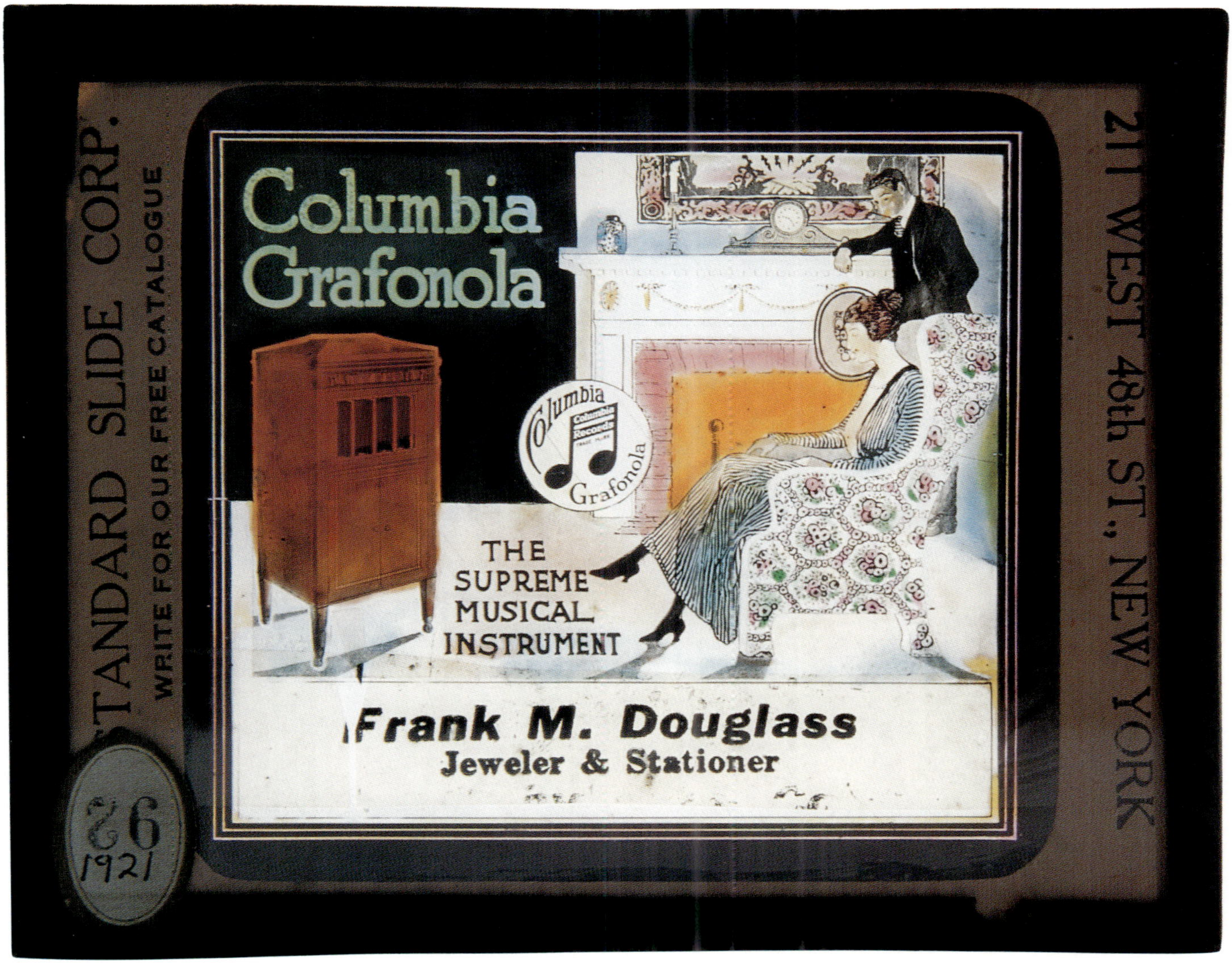


5-60. Lantern slides made to be shown in movie houses and theatres were popular methods of advertising during the first two decades of the twentieth century. *Courtesy of Alan H. Mueller.* (Value code: F)

5-62. Two talking machine advertising fans from the 1920 period. (Value code: F)

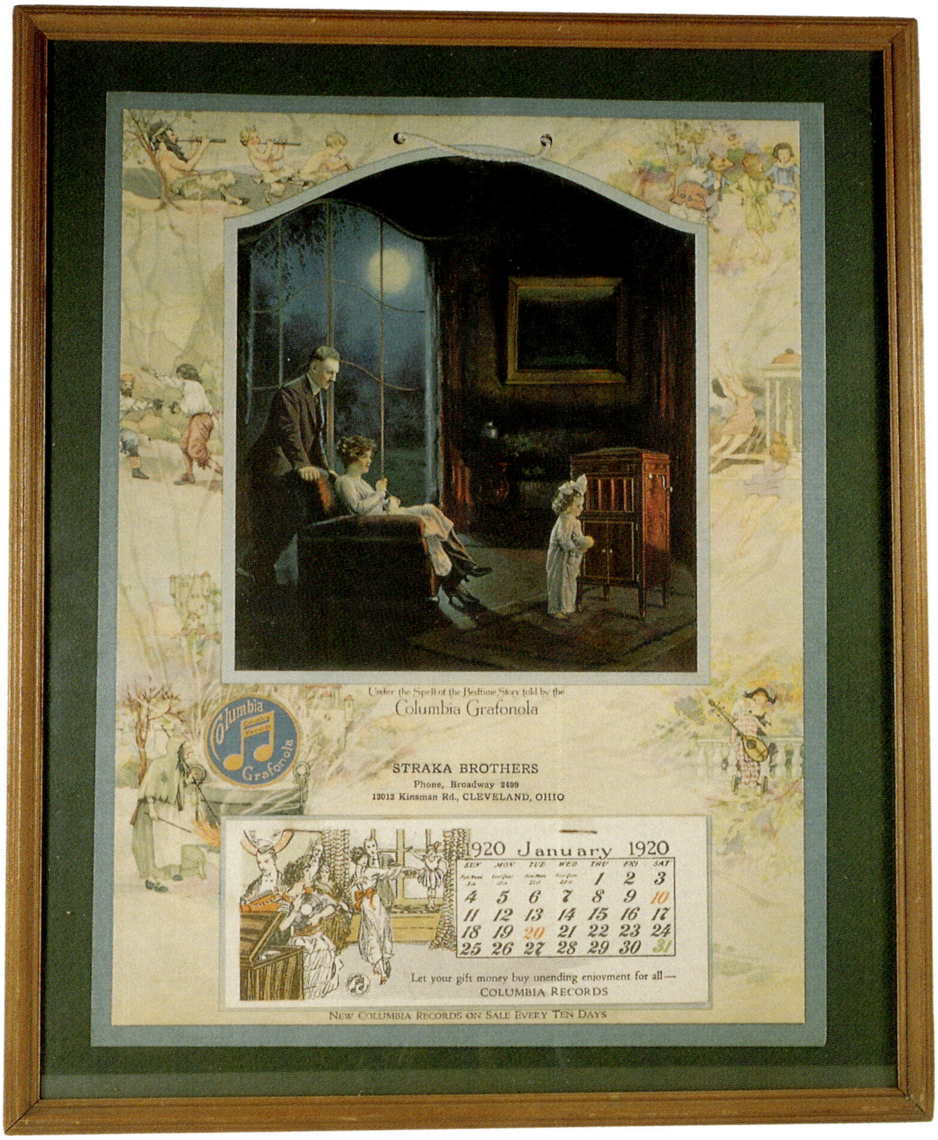


5-61. Calendars have long been effective marketing tools. This richly-designed example from 1920 promoted the Columbia Grafonola. 9 1/2" x 12 1/2". (Value code: F)

5-64. Various Columbia paper items. From left to right: a 1924 disc record catalogue; a small packet of steel needles; a booklet listing Columbia discs suitable for school use; a 1912 catalogue, and another circa 1910. Both Victor and Columbia introduced double-faced discs at the end of 1908, and the companies (Columbia in particular) called close attention to this innovation during the first years of production. *Courtesy of Martin F. Bryan*. (Value code: G, H, G, F, F)

5-63. A 13 1/2" high wood-grained metal counter display for Columbia record supplements, circa 1921. *Courtesy of the Charles Hummel collections.* (VR)

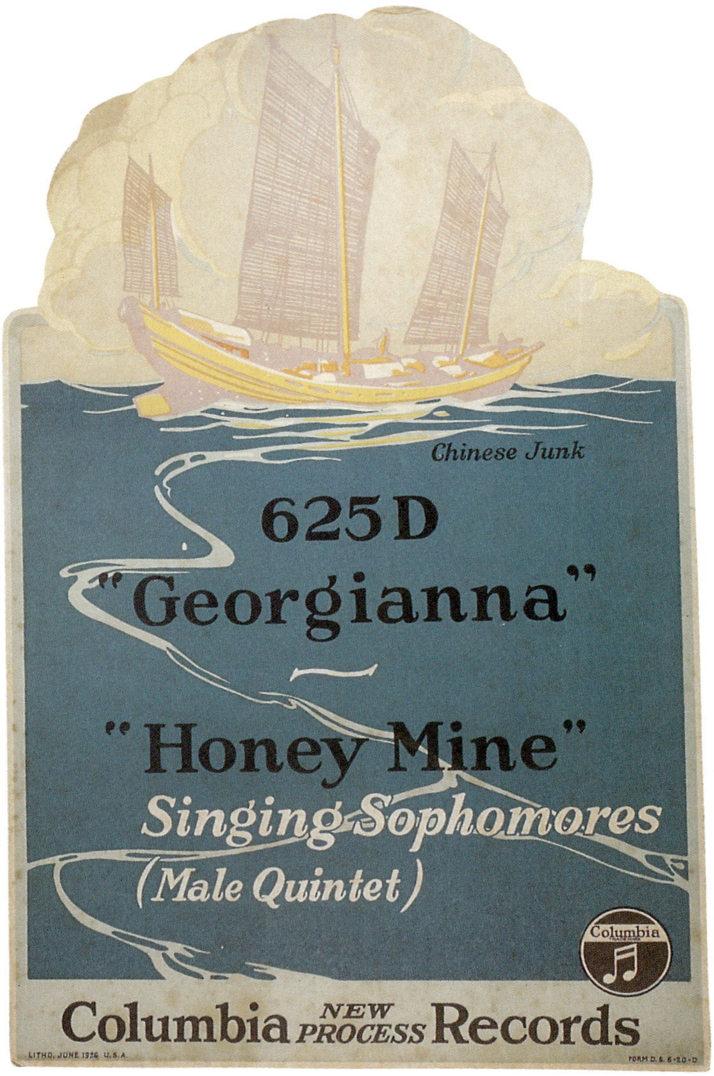


5-65. A Columbia Store display card promoting a record released in June 1926. *Courtesy of Martin F. Bryan.* (Value code: E)

5-66. A desk accessory which combines inkwell, calendar and paperweight in the form of a miniature Columbia "Viva-Tonal" portable, circa 1928. Precise in nearly every detail, it measures only 1 3/8" x 2 1/2" x 3 1/4". The "turntable" acts as an inkwell cover and depicts a Columbia disc in place. *Courtesy of the Charles Hummel collections.* (Value code: C)

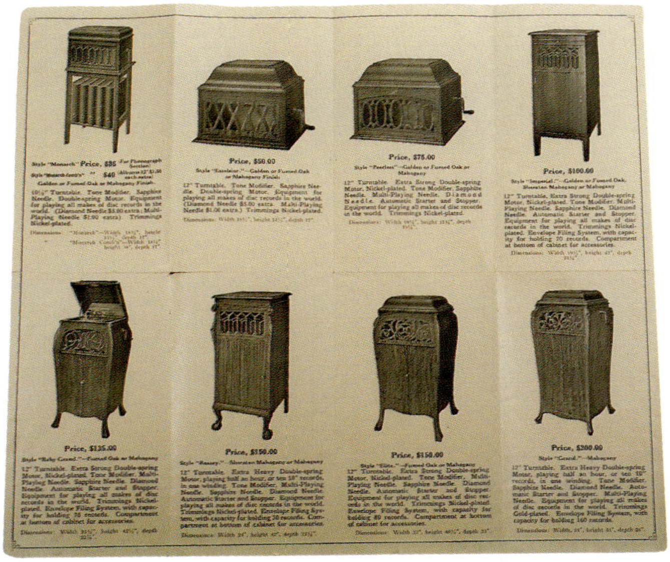


5-67. A catalogue sheet from the 'teens shows the Sonora line of talking machines, culminating in the company's signature bombé models. Having fought the good fight and succeeded in deflecting Victor's legal department in 1911, Sonora went through a complete reorganization before emerging as a formidable force in the industry by the late 'teens. *Courtesy of Martin F. Bryan.* (Value code: G)

5-69. This 9" x 13" store sign was produced in "Chrystoglas," a process which employed a celluloid skin to give the impression of depth. The manufacturer, Whitehead and Hoag Company of Newark, New Jersey, claimed it to be "the highest development of art in indoor signs." *Courtesy of the Charles Hummel collections.* (Value code: B)

5-68. A striking and vivid Sonora metal sign, circa 1920, measuring 13" x 19". *Courtesy of the Charles Hummel collections.* (Value code: B)

5-70. This large sheet metal Sonora sign measuring 28" x 48", features a Queen Anne console. A variety of dealers' names have been seen painted at the bottom. *Courtesy of Michael and Suzanne Raisman.* (Value code: B)

5-71. The sheet music of a promotional Sonora rhapsody, along with a flyer rhapsodizing the merits of the Sonora phonograph. *Courtesy of Martin F. Bryan.* (Value code: F, H)

5-72. Store advertising signs seldom seem to have been made of wood, like this one. It may be that wooden signs have deteriorated faster than sheet metal ones. This Sonora sign, painted in the brand's distinctive colors, is an unusual survivor from the late 'teens. (Size: 19" x 36".) *Courtesy of Norm and Janyne Smith.* (Value code: B)

5-73. A trick trade card from around 1920, showing an elegant lady with features in repose. *Courtesy of Walter and Carol Myers*. (Value code: F)

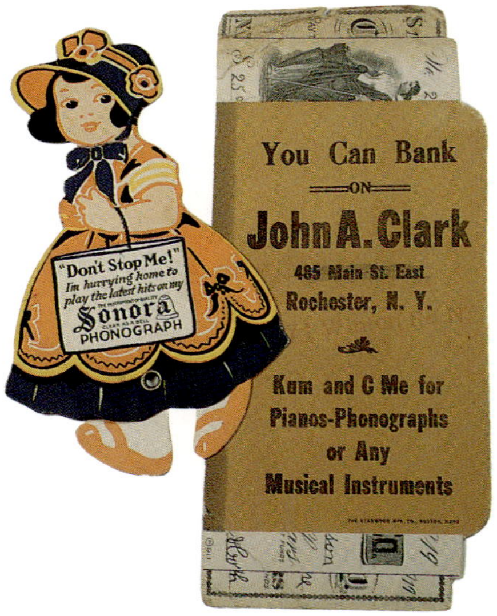


5-75. A charming "walker" trade card promotes the "Sonora." To the right, a *trompe l'oeil* bank book, complete with protruding checks, attracts the interest (pun intended) of potential customers. (Value code: G)

5-74. Holding the trick card to the light makes a Sonora phonograph appear before a suddenly alert "Mrs. Brown." *Courtesy of Walter and Carol Myers.*

5-76. "The Phonograph Game," circa 1899, was manufactured by Selchow and Righter of New York City. More a parlor amusement than a competitive game, it was predicated on making proper people say silly things. Popular song titles, drawn at random, were inserted into a stock story line—with nonsensical results! (Value code: D)

A typical sample of the game with random song titles in italics:

Dear Mother:
Uncle Reuben arrived safely last Monday. I met him at *The House Of Too Much Trouble*. After shaking hands the first thing he said to me was *How'd You Like To Be the Iceman*. Of course I was surprised and answered *I Guess I'll Have To Telegraph Ma Baby*. He said, I want you to show me around the town; I want to see *A Bird In a Gilded Cage, The Girl I Left Behind Me* and *Old Black Joe*. As we walked along I met my old friend *My Jersey Lily* in company with *Sarah From Syracuse* and I called out *Strike Up the Band! Here Comes a Sailor* and they said *I Don't Care If You Nebber Come Back*. Uncle said, "Is that *The Church Across the Way* where you get *Love's Magic Spell* and see *The Old Folks At Home*?" I said in reply, "*Go Way Back and Sit Down*, you must go to *My Old Kentucky Home* if you want to see *Rhoda and Her Pagoda* and hear *The Village Blacksmith*."

5-77. Topical and souvenir plates were popular around the close of the Nineteenth Century. This 8" diameter French plate in the "Great Discoveries of the Century" series reads, "Listen: it's Grandfather that you are hearing." *Courtesy of Jean-Paul Agnard.* (Value code: D)

5-79. Business envelopes were decorated with advertising to lure the recipient into looking within. Above, a novelty firm promotes the toy we know as the "penny phonograph" (see illustration 3-97). Middle, the "His Master's Voice" trade mark attracts the eye. Below, the Duplex Phonograph Company tells you everything you need to know before you open the envelope! (Value code: H)

5-78. The American Record Company (associated with Hawthorne & Sheble) introduced its "Indian" discs in 1905. A catalogue similar to the one shown on the left was described in the March 1905 issue of *Talking Machine World* as follows: "The cover is one of the most artistic which has appeared in a long time. The body color is light buff. On the front page is a deerskin spread out surrounded by eagle feathers, spears, arrows, Indian pipe, bull skin shield and other Indian trappings." The flyer to the right refers to the "Imperial" disc, which was the house brand of the Leeds & Catlin Company during the same period. (Value code: E, H)

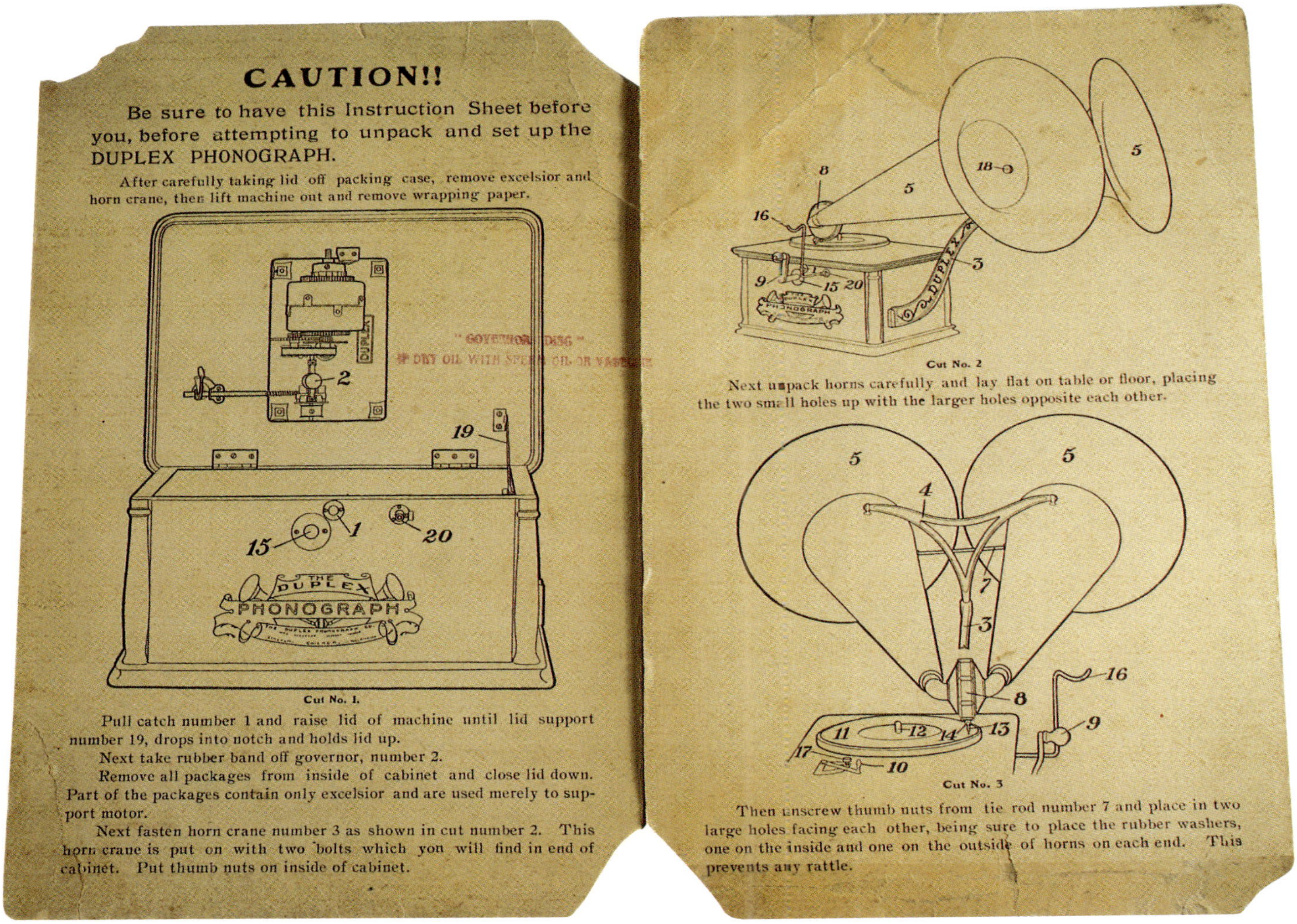

**CAUTION!!**

Be sure to have this Instruction Sheet before you, before attempting to unpack and set up the DUPLEX PHONOGRAPH.

After carefully taking lid off packing case, remove excelsior and horn crane, then lift machine out and remove wrapping paper.

Cut No. 1.

Pull catch number 1 and raise lid of machine until lid support number 19, drops into notch and holds lid up.

Next take rubber band off governor, number 2.

Remove all packages from inside of cabinet and close lid down. Part of the packages contain only excelsior and are used merely to support motor.

Next fasten horn crane number 3 as shown in cut number 2. This horn crane is put on with two bolts which you will find in end of cabinet. Put thumb nuts on inside of cabinet.

Cut No. 2

Next unpack horns carefully and lay flat on table or floor, placing the two small holes up with the larger holes opposite each other.

Cut No. 3

Then unscrew thumb nuts from tie rod number 7 and place in two large holes facing each other, being sure to place the rubber washers, one on the inside and one on the outside of horns on each end. This prevents any rattle.

5-80. A set of instructions for the "Duplex" phonograph which used two linked horns. This machine was originally envisioned as the "Duplexaphone" when the company was organized in Lincoln, Nebraska, in the spring of 1905. The firm expected to make both cylinder and disc talking machines using the patents of Charles E. Hill. The model pictured was introduced in 1906 as the "Duplex" and was the only style the company made, with slight variations. (Value code: F)

5-81. Chicago was home to a number of the independents who braved the talking machine market during the Twentieth Century's first decade, when the litigious breath of Victor and Columbia could frequently be felt on the back of their necks. Veteran entrepreneur Arthur J. O'Neill's two brands, "Busy Bee" and "Aretino," are represented by the left and right catalogues. In the middle is a catalogue of "D & R" ("Double and Reversible") discs, which were being sold as the 'teens were about to begin. *Courtesy of Martin F. Bryan.* (Value code: E, F, E)

5-82. The O'Neill-James Company sold cylinder records (left) and machines under the "Busy Bee" brand, as well as other talking machine equipment. The Englewood company sold a disc instrument called the "Musicalphone," shown in an advertising sheet to the right. Below, a postcard depicts Dearborn Street, in Chicago's commercial district, as it appeared when firms like the Standard Talking Machine Company made it their home. (Value code: F, G, H)

5-83. This 1904 flyer promoting the "Busy Bee" cylinder Graphophone evokes the hand of an "advertising specialist" such as Arthur J. O'Neill. Before O'Neill's company began marketing "Busy Bee" machines, it was already in the premium scheme and retail promotion racket. Clearly shown here are the terms under which the "Busy Bee" was offered by various retail establishments: the customer received coupons when making cash purchases. The coupons could then be saved up and redeemed for a talking machine or records. Equally interesting is the topical (and rather jingoistic) reference to the Russo-Japanese War. (Value code: G)

5-84. More ephemera from Chicago. At the top, an invoice from the Great Northern Manufacturing Company shows that it returned to the domestic ware business, in which it began, after spending more than five years selling talking machines ("Harmony" was one of its brands). Below, a catalogue of "Busy Bee" discs distributed by the rival O'Neill-James Company. (Value code: H, F)

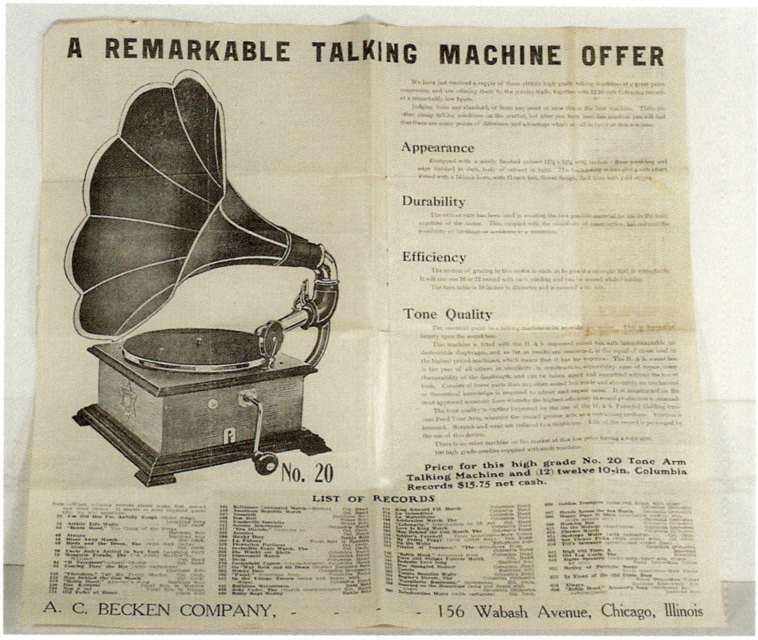


5-85. Hawthorne & Sheble Manufacturing Company of Philadelphia offered an ingenious line of disc talking machines under the "Star" brand. Shown in this flyer from 1908 is the Model "20," which reflected the retail price in dollars. Horn and elbow used convenient slip fittings, the soundbox diaphragm could be replaced without touching a screw, and the tone-arm was acted upon by the patented "Yielding Pressure Feed" (a gizmo intended to discourage charges of infringement by Victor). (Value code: G)

5-87. The designer of this cylinder box label from Robinson's of Manchester, England, must have suffered from *horror vacui*, or a fear of empty space. Crammed to the limits of its borders was an incredible array of information, including some pertaining to disc talking machines! (Value code: G)

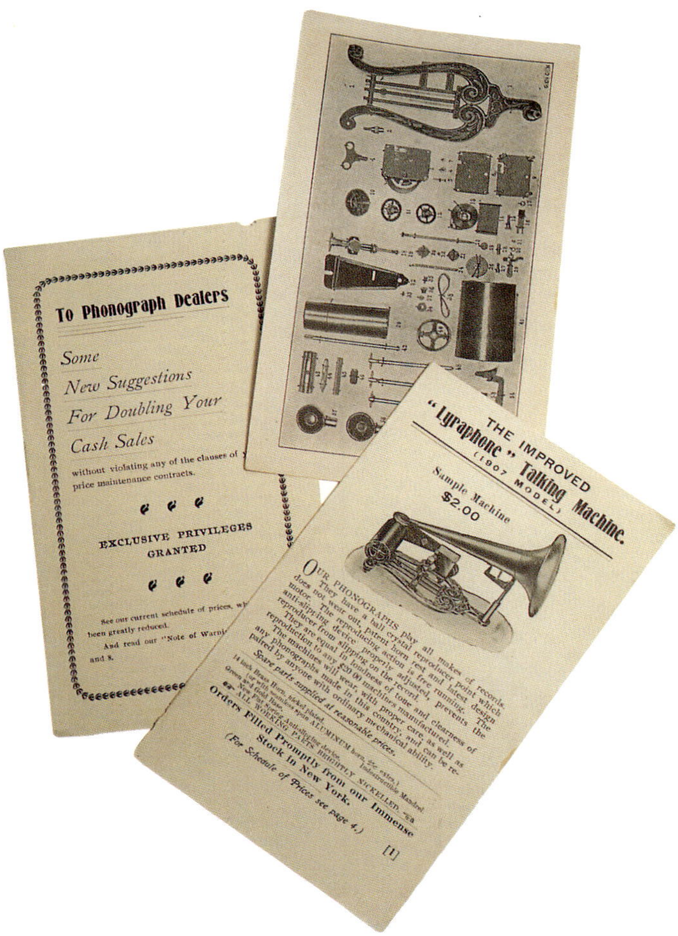


5-86. The "Lyraphone" was one of the "Puck" style of inexpensive cylinder talking machines which were produced primarily in Germany. Although ubiquitous in Europe and Britain, such marginally-equipped machines were not popular in the United States. One firm which did take a stab at marketing them was the Edwin A. Denham Company, Incorporated, of New York City. These flyers from 1906 were intended to interest dealers in carrying the "improved...1907 model." *Courtesy of Walter and Carol Myers*. (Value code: F)

5-88. This German collapsible die-cut novelty valentine measures 3 1/4" x 6 1/2" x 10 1/2", circa 1910. *Courtesy of Alan H. Mueller.* (Value code: D)

5-89. The "Multiphone" was a coin-operated entertainment device which selectively played 24 cylinders. The original company was organized late in 1906 and continued in fits and starts for about four years. Although various models were made, the version most commonly associated with the company was the "rococo" style shown in this 1909 catalogue. *Courtesy of John Woodward.* (Value code: D)

5-90. The U-S Phonograph Company of Cleveland, Ohio, produced a high-quality line of cylinder talking machines and records from 1910 through 1913. Pictured in this catalogue are examples of both external and internal-horn U-S models. Above is a slip which sometimes accompanied U-S "Everlasting" cylinder records. (Value code: E)

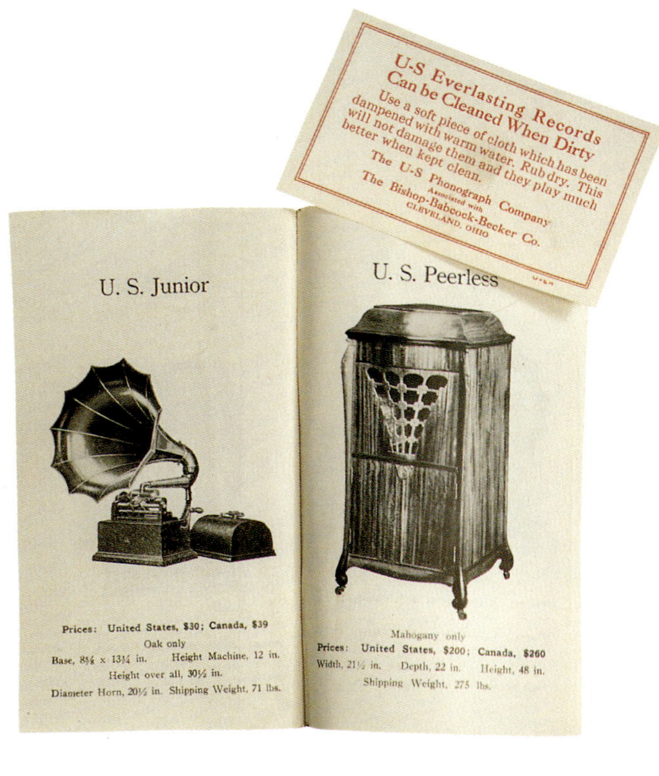

PIANOS:
MASON & HAMLIN, SOHMER, HARDMAN, CHAPMAN, BEHNING, KURTZMANN, KROEGER, KOHLER & CAMPBELL, FLEISHER, SOHMER CECILIAN, BEHNING PLAYER, HARDMAN AUTOTONE AND OTHER WORLDS BEST PIANOS.

PHONES: HOME 2846 - BELL 3593

E. J. Chapman

HIGH GRADE PIANOS

GENERAL DISTRIBUTOR FOR Victor Talking Machines

WHOLESALE AND RETAIL

EVERYTHING IN MUSIC

63 STATE STREET Rochester, N.Y.

May 15-1915.

Clark Music Co.,

Syracuse, N. Y.

Gentlemen:-

Enclosed herewith find note covering the two XVI's mahogany, we shipped you, which please sign and return. It is not convenient for us to make the note payable at your office, we prefer to have it payable at

5-91. Beginning in the mid-nineteenth century with the advent of affordable lithography, American business letterheads became complex and ornate. By the time this richly detailed example, with its delicate classical elements, was mailed in 1915 the trend was nearly over. In a few years, this much "gingerbread" would be looked on as silly. (Value code: H)

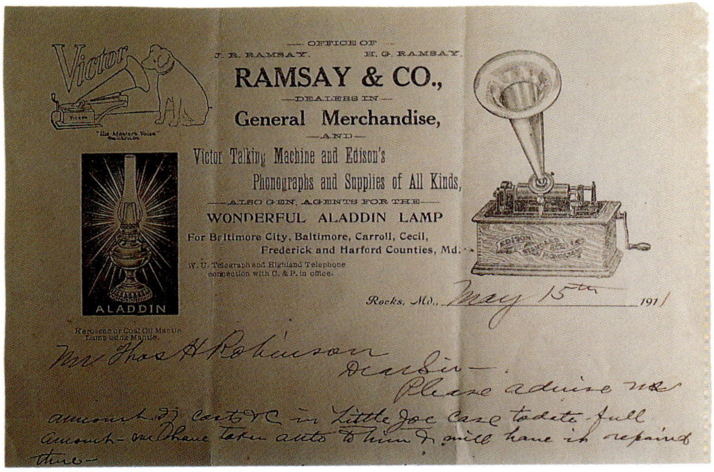
—OFFICE OF—

J. R. RAMSAY. H. G. RAMSAY.

RAMSAY & CO.,

—DEALERS IN—

General Merchandise,

—AND—

Victor Talking Machine and Edison's Phonographs and Supplies of All Kinds,

—ALSO GEN. AGENTS FOR THE—

WONDERFUL ALADDIN LAMP

For Baltimore City, Baltimore, Carroll, Cecil, Frederick and Harford Counties, Md.

W. U. Telegraph and Highland Telephone connection with C. & P. in office.

Rocks, Md., May 15th 1911



5-92. The letterhead of a general merchandise dealer illustrating the principal money-makers. (Value code: H)

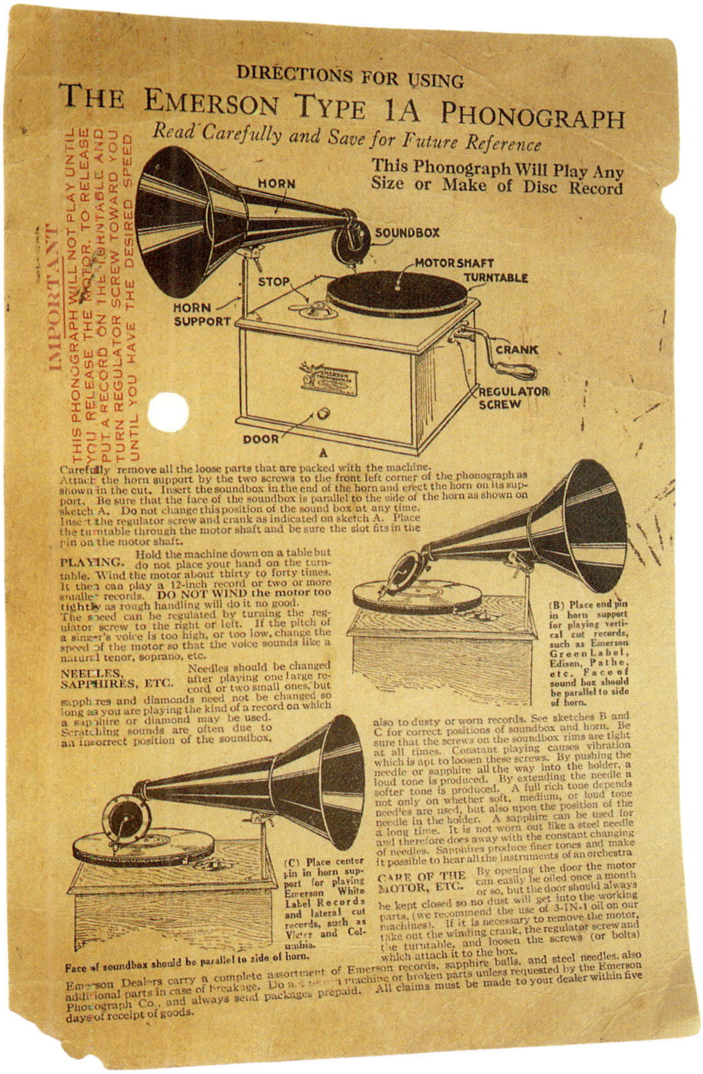
DIRECTIONS FOR USING

THE EMERSON TYPE 1A PHONOGRAPH

*Read Carefully and Save for Future Reference*

This Phonograph Will Play Any Size or Make of Disc Record

IMPORTANT

THIS PHONOGRAPH WILL NOT PLAY UNTIL YOU RELEASE THE MOTOR. TO RELEASE PUT A RECORD ON THE TURNTABLE AND TURN REGULATOR SCREW TOWARD YOU UNTIL YOU HAVE THE DESIRED SPEED



Carefully remove all the loose parts that are packed with the machine. Attach the horn support by the two screws to the front left corner of the phonograph as shown in the cut. Insert the soundbox in the end of the horn and erect the horn on its support. Be sure that the face of the soundbox is parallel to the side of the horn as shown on sketch A. Do not change this position of the sound box at any time. Insert the regulator screw and crank as indicated on sketch A. Place the turntable through the motor shaft and be sure the slot fits in the pin on the motor shaft.

**PLAYING.** Hold the machine down on a table but do not place your hand on the turntable. Wind the motor about thirty to forty times. It then can play a 12-inch record or two or more smaller records. **DO NOT WIND the motor too tightly** as rough handling will do it no good. The speed can be regulated by turning the regulator screw to the right or left. If the pitch of a singer's voice is too high, or too low, change the speed of the motor so that the voice sounds like a natural tenor, soprano, etc.

**NEEDLES, SAPPHIRES, ETC.** Needles should be changed after playing one large record or two small ones, but sapphires and diamonds need not be changed so long as you are playing the kind of a record on which a sapphire or diamond may be used. Scratching sounds are often due to an incorrect position of the soundbox, also to dusty or worn records. See sketches B and C for correct positions of soundbox and horn. Be sure that the screws on the soundbox rims are tight at all times. Constant playing causes vibration which is apt to loosen these screws. By pushing the needle or sapphire all the way into the holder, a loud tone is produced. By extending the needle a softer tone is produced. A full rich tone depends not only on whether soft, medium, or loud tone needles are used, but also upon the position of the needle in the holder. A sapphire can be used for a long time. It is not worn out like a steel needle and therefore does away with the constant changing of needles. Sapphires produce finer tones and make it possible to hear all the instruments of an orchestra

(B) Place end pin in horn support for playing vertical cut records, such as Emerson Green Label, Edison, Pathe, etc. Face of sound box should be parallel to side of horn.

(C) Place center pin in horn support for playing Emerson White Label Records and lateral cut records, such as Victor and Columbia.

Face of soundbox should be parallel to side of horn.

**CARE OF THE MOTOR, ETC.** By opening the door the motor can easily be oiled once a month or so, but the door should always be kept closed so no dust will get into the working parts. (we recommend the use of 3-IN-1 oil on our machines). If it is necessary to remove the motor, take out the winding crank, the regulator screw and the turntable, and loosen the screws (or bolts) which attach it to the box.

Emerson Dealers carry a complete assortment of Emerson records, sapphire balls, and steel needles, also additional parts in case of breakage. Do n[illegible] machine or broken parts unless requested by the Emerson Phonograph Co., and always send packages prepaid. All claims must be made to your dealer within five days of receipt of goods.

5-94. In 1915, the Emerson company introduced a minimally-designed disc talking machine to play both lateral and vertical cut records. Priced at about $3.00, the machine was heralded in contemporary advertising as "The Ford of the Phonograph Industry." Although it was short-lived, the "Emerson" shared the distinction with the "Keen-O-Phone" model "IV" of being American external-horn talking machines designed to play both types of disc record. (Value code: G)

5-93. An assortment of advertising rulers from the 'teens and twenties. (Value code: G, each)

# A Fine Disc Phonograph Free

## TO RIP-SAW CLUB RAISERS

By arrangements with one of the largest factories and by making a contract for several thousand phonographs, the RIP-SAW is able to provide every comrade who will do a little work for Socialism with a wonderful new Emerson Phonograph that will bring into his home all the music of the masters, grand opera, ragtime, classical selections or the songs and tunes we all love; the songs our mothers used to sing, as well as the latest "hits."

Comrade Phil Wagner and Comrade Frank O'Hare each took an Emerson phonograph home and each played Victor and Columbia records on it and compared it with the finest Victor and Columbia graphophones. The Emerson model phonograph plays every record in perfect tune, loudly and clearly and if a person were in another room he would be unable to tell but what it was a $50.00 or $100.00 phonograph.

The Emerson will play any Columbia, Victor, Edison or Pathe Disc record, the largest twelve-inch size or the seven-and-a-half or five-inch sizes. It will play Edison and Pathe Disc records when supplied with a special sapphire point.

### The Emerson Record

This record is a recent invention of Mr. Victor H. Emerson, one of the pioneers in the phonograph industry, and for seventeen years General Manager of the Record Department of the Columbia Graphophone Company.

Emerson Disc Records (Patent Pending), represent a distinct advance in the art of recording musical sounds, for they can be played on all disc talking machines, such as Victrola, Grafonola, Emerson or Pathe without an attachment, and on the Edison with an attachment.

Either a needle or an Emerson Sapphire can be used. The Sapphire costs 25 cents extra.

Here are the thirty splendid Emerson Records which the RIP-SAW sends you free.

POPULAR SONG HITS—VOCAL AND ORCHESTRA

**My Sweet Adair**—(L. Wolfe Gilbert)
**If We Can't be the Same Old Sweethearts**—(Monaco and McCarthy)
**Painting That Mother of Mine**—(Sturgis and Gilbert) Henry Burr, Tenor
**The Little Grey Mother**—(de Costa and Grossman) J. W. Myers, Baritone.
**Scaddle de Mooch**—(Chris Smith) Arthur Collins, Baritone
**Hello 'Frisco**—(Buck and Hirsch)
**My Little Dream Girl**—(Gilbert and Friedland)
**Tulip Time in Holland**—(Radford and Whiting) Henry Burr, Tenor
**Norway**—(McCarthy and Fischer)
**Queen of the South Sea Isles**—(Henry and Gilbert) J. W. Myers, Baritone
**When I Was a Dreamer**—(Little and Van Alstyne)
**Open Up Your Heart**—(L. Wolfe Gilbert)
**Put Me to Sleep with an Old-Fashioned Melody (Wake Me Up with a Rag)**—(Lewis, Howard and Jentes)
**Sweet Little Mary Pickford**—(Edna Williams)
**When I Leave the World Behind**—(Irving Berlin) Henry Burr, Tenor
**When You're in Love With Someone**—(Al. Piantadosi) Henry Burr, Tenor

DANCE MUSIC—METROPOLITAN MILITARY BAND

**Georgia Grind**—(Ford T. Dabney)
**Trilby Rag**—(Cary Morgan)
**Illusion Waltz**—(Carlo Neve
**Music Box Rag**—(C. Luckyth Roberts)
**Miniature Waltz**—(D. Onivas)
**By Heck Fox Trot**—(S. R. Henry)
**The Castle Walk**—(Europe and Dabney)
**Castle Valse Classique**—Arranged by Ford T. Dabney from the famous Humoresque by Dvorak.
**Shakesperian Love** (Fox-Trot)—(Hugo Fry)
**Omar Khayyam** (One-Step)—(S. Romberg)

STANDARD AND CLASSIC METROPOLITAN SYMPHONY ORCHESTRA

**Barcarolle** (Tales of Hoffman)—(Offenbach)
**Spring Song, Op. 62, No. 30**—(Mendelssohn)
**Blue Danube Waltz**—(Strauss)
**Over the Waves** (Sobra Las Olas)—(Rosas)

To secure one of these wonderful Emerson Phonographs and thirty different pieces free, merely send in a club of 100 yearly RIP-SAW subscribers at 25c each ($25.00) and we shall ship you by express, the outfit described on this page.

You all love music. What is home without music—what else drives away dull care as does a rollicking song or a brilliant march?

If the young people want to dance, the Emerson will supply the music.

If you have company at the house they will all enjoy a few fine selections on the phonograph.

If you want to hear the finest classical music it is not necessary to invest $60.00 or $100.00 to do so—the Emerson will play the very finest records in a way that will amaze you!

While we were trying out the Emerson Phonograph at the RIP-SAW office some of the young ladies employed in the RIP-SAW asked office how many subscriptions were necessary to secure a phonograph as they wanted one to play during the noon hour. So the very first club will be raised by RIP-SAW employes themselves and the first premium phonograph will be secured by the young ladies who handle your subscriptions in the RIP-SAW subscription department.

The RIP-SAW places the Emerson phonograph and thirty splendid records within reach of every comrade who is willing to do a little work for the cause of Socialism by extending the circulation of the National Rip-Saw. Here is a fine prize for your boy or your girl, (if the older folks themselves do not have time to work at the job.)

Any twelve-year-old boy or girl can easily canvass his or her neighborhood and secure 100 subscribers for the RIP-SAW at 25c each. So, boys and girls, go to work at once.

You do not need any special order blanks or subscription blanks. Any kind of writing paper will do—just write down the name and address of each subscriber and sign your own name and mention your nearest express office. Send the list to us—100 names accompanied by $25.00 and we will ship you the complete outfit to your nearest express office. Or, you can send us ten names at a time if you prefer.

Do not delay; start in at once raising your club of RIP-SAW subscribers and let us send you the Emerson phonograph and thirty fine selections at once.

### The Emerson Phonograph

Will play one twelve-inch record with one winding. It has a good strong motor, the governor is adjustable to different speeds, so that you can tune up the Emerson Phonograph the same as any of the fine makes. No Expense wasted on finish. It is all in the reproducer and the motor—the essential parts of a phonograph; the base measures 9½ x 9½ inches. Even if you have a fine $200 machine, the Emerson will come in handy, as it can be carried on excursions and camping trips, in a buggy or automobile, and there is no danger of injuring it. It will be a boon to thousands of music lovers who do not wish to invest a large sum in ornamental cabinet work, but want a phonograph that will produce MUSIC.

### You Have Six Months to Get the 100 Subscribers

Send in the names, not less than ten at a time.

If you can send us the hundred subscriptions all at once, so much the better, but you may need more time, hence you are allowed six full months from the day we receive your first installment of names.

Note—If you should find after sending in not less than fifty names and $12.50 that you cannot see your way clear to get the balance of the names you may get the Phonograph outfit as described by enclosing a small amount of cash extra, thus:

50 subs ($12.50) and $3.50 extra—$16.00 in all
60 subs ($15.00) and $2.50 extra—$17.80 in all
70 subs ($17.50) and $2.10 extra—$19.60 in all
80 subs ($20.00) and $1.40 extra—$21.40 in all
90 subs ($22.50) and $0.70 extra—$23.20 in all
100 subs ($25.00) and no extra—$25.00 in all

Comrade-- is there any bigger and finer way to work for the cause of Socialism than to get one hundred families in your locality reading the RIP-SAW, with its message every month from the pens of the members of the editorial staff--Debs--Tichenor--Kate O'Hare--Ameringer--Morgan--and the special articles by Walter Thomas Mills! Will you personally see that this blank is not wasted, but that someone in your family or some comrade uses it for the first installment of a list of 100 subscribers

*Why not get an Emerson Phonograph and thirty selections for your local; a little music will brighten up the meetings.*

5-95. A Communist conspiracy? In 1916, one could join the Workers' Struggle and earn an Emerson disc talking machine by selling subscriptions to the *Rip Saw*, a Socialist periodical. "Comrade, is there a bigger and finer way to work for the cause of socialism than to get 100 families in your locality reading the *Rip Saw*...Will you personally see that this blank is not wasted, but that someone in your family or some comrade uses it for the first installment of a list of 100 subscribers [?]" With a comrade earning exactly three cents per subscription (the Emerson retailed at $3.00), could worse exploitation be feared from the Capitalist Pigs? *Courtesy of the collection of Howard Hazelcorn.* (Value code: F)

5-96. Emerson disc record supplements below a cardboard store display. During the World War I period, 7" diameter Emerson discs found a ready market among budget-minded consumers. 10" discs of the major brands averaged about 75 cents. *Courtesy of Martin F. Bryan.* (Value code: H, D)

5-97. This plaster effigy of a proud rooster was used as a display piece by Pathé dealers in the 'teens. It measures 23" high and stands astride a Pathé (vertical cut) disc of 12" diameter. There were two versions of this bird: one with advertising slogan ("No Needles to Change") and one (shown) without. (Value code: B)

5-98. Pathé ephemera from the sapphire disc period (1913-1920) of the American branch. Clockwise from the left: spritelike nymphs *en déshabillé* attract the viewer to the recorded delights within a disc catalogue from May 1917; a more circumspect record catalogue from a short time later; an envelope containing a sapphire stylus (which was available in different loudness grades, like the steel needle); a Pathé phonograph catalogue showing two of the "period" cabinet models which many companies offered in the 'teens. *Courtesy of Martin F. Bryan*. (Value code: F, G, G, F)

5-99. Talking machine companies offered their dealers some rather unusual promotional novelties. This "Progressive Pedro" game scorecard advertises the Pathephone, circa 1915. (Value code: G)

5-100. This two foot long Wall-Kane needle was meant to be used in a dealer display, or possibly hung above the counter in a record store, circa 1920. We trust that the moorings of this formidable projectile were kept secure, or at least that it never landed on one of the customers. *Courtesy of Lynn Bilton.* (Value code: C)

5-101. The Brunswick-Balke-Collender Company had been a successful manufacturer of sports equipment and commercial interiors when, in 1916, it began marketing a line of disc cabinet models under its own name. The brand would enjoy a long period of popularity, becoming one of the three biggest firms in the field by 1921. *Courtesy of Martin F. Bryan.* (Value code: H, G, H)

5-102. A sheet metal sign from the mid 1920s, measuring 11 1/4" x 36", advertising the Brunswick phonograph. *Courtesy of the collection of Howard Hazelcorn.* (Value code: C)

5-103. A wood-grained metal revolving rack for Brunswick catalogues and supplements, measuring 12" high, circa 1920. *Courtesy of the Charles Hummel collections.* (VR)

5-104. "Silvertone" talking machines were sold by Sears, Roebuck and Company of Chicago. Judging by the models extant today, most of the clients of this low-priced mail-order house bought the least expensive instruments, like the one on the bottom right. This catalogue dates from around 1920. *Courtesy of Martin F. Bryan.* (Value code: G)

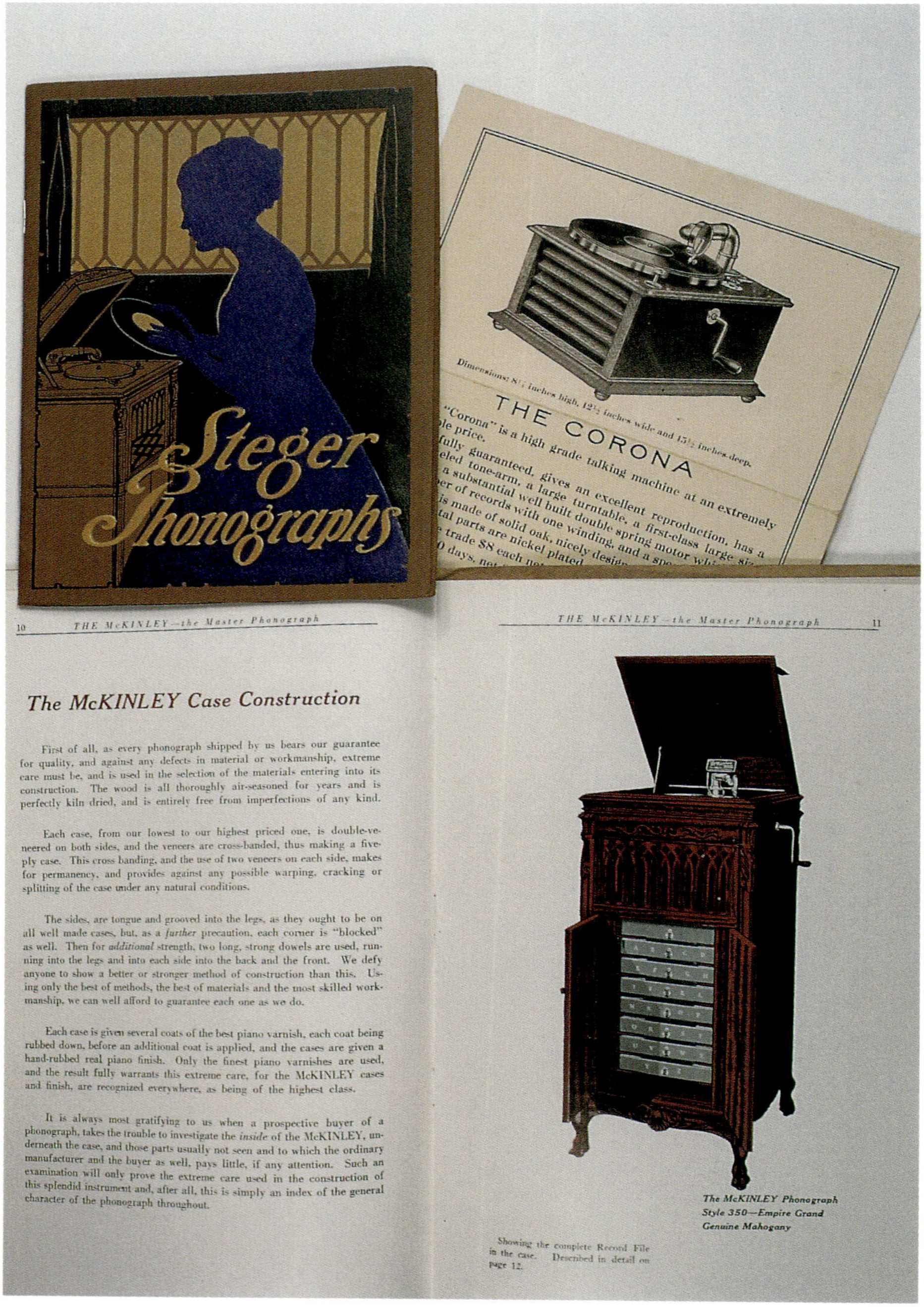


5-105. During the 'teens and twenties, a great many small-time talking machine brands appeared in the United States. In early 1912, a crucial Victor patent (No.534,543), which had effectively controlled the market for over a decade, expired and allowed the disc talking machine business to explode with independent enterprise. As in most other forms of commerce, only a very few of the off-brand machine companies survived past the initial offering. *Courtesy of Martin F. Bryan*. (Value code: G)

5-112. A "Tootsie Toy" model of an upright talking machine, circa 1925. It measures 1" x 1" x 2 1/4". *Courtesy of Alan H. Mueller.* (Value code: H)

5-106. The Cheney disc phonographs were introduced in the 'teens: artistically designed and substantially constructed. This sign, measuring 8" x 30" is stylishly painted over sheet brass. *Courtesy of Bob and Karyn Sitter.* (Value code: C)

5-107. This 10" x 11" metal sign advertised the "Claxtonola," a line of cabinet models introduced in January, 1919. The company's motto ("As Good As The Best, Better Than The Rest") combined two vague sentences which must have left the customer somewhat puzzled. *Courtesy of the Charles Hummel collections.* (Value code: B)

5-111. Comic takes on the raucous or repetitive tendencies of the talking machine were inevitable. On this "pinback" from the 1920s, comic strip characters Mutt and Jeff quarrel over a noisy phonograph. *Courtesy of Michael F. Khanchalian.* (Value code: G)

5-108. The "Mandel" was an independent brand of disc cabinet talking machine from the late 'teens. This charming illuminated sign measures 13 1/2" x 25 1/2". *Courtesy of the Charles Hummel collections.* (Value code: A)

5-109. Record supplements of three brands from the 1920s. "Vocalion" discs were described as red because the shellac from which they were pressed was not tinted and resembled a terracotta color. *Courtesy of Martin F. Bryan.* (Value Code: H)

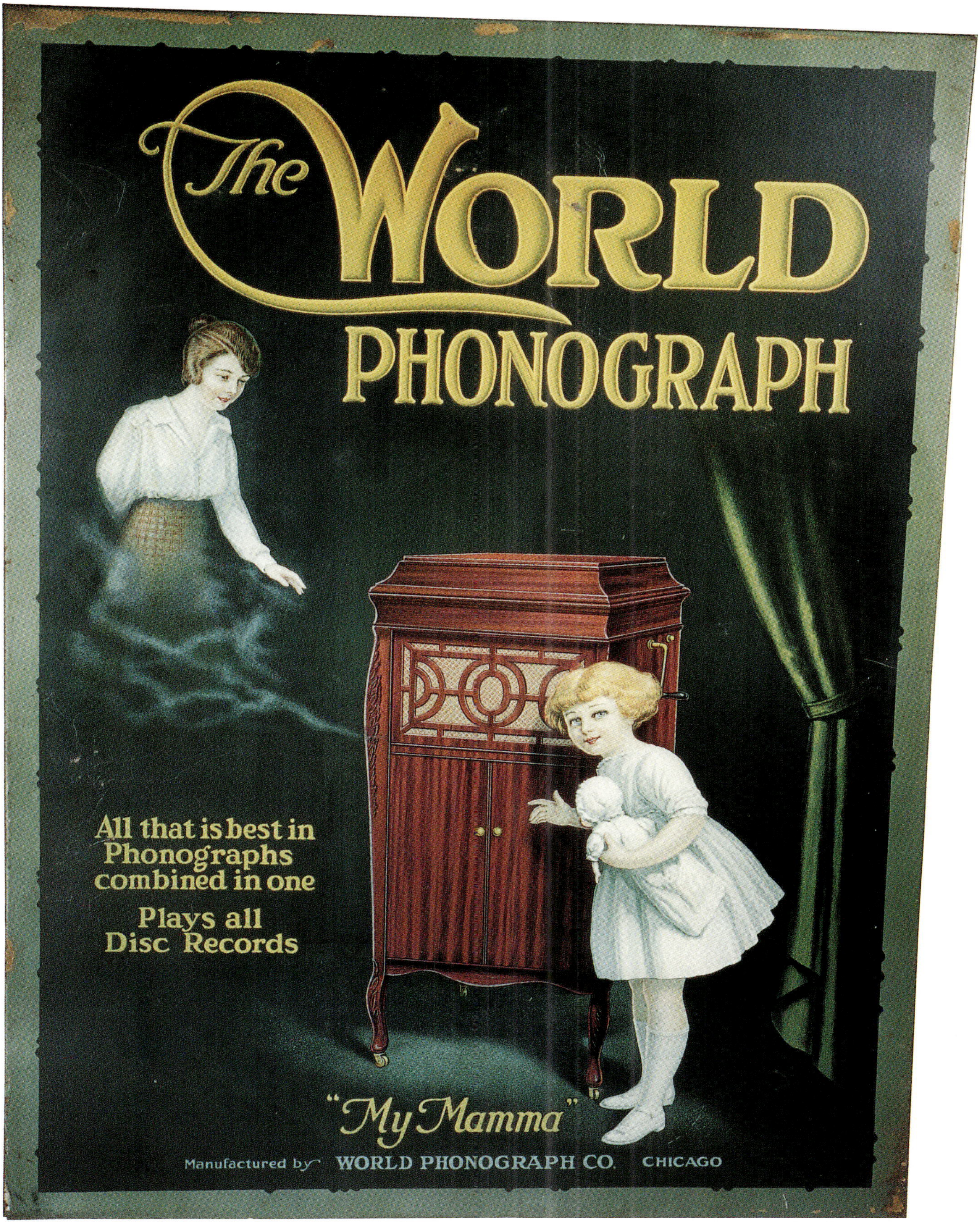


5-110. In the sepulchral gloom of this 17" x 23" World Phonograph Company sign a mother's spirit is conjured by a recording of her voice, in imitation of the famous "His Master's Voice" trade mark. Both logos were predicated on the unlikely premise of a home-recorded disc. *Courtesy of the Charles Hummel collections.* (Value code: B)

5-113. An example of the very first commercial lithograph of the famous "His Master's Voice" painting. In 1899, the picture of the dog "Nipper" and a Gramophone had been only recently acquired from artist Francis Barraud by the Gramophone Company, Ltd, in London. It would eventually become associated with the Victor Talking Machine Company in the United States, but in the fall of 1899 it was simply an untried trade mark for which the Gramophone Company wished to get a return on its money. With this in mind, the firm hired the Rembrandt and Intagalis Printing Company of Lancaster, England, to produce a run of lithographs drawn from the original painting. The example shown is from the group sold in December of 1899, measuring 13 5/8" x 18 3/8". *Courtesy of Rae Ann Rieping.* (VR)

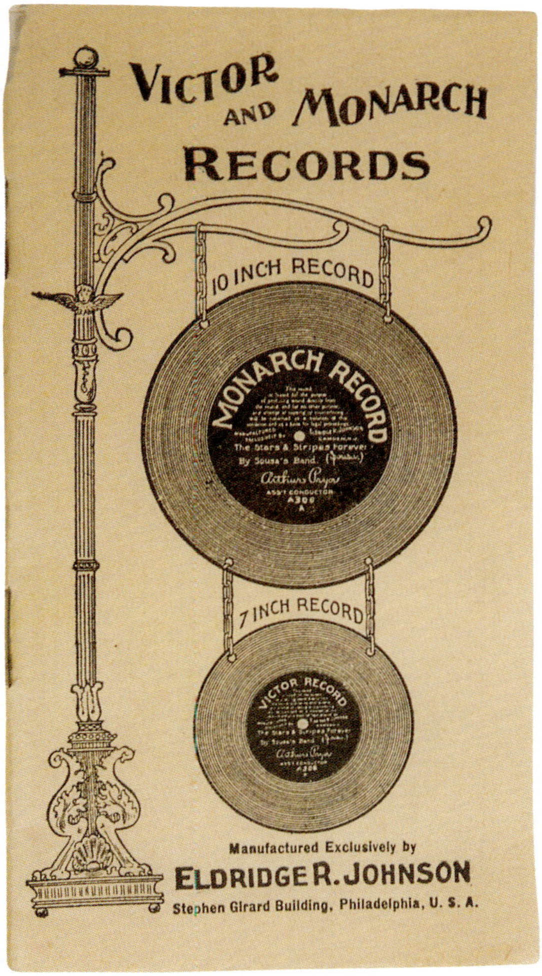


5-114. A very early (1901) catalogue of discs sold by Eldridge R. Johnson under the "Victor" mark. When he began selling his own discs, Johnson scrupulously avoided a specific brand name because his legal affairs were in question. Soon, however, he selected "Victor," which he would also call his company. (Value code: E)

5-115. An unusual invoice from the brief period in 1901 when Eldridge Johnson, for unsettled legal reasons, put his own name above his soon-to-be-famous brand name: "Victor." The discounts to dealers were clearly indicated. A modern collector will find it incredible to imagine that the Victor model "B," rare and costly today, had a wholesale price of only $12.00. *Courtesy of Norm and Janyne Smith.* (Value code: F)

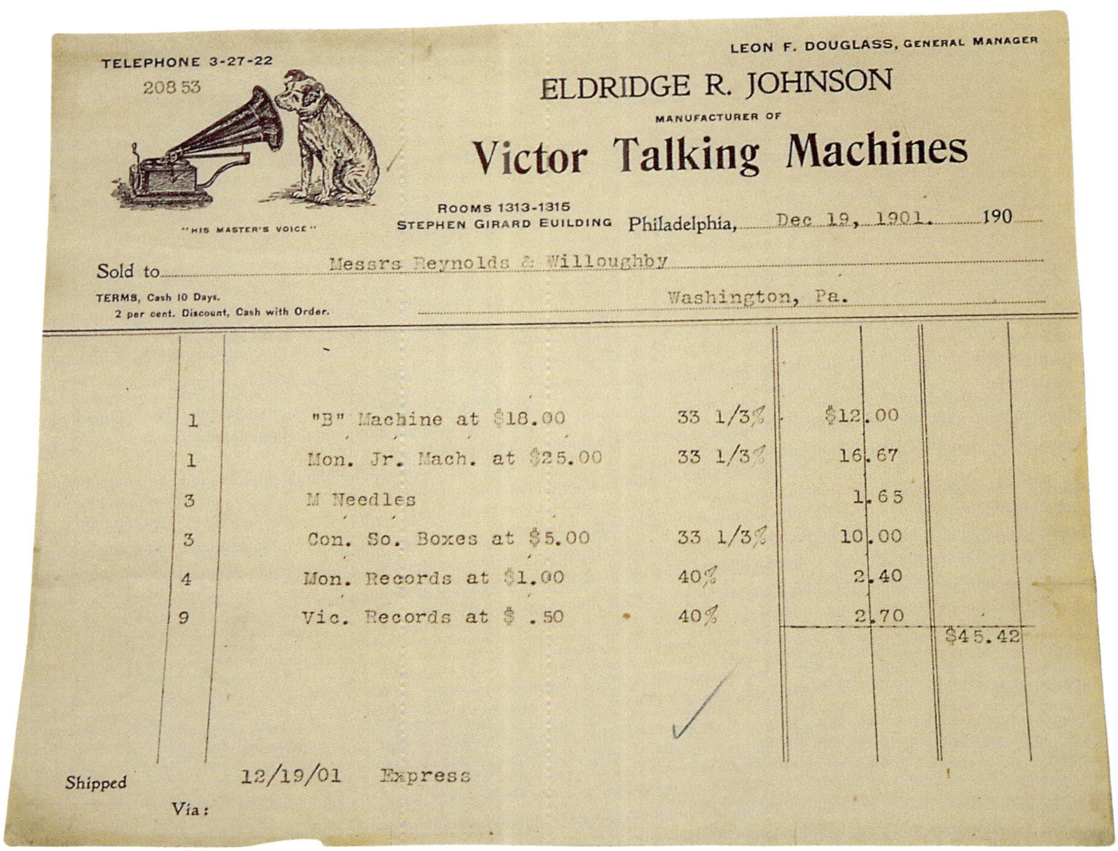

TELEPHONE 3-27-22
208 53

LEON F. DOUGLASS, GENERAL MANAGER

ELDRIDGE R. JOHNSON

MANUFACTURER OF

Victor Talking Machines

"HIS MASTER'S VOICE"

ROOMS 1313-1315
STEPHEN GIRARD BUILDING Philadelphia, Dec 19, 1901. 190

Sold to Messrs Reynolds & Willoughby
Washington, Pa.

TERMS, Cash 10 Days.
2 per cent. Discount, Cash with Order.

| | | | | |
|---|---|---|---|---|
| 1 | "B" Machine at $18.00 | 33 1/3% | $12.00 | |
| 1 | Mon. Jr. Mach. at $25.00 | 33 1/3% | 16.67 | |
| 3 | M Needles | | 1.65 | |
| 3 | Con. So. Boxes at $5.00 | 33 1/3% | 10.00 | |
| 4 | Mon. Records at $1.00 | 40% | 2.40 | |
| 9 | Vic. Records at $ .50 | 40% | 2.70 | |
| | | | | $45.42 |

Shipped Via: 12/19/01 Express

5-116. An amazing departure for the morally restricted world of American advertising, circa 1903. A truly eye-opening articulated trade card. (Value code: E)

5-117. Unfolding the wings of the card defuses the shock value. The figures suggest a European style which was somewhat out-of-date, but the overall impression is effective.

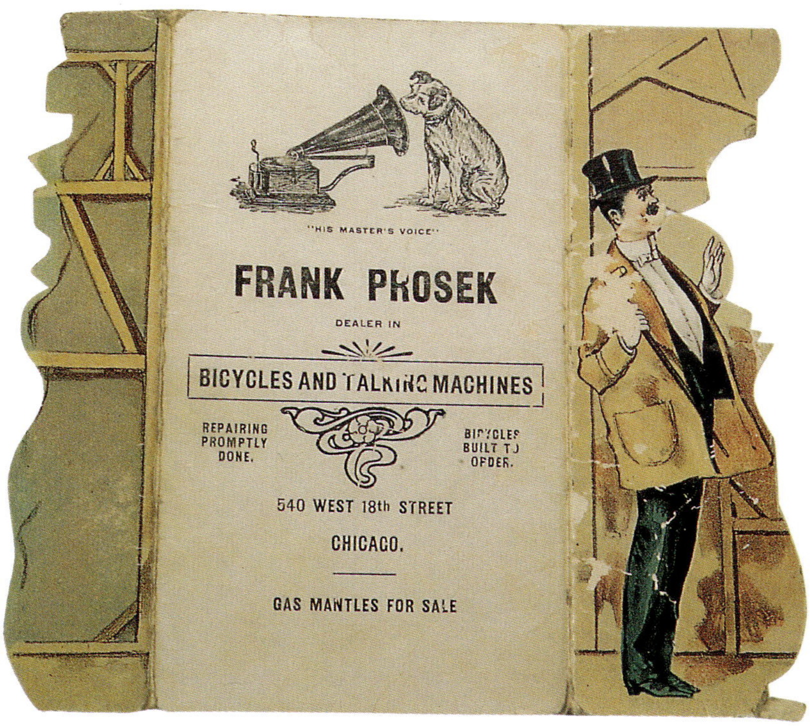


5-118. Reversing the articulated card indicates who the viewer should thank (or condemn) for the momentary titillation. Did the circumspect Eldridge Johnson know how his trade mark was being exploited?

5-119. Various Victor Talking Machine Company catalogues: 1910, 1906, 1905, 1904. (Value code: F, E, E, E)

5-120. An inkwell in the shape of a talking machine, measuring 3 1/2" x 3 1/2". These "No. 3 Inkwells" were sold by the Gramophone Company Ltd., in England between 1901-1903. A contemporary catalogue stated: "A most ingenious and novel design, with solid mahogany base, and heavily plated nickel fittings. It will be found that all the working parts of the Gramophone are carefully copied and adapted to some practical use. The Record Nut, as the lid of the ink Bottle, is held in place by the winding key, and the Trumpet is made the receptacle for a pen wiper. Price...5/- each." *Courtesy of Bob and Karyn Sitter.* (VR)

5-121. In the same Gramophone Company Ltd. catalogue a "No.5 Pen Tray" was offered with an unusual depiction of a standing "Nipper." It sold for 7/6. (VR) Below, a 3" diameter Victor paperweight, circa 1912.

5-122. A 5" diameter ashtray, circa 1905, with advertising for Victor talking machines on the central matchbox holder. (Value code: D)

5-123. A 1907 Zonophone trade card which capitalized on President Theodore Roosevelt, whose characteristic exclamation ("de-lighted!") and eponymous bear were well known at the time. An article in the September 1907 *Talking Machine World* stated: "One of the happiest pictorial postals takes advantage of the prevailing popularity of the Teddy bear. This is the first time this idea has been used in the...trade, and is original with B.G. Royal, the president of this enterprising company." (Value code: F)

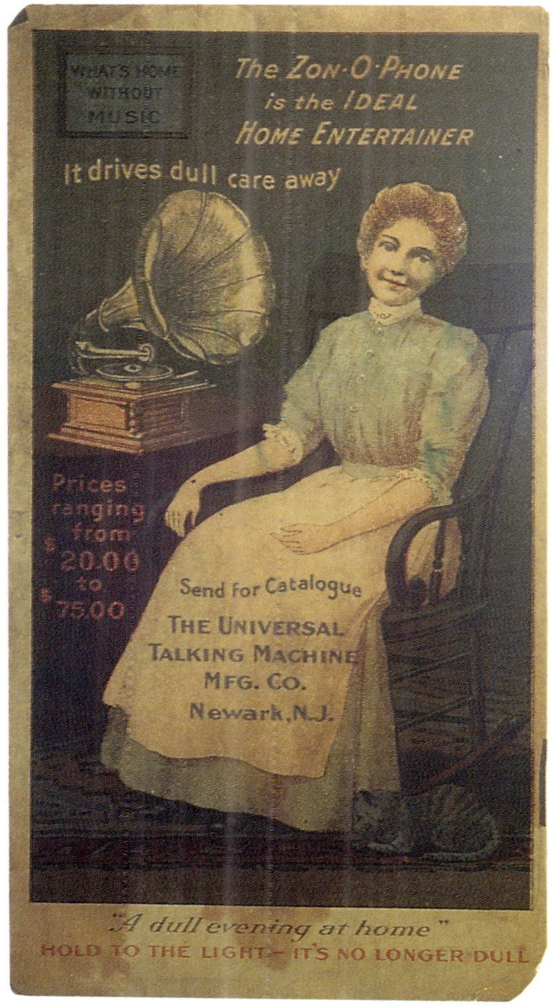


Top left: 5-124. A novelty trade card depicting "a dull evening at home," circa 1908. (Value code: E)

Top center: 5-125. When held to the light, a Zonophone "Grand Opera" appeared, to the delight of the housewife.

5-126. Zonophone record listings, including one cleverly shaped like a disc record. "Zonophone" discs were less expensive than "Victors" (in fact, Victor owned Zonophone and promoted it as a "bargain-priced" line), but appear to have sold in uninspiring quantities. Zonophone supplements and catalogues, too, did not enjoy the widespread distribution of Victor's own series. *Courtesy of Walter and Carol Myers*. (Value code: G, F, H)

5-127. Zonophone machine catalogues. In its first incarnation, the Zonophone was represented by a stylish and technically refined line of talking machines. Beginning in late 1899 and continuing until a short time after the takeover of the company by Victor in 1903, Zonophone instruments were cutting-edge equipment. Victor, however, began to degrade the line and eventually transformed it into the kind of inexpensive goods flogged by mail-order houses. The open pages at the top show Zonophones circa 1905, at the beginning of their descent. *Courtesy of Walter and Carol Myers*. (Value code: E)

5-128. Three seldom-seen pieces of Victor ephemera: a 1908 alphabetical record list, a booklet explaining and promoting the use of Victor steel needles, circa 1910, and a list of Grand Opera discs from 1908, near the beginning of the company's rise to fame as a purveyor of high musical art. *Courtesy of Walter and Carol Myers*. (Value code: F, F, E)

5-129. A 20" high die-cut "Nipper" from the "Ready Made Window Display Department" of the Victor Talking Machine Company. By the end of 1909, this department had up a full head of steam and, as reported in a December 1909 *Talking Machine World* article, "...there can be no doubt that the window display idea recently inaugurated is one of the biggest helps ever rendered the dealer." A die-cut Berliner Gramophone originally accompanied "Nipper." *Courtesy of Walter and Carol Myers.* (Value code: D)

5-130. Monthly Victor record supplements during the century's first decade were issued in two styles: with pictorial cover and with plain cover. As one may see by these examples, the decorated versions represented the best in contemporary color lithography. *Courtesy of Walter and Carol Myers.* (Value code: F)

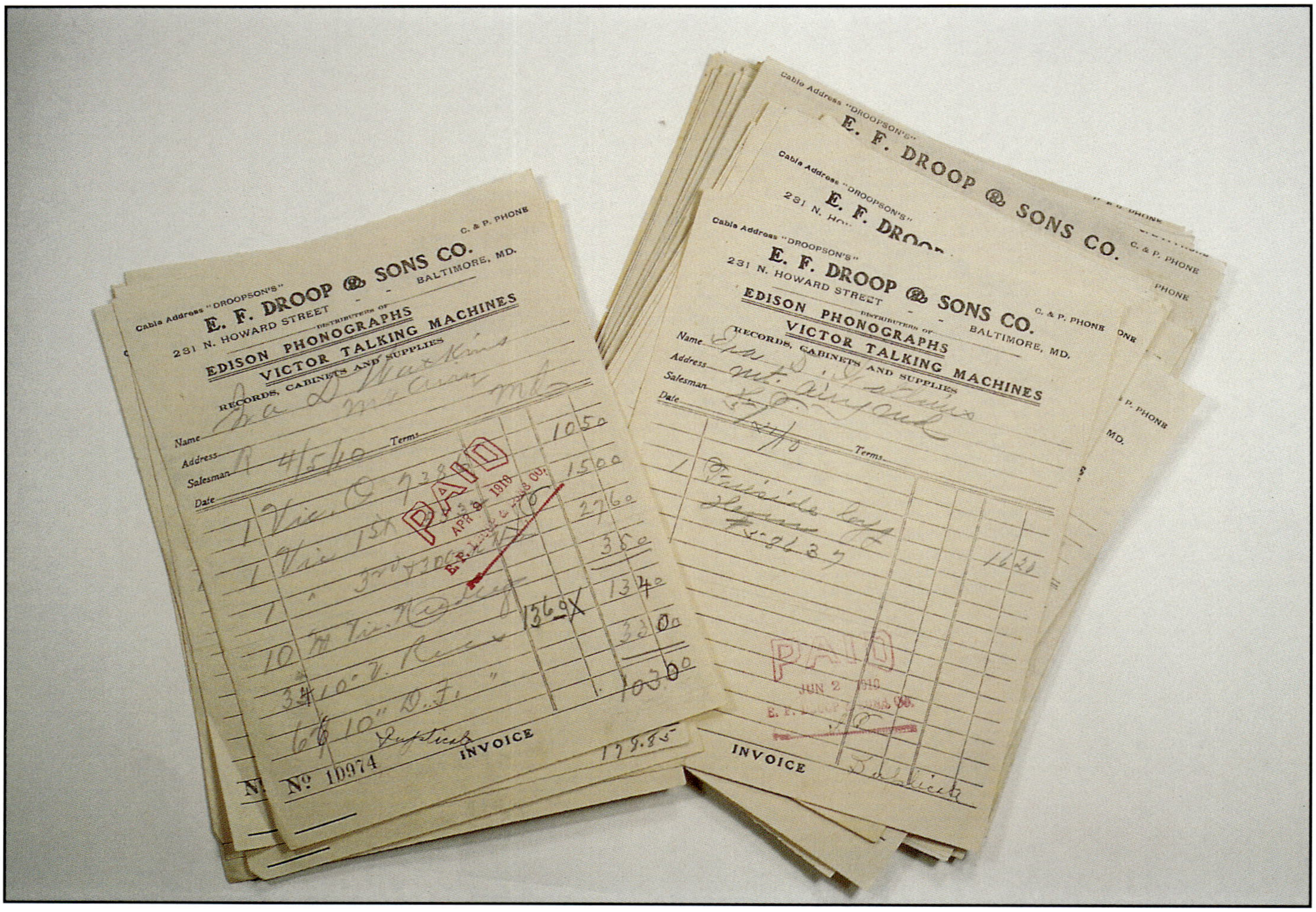


5-131. Billheads like these from talking machine wholesaler E. F. Droop & Sons of Baltimore, Maryland, provide glimpses behind the sales counter. In 1910, a dealer was buying a Victor "III" for $27.60 (not including freight) which he would retail for $45.00, and a Victor "0" for $10.50 (before freight) which retailed at $17.50. This would have been considered a "full" discount. In the talking machine business, a dealer could usually expect to make about 30% - 35% after freight charges. *Courtesy of Martin F. Bryan*. (Value code: H, each)

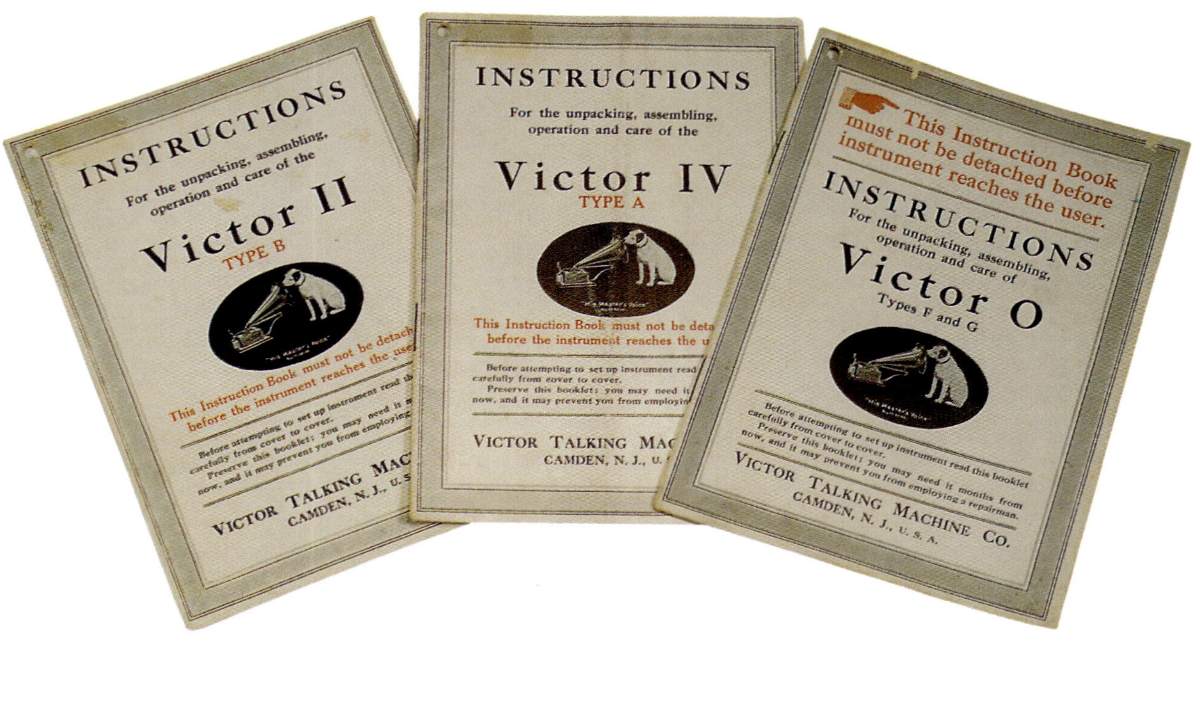


5-132. These instruction booklets were originally delivered with external-horn Victor talking machines. They contained operating information, diagrams and maintenance instructions. The examples here are from the post-1909 era, when Victrola (cabinet model) booklets were issued in the same format. (Value code: F)

5-133. Items with the famous "His Master's Voice" logo. Left a celluloid-backed advertising mirror featuring the popular Victrola "XI." Above, another celluloid mirror. Below, a rectangular metal tip tray from the Berliner Gramophone Company of Canada, measuring 3" x 4". *Courtesy of Bob and Karyn Sitter.* (Value code: D)

5-134. *The Voice of Victor* was the company's monthly dealer magazine (8 1/2" x 11 1/2"). An issue from 1915 is shown. (Value code: G)

5-135. A 4" diameter metal tip tray from the Berliner Gramophone Company of Canada, circa 1915. *Courtesy of Steve and Ellie Saccente.* (Value code: D)

5-137. This fold-out flyer issued by Victor in 1915 illustrated the Victrola line which devastated the competition and established the company as the premier talking machine manufacturer of the 'teens. (Value code: G)

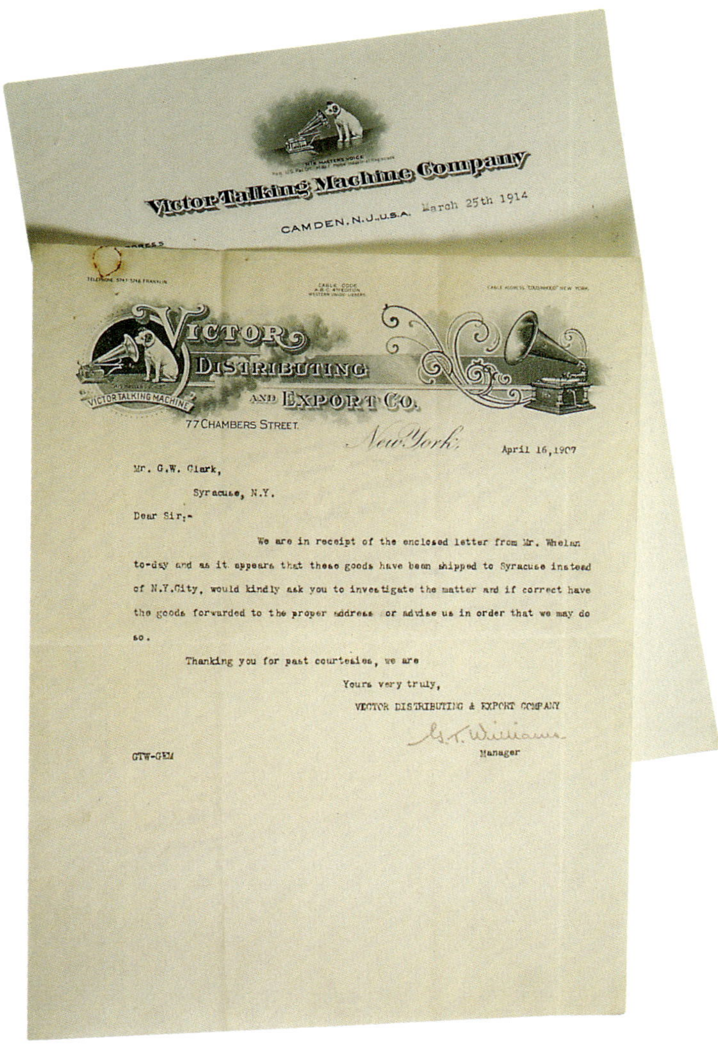
Victor Talking Machine Company

CAMDEN, N.J., U.S.A. March 25th 1914

VICTOR DISTRIBUTING AND EXPORT CO.

VICTOR TALKING MACHINE

77 CHAMBERS STREET.

New York, April 16, 1907

Mr. G.W. Clark,

Syracuse, N.Y.

Dear Sir;-

We are in receipt of the enclosed letter from Mr. Whelan to-day and as it appears that these goods have been shipped to Syracuse instead of N.Y.City, would kindly ask you to investigate the matter and if correct have the goods forwarded to the proper address or advise us in order that we may do so.

Thanking you for past courtesies, we are

Yours very truly,

VICTOR DISTRIBUTING & EXPORT COMPANY

G.T. Williams

Manager

GTW-GEM

5-136. Two letterheads showing the "His Master's Voice" logo. Above, the ordinary business stationery of the Victor Talking Machine Company from 1914. Below, an earlier (1907) and more elaborate letterhead from the Victor Distributing and Export Company. (Value code: H)

5-138. A theatrical lantern slide (3 1/4" x 4") used to advertise the Victrola. The figures and the reference to dance music suggest a date of 1914. *Courtesy of Steve and Ellie Saccente.* (Value code: E)

5-139. Another Victor lantern slide from about 1915. *Courtesy of Steve and Ellie Saccente.* (Value code: E)

5-140. The "His Master's Voice" trade mark gracing a Victor pocket watch and fob. *Courtesy of Norm and Janyne Smith.* (Value code: C)

5-141. Small Victor celluloid items. Clockwise from left: a mirror in the image of a "Red Seal" record; an ID button for a music store clerk; a lady's compact and mirror with imitation record top; a mirror from a store in Brooklyn, New York. (Value code: F, E, F, E)

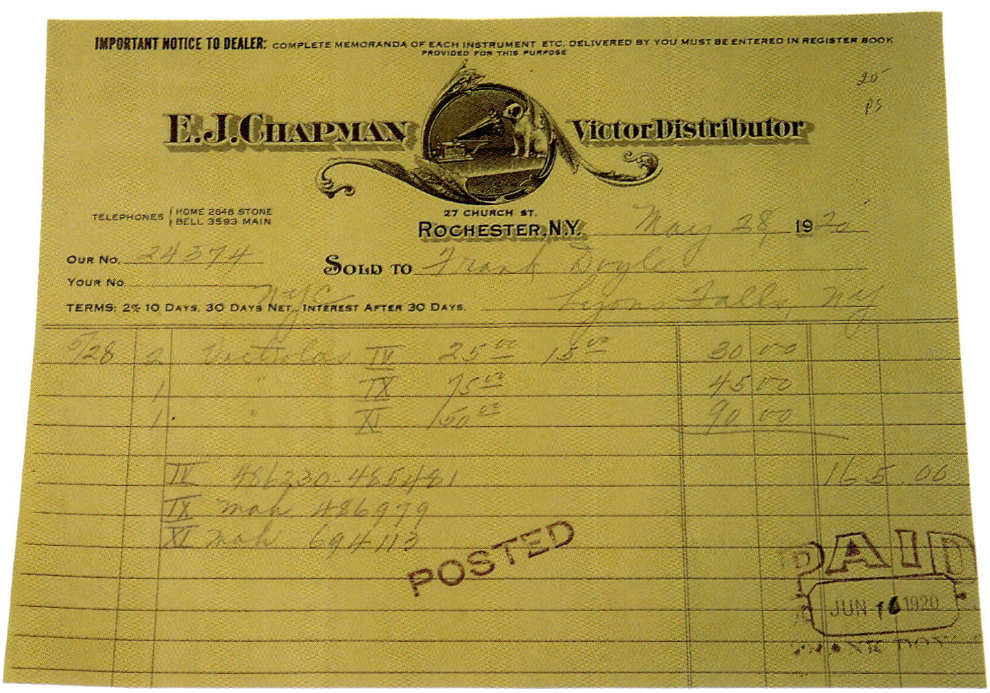

IMPORTANT NOTICE TO DEALER: COMPLETE MEMORANDA OF EACH INSTRUMENT ETC. DELIVERED BY YOU MUST BE ENTERED IN REGISTER BOOK PROVIDED FOR THIS PURPOSE

E. J. CHAPMAN Victor Distributor

TELEPHONES HOME 2648 STONE / BELL 3593 MAIN

27 CHURCH ST.
ROCHESTER, N.Y. May 28 1920

OUR NO. 24374 SOLD TO Frank Doyle
YOUR NO.
TERMS: 2% 10 DAYS, 30 DAYS NET, INTEREST AFTER 30 DAYS. Lyons Falls, NY

| 5/28 | 2 | Victrolas IV 25.00 15.00 | 30.00 | |
|---|---|---|---|---|
| | 1 | " IX 75.00 | 45.00 | |
| | 1 | " XI 150.00 | 90.00 | |
| | | IV 486230-486481 | | 165.00 |
| | | IX mah 486979 | | |
| | | XI mah 694113 | | |

POSTED

PAID JUN 16 1920

5-142. An invoice from a Rochester, New York, wholesaler illustrates the kind of profit that could be made in Victrolas. At this time (1920), the mainstay-of-the-line Victrola "XI" would earn the dealer $60.00, minus freight charges. Listed to the lower left are the serial numbers (and type of cabinet wood) of the machines being sold. (Value code: H)

5-143. A Victor advertising fan from the early 1920s, emphasizing the tasteful and refined quality of the Victrola. (Value code: F)

5-144. These die-cut figures of Victor artists from the late 'teens through the twenties stood about 14" high. They were used by dealers in store displays. Front, left to right: Lou Holtz, Will Rogers, Fannie Brice and Paul Whiteman. Rear, left to right: Classical artists Ruffo, Tetrazzini, Schipa, Schumann-Heink, Melba, Fleta and Gluck. *Courtesy of Alan H. Mueller.* (Value code: H, each)

5-145. An illuminated, double-sided Victor dealer's sign from the early 1920s, measuring 23" x 31 1/4". *Courtesy of the Charles Hummel collections.* (Value code: A)

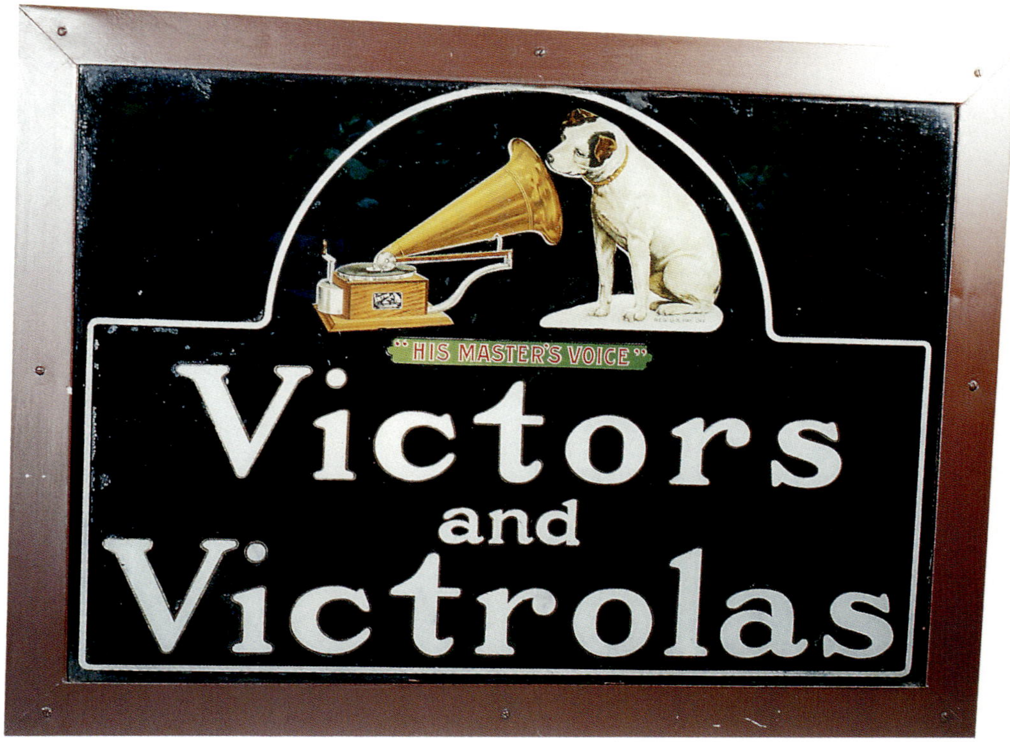

5-147. Two papier-mâché "Nippers" of the King Cole company type, approximately 14" high. *Courtesy of Alan H. Mueller.* (Value code: C)

Opposite page:
5-146. A grouping of "Nippers." In order of size: 3" high salt and pepper shakers, very popular throughout the RCA era. 12" high RCA era dog found in hard rubber or composition. 14" high papier-mâché dog from the King Cole company. An earlier, 1920s Victor era 18" high King Cole dog most commonly seen in papier-mâché. This particular example is the seldom-found version pressed out of sheet zinc. *Courtesy of Bob and Karyn Sitter.* (Value code: G, C, C, VR in zinc)

5-148. A colorful flyer from the mid-1920s emphasizing the easily portable quality of the smaller Victrolas. *Courtesy of Martin F. Bryan*. (Value code: G)

1-150. Items with the Victor trade mark. Left, a celluloid stick-pin. Center, matches from the post-1929 RCA era. Right, A "Victor" cigar. *Courtesy of Rae Ann Rieping*. (Value code: E, H, F)

5-149. This stylish clock, measuring 11 1/2" high, fairly floats atop an accurate miniature of the Victrola "330," circa 1924. The talking machine opens to suggest a jewel case. There was no attribution to the Victor company, or any other marking to suggest a promotional purpose. *Courtesy of Walter and Carol Myers*. (Value code: C)

5-151. With the advent of the electrical recording era in 1925, the Victor Talking Machine Company experienced a great flowering of its fortunes. Integral to this period of success was Victor's line of "Orthophonic" Victrolas, which represented the company's highest achievement in acoustical reproduction. Although the records were "electric," Victor did not exploit electric amplification until a few years later. As the 1920s faded, the "Orthophonic" nomenclature blended into the use of the term "Electrola." This was actually a revival of an earlier name the company had applied to electric motor, acoustic Victrolas. In its renewed definition, the term referred to electrically operated and amplified machines. Shown with this late-1920s portfolio of Victor instruments is a tin of "Tungs-tone" (multi-use) needles. *Courtesy of Martin F. Bryan*. (Value code: F portfolio, H tin)

5-152. This cut-away miniature, 9 1/2" high, was used by Victor dealers to illustrate the design of the "exponential" internal horn used in the Victrola "Credenza" (or "8-30") and other "Orthophonic" models. A revolutionary method of "folding" the horn within the Victrola cabinet allowed a longer and more properly shaped horn to be used, resulting in greatly improved sound. *Courtesy of Walter and Carol Myers*. (Value code: D)

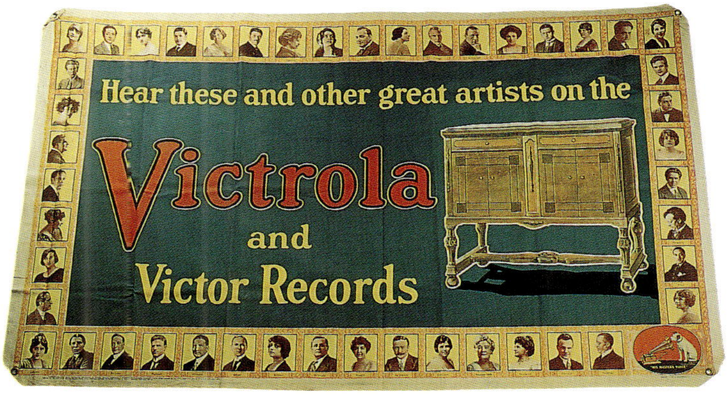


5-153. A colorful canvas banner from the "Orthophonic" era displaying the portraits of Victor artists around the periphery. It measures an impressive 35" x 58". (Value code: C)

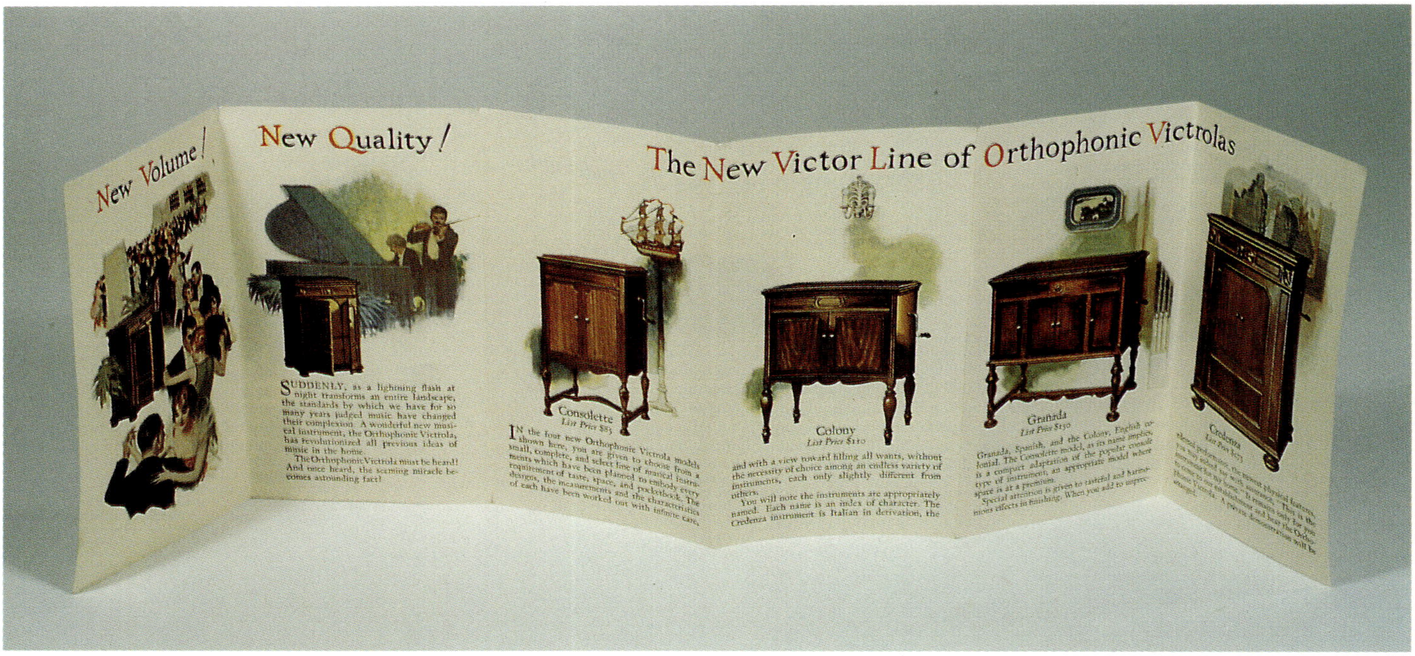


5-154. A fold-out flyer from 1925 measuring 6 1/4" x 20", which advertised Victor's "Orthophonic" line of Victrolas. (Value code: F)

5-156. A trolley sign from the "Orthophonic" era, which advertised a Victor record release. *Courtesy of Norm and Janyne Smith.* (Value code: C)

5-157. A political cartoon from the humor magazine *Judge*, during Theodore Roosevelt's Presidency. The artist suggested that it was the American People who demanded the reforms and better government which Theodore Roosevelt (depicted as a rapt youngster) had made the rallying points of his political agenda. On cylinder and disc records in 1912, Roosevelt expounded upon his anti-big business, pro-social reform views. *Courtesy of Mark E. Lynch.* (Value code: H)

Opposite page:
5-155. A Victor poster from 1927, measuring 28" x 40 1/2". Victor spared no expense to create lush artwork, even when promoting a single record. *Courtesy of Martin F. Bryan.* (Value code: D)

Victor Light Opera Company
Gems from The
DESERT
SONG
and
COUNTESS
MARITZA
35809

Chapter Six:

# Ordinary People: The Talking Machine in Real Life

6-1. "Snowing like hell" was the photographer's wry comment about this March 1914 blizzard which hit Philadelphia. Nearly buried at the exact center of the frame was the darkened electric sign of the Victor showrooms on South Broad Street. One block further along Broad, the Keen-O-Phone Company was lost in white. *Courtesy of the Philadelphia City Archives*. (Value code: G)

"There are two classes of trade that are comparatively easy to sell," wrote Horace Sheble, the talking machine entrepreneur, in 1908. "First, the very rich, who buy anything new that appeals to them; and, second, the very poor, who purchase the cheapest class of talking machines as their one possible form of amusement." Mr. Sheble, at the height of his success as the co-proprietor of the Hawthorne & Sheble Manufacturing Company of Philadelphia, was quoted in the October 3, 1908 issue of *The Music Trades*, excerpted from the British publication *Phono Trader and Recorder*. He continued:

> All this business is very good, very profitable...but there is another class which in its combined purchasing strength...eclipses them all, namely the middle class...In America the methods employed in selling machines have directly appealed to the middle classes, and a very large percentage of the business done has been with such people...

It follows, then, that successful marketing would be focused at the social center, where the biggest gains could be made. In the vast number of surviving talking machines originally located in the middle price range, we see evidence of this today. Though many of the cheapest machines are also extant, the poor were confined by circumstance to these inexpensive models and could seldom aspire to anything better. Likewise, the rich, because they were able to buy any instrument however costly, quickly exhausted the field of choice. The members of the middle class, on the other hand, represented the broadest commercial possibilities, especially if a clever salesman could convince them to stretch for an instrument they could barely afford.

This information is better appreciated if we place it within the developmental context of recorded sound. A period of nearly twenty years elapsed between the invention of sound recording/replay and the point at which the majority of Americans could afford to buy a talking machine. During this time many, many people had read or heard about the talking machine, and a good number had actually attended an exhibition or put a nickel in a coin-operated model. These contacts, especially with public demonstrations and arcade machines, would have piqued an interest which for a long time could be only fleetingly satisfied. This was a situation that persisted from the days of the Edison Speaking Phonograph Company in 1878, when full-sized "Tinfoil Phonographs" sold for $95.50, to just after the end of the North American Phonograph Company in the 1894, when electrically-driven Edison Phonographs were selling for $150.00.

Throughout most of 1895, talking machine buyers needed to spend at least $75.00 (a sizeable sum—about a month's salary for the average working man). Late in 1895, however, the first more affordable talking machines appeared, beginning with the spring-driven Columbia Type "N" Graphophone ("Bijou") at $40.00. Edison would attempt to meet the challenge by haltingly introducing a comparably-priced "Home" Phonograph early the next year. Yet a clever fellow named Edward H. Amet, working independently, got the jump on both major forces. He created a little cylinder talking machine known through most of its short life as the "Echophone." This diminutive but effective instrument, with its spring motor right out of a clock, dramatically thrust the talking machine into the world of the common man. The price tag was only $5.00. Sadly, Amet would not enjoy the fruits of the courage it took to shake up the established forces. He lost in court over patent infringement and Columbia was awarded the stock of "Echophones," which were disposed of through various sales promotions. Thus was the promise of the "Echophone" finally and ironically fulfilled.

Columbia very rapidly introduced its own lesser-priced models: The "A" or "Columbia" ($25.00) in late 1896; the "B" or "Eagle" ($10.00) in 1897; and the "Q" ($5.00) in 1898. Amet had stolen a march on Columbia by more than a year, but Edison lagged even farther behind. He failed to offer a machine under $20.00 until 1899: the $7.50 "Gem." Emile Berliner's Gramophones were value-priced during the late nineties, with the hand-driven model selling for $15.00 and the spring-motored version for $25.00. An $18.00 spring motor Gramophone arrived too late to prevent the scuttling of Berliner's company in 1900 from an internal upset largely driven by matters of price. Price positioning was important in the waning years of the century, and those who failed to recognize this were left behind.

By the turn of the century, the talking machine market would continue to represent a full range of retail prices, from the cheapest to the most expensive. Even in the inflationary mid-1920s, the bargain shopper could find satisfaction, with Victor's least expensive table model VV "1-1" selling for only $17.50, and various off-brands for even less.

The results of the Thirteenth Census had shown that the capital invested in the talking machine industry was 64% greater in 1909 than in 1904. Previous forms of home amusement, like music boxes, had already sagged before the talking machine's unstoppable march into a vast number of homes. Swiss music box exports fell by nearly 48% between 1893 and 1904, according to a report excerpted in the January 1906 *Talking Machine World*. Summing up the situation, the United States Consul to Switzerland said, "Musical boxes have found in phonographs, gramophones and pianolas of all kinds keen competition." With a few brief sputterings, the talking machine industry would continue to grow until blind-sided by the Great Depression. However, even this economic catastrophe again underscored the importance of the low-cost phonograph.

The collector of today harbors his or her private relationship with the talking machine, and this intimate lens uniquely filters objects and events. If it is difficult to say exactly what the hobby means to each of us, at least we have the chance of articulating our feelings. It seems far more daunting to imagine what the talking machine might have meant to people in times past—but we are tempted to ask questions. Indeed, many collectors long for a folksy provenance to accompany their acquisitions ("It belonged to my old Aunt Maude from Mecklenburg..."), though by this writing machines have changed hands so frequently that such comforting pedigrees are rarely possible.

The historically-minded, however, seek resources for sorting out the talking machine's true place in the lives of the original owners. We have sales figures, census figures, statistics about income levels and so on—but most tellingly we have actual photographs which provide countless clues to be interpreted. In some cases these are stiff-backed and static, like vacation snapshots posed before the Washington Monument. In other photographs we see the talking machine captured in some revealing way, either by its direct connection with a person in the same picture or by the context in which it appears.

Often, the talking machine is the focus of the picture: showing off the new (frequently expensive) possession. Sometimes it is peripheral: a horn protruding from the shadows, suggesting a transition to ordinary household object. Other times, we see only traces of the talking machine's presence: a perfectly average street scene in which a banner can be discerned in the distance, advertising Edison Phonographs. Yet if we are lucky, something about the photograph, hidden or obvious, will inform our understanding of the talking machine as it existed in the real world of the vanished past.

6-2. This is how the world ends: not with a bang, but with a splinter. A wrecking yard for acoustic talking machines, around 1930. The closer you look at this photograph, the more horrifying it becomes. At first you see only the cabinet models, splayed willy-nilly or being bashed upside-down as the man in the foreground is doing. Then you begin to see the horn-machines sitting akimbo, about to join the heaps of scrap. An *incidental* photograph of people at work. In motion. The photographer certainly was unaware he was documenting an "atrocity." This was the final stop in the history of many talking machines. Yet, from where did they come, and for whom were they once the *newest thing*? (Value code: G)

Opposite page:
Top: 6-3. Where's the party? A festively-decorated room circa 1910 waiting for people. Everything is in place, so crisply arranged. We feel as if we could step into the frame, feel the *shoosh* of the carpet under our feet as we walk over and settle down on the lumpy, squeaky springs of the sofa. Everybody else will be here soon. May we be in charge of playing the Edison? A box brimming with records is at our feet, and we're ready to enter the original world of the talking machine. (Value code: G)

Bottom: 6-4. American gothic. A sedate couple in their front room circa 1915. Posing, but politely averting their gaze from the lens. Here, the Edison Diamond Disc Phonograph is an incidental part of the room. It just happens to be next to the settee. It makes a pretty good hat stand, too. But the lid is *open*- what does this suggest? It implies that although the machine was ordinary-enough to rest a hat on, it was being frequently played. It was such a part of the everyday life of this home that the lid was simply left up, allowing the machine to be enjoyed at any time. It would have made a slightly better hat stand with the lid down, but this talking machine was a contributing part of this home. (Value code: G)

HOW DO YOU DO

6-5. The talking machine in a social context: an "ice cream social" to be exact. This photo, circa 1906, shows the pretty, public world of a festive gathering: the cavernous, echo-y Masonic Hall; the smell of floor polish; the smell of coffee; the tempting aroma of pies; the creak of wooden chairs; the creak of children's brand new shoes—and the Zonophone ready to entertain. An ordinary object, but a necessary one, necessary to complete the amusement and diversions of a summer's day in the cool shadows of the grand hall. (Value code: G)

6-6. Another grand hall, rather, a lodge circa 1912. Again we feel the coolness of the room. It is big, darkly paneled and well-polished. The figures were caught in an unsuspecting fashion. They were really too far away from the camera to be properly recognized. One figure is only a blur: a waiter carrying a tray? The room itself was the subject of this photo. The people were incidental, as "by-the-way" as the Victor talking machine to which they were probably listening. (Value code: G)

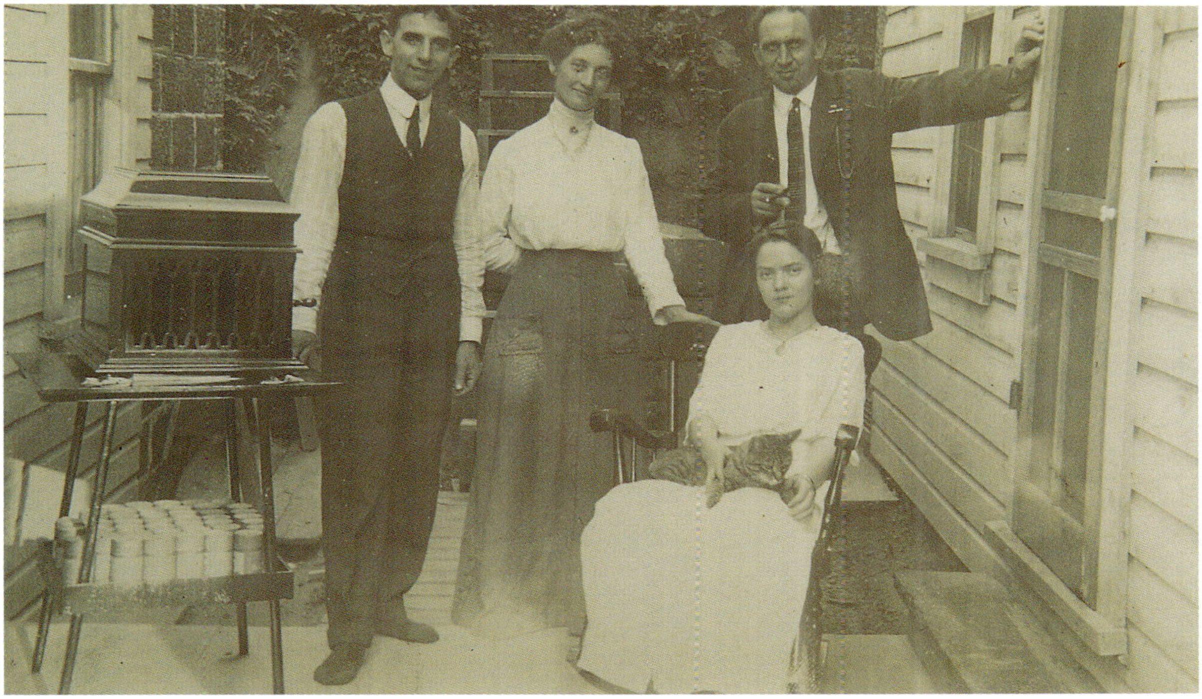

6-7. Home. It was summer, hot. Out back on a lazy evening. The cat was purring. It was 1913. They kept their Edison out there, under the covered arbor, all summer. It was so nice to hear the music after dinner. They were playing a waltz when this picture was taken. A pretty waltz at the close of a lovely day. (Value code: G)

6-8. Pretty small, isn't it? 1907. A lady with her chickens in front of a shack, and a brand new Edison "Home" Phonograph. Was she playing a record for the benefit of her brood? The nearby chair is a necessity born of records which lasted only two minutes. So, this Phonograph wasn't put there for the picture. It sat there *by custom*, with its customary chair. It was a *customary* part of this world, like the clucking of the chickens, and the pungent dust of the yard. (Value code: G)

6-9. Camping. Cool air and refreshing forest breezes. The summer of 1911. The tent was so still, except for the soft *flap, flap, flap* of some loose material. The young woman was smiling, really beaming, next to a camp bed fitted out in chenille to make it feel just like home. Later, she'd play some records on the Edison, "What did Mom and Dad do out here before they had a phonograph? A phonograph and *plenty* of new records!" (Value code: G)

6-10. Mom, Dad and the whole family, August 20, 1906. Dad believed in the value of sleeping out where the fresh air could get at your lungs. He claimed he never had a cold in his life. Looking back, we all seemed pretty robust. I thank heaven we had that talking machine. Peeking out, it looked insignificant. True, it didn't take up much room. But it sure made a lot of wonderful noise! (Value code: G)

6-11. An open-air recital, 1917. The charming-faced girl to the right of the Edison "Fireside" waits awkwardly. As staged as this picture seems, the machine was not hauled out in the sun just to be photographed. The table had been carefully leveled. Though no cylinders were visible, we may imagine that the Edison was there to be played. (Value code: G)

Opposite page:
Bottom: 6-13. Here's Tom serenading the ladies in 1919. He couldn't sing, so he concentrated on winding up the Grafonola. Out over the river would echo the sounds of "Row, Row, Row" or "Moonlight Bay." It seems so obvious now what would happen. A canoe was not a very wise place to put a shiny new talking machine. It was toward the end of that summer, late August. In the middle of the stream, Tom got up to change the needle. Someone must have leaned the wrong way and over went the lot of them. They were all good swimmers, thank God... except the Grafonola. I expect the fish might have used it to play "At the Codfish Ball" after that. (Value code: G)

Top: 6-12. A school picnic, 1903. The solemn-faced boys were posing. But you can feel their energy—as if they were ready to jump up as soon as the picture was taken—and they probably did. They jumped up and got the lunches their mothers had packed, sat down on the long boards, leaned their elbows on the oil-cloth of the table and played the Edison. (Value code: G)

6-14. People bought their talking machines in different places. There were big-city music stores with paneled booths and fancy carpets. There were smaller shops, too. The talking machine was good business. Here is a small American town in 1907. The street isn't paved. The sidewalks are wooden. You can hear the creak and rattle of the horse-drawn buggy and the noisy chugging of the automobile as they make their way up Main Street. (Value code: G)

6-15. Crisp winter light. A mother and her child pass the little shop that sells Edison Phonographs on their way home. The child's eyes were attracted to the bright barber pole just up the street. Two people passing under the tin-smith's handiwork: a sign representing a phonograph horn, the shop window with its neat rows of cylinder records, the faint music from within. Someone was playing a record, barely audible above the clanking of the motor car. (Value code: G)

6-16. Inside a shop in 1907. The proprietor and his little family. Edisons, Victors and Columbias, clocks, musical instruments and you-name-it dispensed from the rough brick and wooden interior of a "boom town." They promoted the healthful, hygienic effects of music in the home. Now you could hear a good orchestra in your own front room, even if you didn't have plaster on the walls. (Value code: G)

6-17. Small enterprise. Mr. Brewer's grocery store. It used to be a home, but it got converted over to business. Out in the middle of nowhere; yet, prosperous and clean. They put in a line of Victors and Edisons. In 1910 lots of people were buying talking machines. (Value code: G)

6-18. "Pretty small, isn't it?" Shopkeeper Fred probably wouldn't have liked his friend's handwritten comment. Yet, in 1908 there was plenty of room for everybody, even the smallest, in the expanding talking machine trade. It *is* amusing, though. The photographer had to include half an empty lot to avoid showing the cottage next door. Fred probably thought it wasn't quite right to put the neighbors in his picture. And that empty lot? He was waiting for a house to be built on it. He'd be over there right away: trying to sell them an Edison. (Value code: G)

6-19. A music shop virtually packed with delightful contraptions, circa 1909. A Victor "Junior" is on the counter. An Edison "Gem" Model "D" sits atop a piano. There are pianos, musical instruments, a push-up piano player, even a sewing machine supporting an Edison "Standard." The bright, beautiful ingenuity of a world squeaking and whirring with progress. (Value code: G)

6-20. Gibson City, Illinois, 1908. Mr. Vreeland's store with its big, painted sign. The frontier between the small shop and the big store. Mr. Vreeland lives in a large house on the main road out of town. He's got several clerks and a general manager. No more long hours for Mr. Vreeland. He's earned his success. He really knows phonographs. (Value code: G)

6-21. The big store. A purposefully-designed place for the music lover in 1912. The plush, paneled booths are at the back, for auditioning records. The clerks are neatly dressed, ready to demonstrate the latest in Victors, Victrolas, or Grafonolas. They applied modern, scientific principles to selling here. The customer was put at ease. Capacious wooden armchairs awaited him—without cushions, though, so the client would not lose his concentration on the merits of good music. (Value code: G)

6-22. The work of a poor photographer? It's odd how accidents can produce a revealing picture. The great hazy mass of foliage above this petulant boy with an Edison Phonograph suggests the brush work of an Impressionist. The tall grass and leaves make a hushed *swoosh*. The sun beaming down on the boy's face makes him close his eyes, waiting for the shutter to click. Waiting to leap up and hop to the music. *Courtesy of Steve and Ellie Saccente.* (Value code: G)

6-23. Not a very happy bunch. What energetic kid wants to be told to sit still until the picture is taken—especially when the Edison "Gem" is playing "Waltz Me Around Again, Willie?" (Value code: G)

6-24. Studying with the talking machine, 1907. This young man's family owns a Victor "III" for entertainment. However, the little cylinder "Languagephone" was there for personal edification. He spread out the whole kit on the dining room table: instruction books, homework, and a set of "Dr. Rosenthal's" famous language-teaching records. He was playing one when the shutter clicked. A serious activity. No need to interrupt his studies for the picture. *Courtesy of Todd Emery.* (Value code: G)

6-25. Dr. Hoopes was a man of means and taste, 1909. An eclectic mix of furniture and decoration gave underlying impressions of classical schooling, military training and travels in the East. No plebian oak talking machine for him. A Victor "IV" with its lustrous mahogany cabinet blended better with the decor. (Value code: G)

Top: 6-26. A quiet interior, January, 1910. A aesthetic-looking young man poses in an amusing imitation of sophistication. What cylinder might he have played on the Edison? A sentimental ballad perhaps. (Value code: G)

Bottom: 6-27. Hong Kong, 1915. The melding of China and the West. Locals in Chinese dress stand before an imposing row of European-style buildings. Plenty of expatriates in the Territory, though, to buy the newest in talking machines. (Value code: H)

Top: 6-28. A sailor with a somewhat reluctant best friend. There was a Victor talking machine on board ship to entertain the men. This fellow got the dog to sit up next to it, as in the famous trade mark. But the mutt didn't like it when the record played, so the sailor just tapped his fingers on the outside of the horn. Then the dog would put his chin up, head to the side. Just like Nipper. (Value code: G)

Bottom: 6-29. Europe, wrecked by war, 1917. Stinking, smoking trenches and the pounding of shells. How far away those suffocating scenes must have seemed on this sunny day when men paused in the dappled shade of a summer grove to enjoy a tune from a Pathé disc machine. (Value code: G)

6-30. A commercial card, but one with the immediacy of a snapshot. World War I soldiers. What attracted their interest the most, at this moment? The tempting pile of doughnuts? The closeness of a pretty girl? Or the photographer's camera? Temporarily, the Victrola "VI" was ignored. When all those "sinkers" were gone, then they'd play it. *Courtesy of Todd Emery.* (Value code: H)

6-31. A World War I soldier playing a vertical cut disc machine with a "reflex" internal horn. Why pose with a talking machine? Perhaps to show the folks back in the States that he had all the comforts of home. (Value code: G)

6-32. An odd trio of swells posing circa 1912. Here, any hypothesis is probably as good as the next. The famous dog Nipper intrudes on this antic scene. Was this die-cut display figure the only thing that could be located on which to write "At Milwaukee?" (Value code: G)

6-33. Although these young men are posed as gypsies, in front of a house-wagon, they are really more suggestive of a sports team. Did they play these instruments, the trappings of real Romany wanderers? Probably not. A Victor talking machine was there to provide musical diversion. It was almost hidden from view. But you didn't need to *see* it did you? You *listened* to a talking machine. This one was rather old and battered; the horn dented. 1910, and it was almost ready for the junkyard. (Value code: G)

# KEY TO VALUE CODES

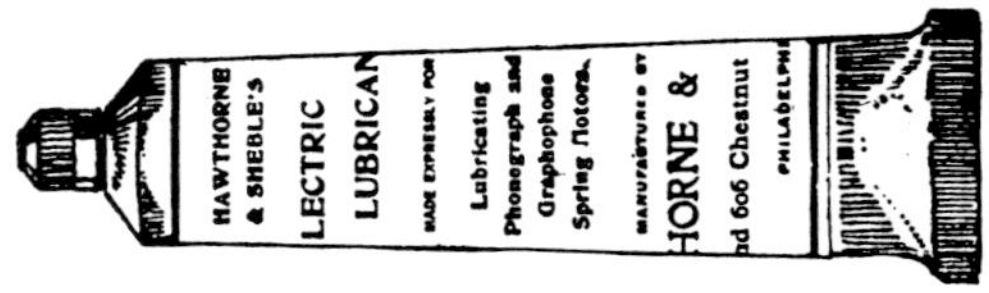

Preparing a value system for a large number of diverse items is a task fraught with concerns. Out of a need to simplify this system and make it as easy to use as possible, we designate prices *only* for the "peripheral" items which are the specific focus of this book. Though some talking machines are pictured, they do not receive values. Items which are extremely uncommon are rated "very rare" (VR).

Values are expressed *in the individual captions* by the following letter codes:

A. $1000 and up
B. $500 to $999
C. $250 to $499
D. $150 to $249
E. $100 to $149
F. $50 to $99
G. $25 to $49
H. $5 to $24

This might seem to be a long list of prices. However, you will find that most of the values actually fall within categories D, E, F and G. Many illustrations contain a selection of objects. If these items are similar enough, a general value code is shown. If there is sufficient disparity in the prices, they are individually valued: always listed from left to right and clockwise, if applicable.

By employing price categories instead of specific dollar amounts, we leave ourselves open to various "slings and arrows" of discontent. It is our feeling that ours is the only effective approach to the subject. However, this does add an element of discretion to the use of our book.

In using the value codes, we advise *conservatism*. If you are trying to establish the value of an object in your possession, the natural instinct is to seize upon the highest price in the given range, regardless of condition. This can be a mistake. The condition of the items in the book is nearly always excellent, but the condition of *your* item is the important issue. Condition can affect the value by up to 50%—and occasionally more. The bottom end of a price range has as much validity as the top, though it seems a less attractive prospect. Different examples of the same type of object may represent the entire range of a certain price category, due to condition. The ranges are also intended to be *comparative*. Certain objects in the "C" category, for instance, may *never* reach $499 no matter how perfectly preserved they are.

Beyond condition, many, many factors affect the price of an "antique." Exact worth is something that can not be fixed precisely in time. We can only hint at it. Our guide is intended to help you understand the value of the objects illustrated, but we vigorously discourage the use of the phrase, "It *books* for such-and-such a price." True worth is what the market will bear. Quoting books, auction results or what a shop is asking will probably not elevate the price higher than the general market will currently support.

# Bibliography

Association for Recorded Sound Collections, various ed.s: *ARSC Journal*, various issues to 1999.

Barnum, Frederick O. III: *His Master's Voice in America*, Camden, General Electric Company, 1991.

Barr, Steven C.: *The Almost Complete 78 RPM Record Dating Guide (II)*, Huntington Beach, Yesterday Once Again, 1992.

Baumbach, Robert W.: *Columbia Phonograph Companion, Vol. II (Disc Graphophones and the Grafonola)*, Woodland Hills, Stationery X-Press, 1996.

Baumbach, Robert W.: *Look for the Dog*, Woodland Hills, Stationery X-Press, 1996.

Bayly, E., ed.: *The EMI Collection*, Bournemouth (GB), Talking Machine Review, 1977.

Bayly, E., ed: *The Talking Machine Review International*, Bournemouth (GB), various issues beginning 1970.

Bill, Edward Lyman, ed.: *The Talking Machine World*, New York, various issues 1905-1929.

Bryan, Martin, ed.: *The New Amberola Graphic*, St. Johnsbury (VT), various issues 1973-1999.

City of London Phonograph and Gramophone Society, various ed.s: *The Hillandale News*, various issues 1960s to present.

Conot, Robert: *A Streak of Luck,* New York, Seaview Books, 1979.

Dethlefson, Ronald, ed.: *Edison Blue Amberol Recordings, 1912-1914*, Brooklyn, APM Press, 1980.

Dethlefson, Ronald, ed.: *Edison Blue Amberol Recordings, 1912-1914* (paper cover), Woodland Hills (CA), Stationery X-Press, 1997.

Dethlefson, Ronald, ed.: *Edison Blue Amberol Recordings, 1915-1929*, Brooklyn, APM Press, 1981.

Edge, Ruth and Petts, Leonard: *The Collector's Guide to "His Master's Voice" Nipper Souvenirs,* London, EMI Group, 1997.

Fabrizio, Timothy C. and Paul, George F.: *The Talking Machine, an Illustrated Compendium 1877-1929*, Atglen (PA), Schiffer Publishing, Ltd., 1997.

Fagan, Ted, compiled by: *The Encyclopedic Discography of Victor Recordings, Pre-Matrix Series,* Westport, Greenwood Press, 1983.

Fagan, Ted, compiled by: *The Encyclopedic Discography of Victor Recordings*, Westport, Greenwood Press, 1986.

Frow, George L.: *Edison Cylinder Phonograph Companion*, Woodland Hills, Stationery X-Press, 1994

Frow, George L.: *The Edison Disc Phonographs and the Diamond Discs*, Sevenoaks, Kent (GB), George L. Frow, 1982.

Gaisberg, Frederick W.: *The Music Goes Round*, North Stratford (NH), Ayer Company Publishers, Inc. 1977 (1942 reprint).

Gelatt, Roland: *The Fabulous Phonograph, revised* New York, Appleton-Century, 1965 (three ed.s 1955-1977).

Gracyk, Tim, ed.: *Victrola and 78 Journal*, Granite Bay (CA), various issues 1994-1998.

Hatcher, Danny, ed.: *Proceedings of the 1890 Convention of Local Phonograph Companies*, Nashville, Country Music Foundation Press, reprint, 1974.

Hazelcorn, Howard: *A Collector's Guide to the Columbia Spring-Wound Cylinder Graphophone, 1894-1910*, Brooklyn, APM Press, 1976.

Hazelcorn, Howard: *Columbia Phonograph Companion, Volume I: Hazlecorn's Guide to the Columbia Cylinder Graphophone*, Woodland Hills (CA), Stationery X-Press, 1999.

Hunting, Russell, ed.: *The Phonoscope*, New York, Phonoscope Publishing Company, various issues 1896-1900.

Johnson, E. R. Fenimore: *His Master's Voice Was Eldridge R. Johnson,* Milford (DE), State Media, Inc., 1975.

Koenigsberg, Allen, ed.: *The Antique Phonograph Monthly*, Brooklyn, APM Press, various issues 1972-1993.

Koenigsberg, Allen: *Edison Cylinder Records, 1889-1912, 2nd ed.*, Brooklyn, APM Press, 1988.

Koenigsberg, Allen: *The Patent History of the Phonograph, 1877-1912*, Brooklyn, APM Press, 1991.

Lorenz, Kenneth M.: *Two-Minute... Cylinders of the Columbia Phonograph Company*, Wilmington (DE), Kastlemusick, Inc., 1981.

Maken, Neil: *Hand-Cranked Phonographs*, Huntington Beach, Promar Publishing, 1995.

Marco, Guy A. and Andrews, Frank, eds.: *Encyclopedia of Recorded Sound in the United States*, New York, Garland Publishing, Inc., 1993.

Martland, Peter: *Since Records Began: EMI: the First Hundred Years*, (distributed by Timber Press, Portland, OR), Amadeus Press, 1997.

Marty, Daniel: *Histoire Illustrée du Phonographe (Illustrated History of the Phonograph),* Lausanne/Paris, Edita/Lazarus, 1979, (reprinted in various English language editions with slight modifications of the title).

Moore, Jerrold Northrop: *A Matter of Records*, New York, Taplinger Publishing Company, 1977.

Moore, Wendell, ed.: *The Edison Phonograph Monthly*, various anthologies 1903-1916, New Albany (IN), Wendell Moore Publications.

Proudfoot, Christopher: *Collecting Phonographs and Gramophones*, New York, Mayflower Books, 1980.

Read, Oliver and Welch, Walter L.: *From Tinfoil to Stereo*, Indianapolis, Howard W. Sams and Company, Inc., 1959.

Reiss, Eric L.: *The Compleat Talking Machine*, Chandler (AZ), Sonoran Publishing, (revised)1998.

Rust, Brian, compiled by: *Discography of Historical Records on Cylinders and 78s*, Westport, Greenwood Press, 1979.

Sherman, Michael W. (with Moran, William R. and Nauck, Kurt R. III): *Collector's Guide to Victor Records*, Dallas, Monarch Record Enterprises, 1992.

Sherwin, Michael W. and Nauck, Kurt R. III: *Note the Notes, An Illustrated History of the Columbia 78 rpm Record Label, 1901-1958*, New Orleans, Monarch Record Enterprises, 1998.

Sutton, Allan: *Directory of American Disc Record Brands and Manufacturers, 1891-1943*, Westport, Greenwood Press, 1994.

Welch, Walter L. and Burt, Leah Brodbeck Stenzel: *From Tinfoil to Stereo, 1877-1929*, Gainesville, University Press of Florida, 1994.

Wile, Raymond R.and Dethlefson, Ronald: *Edison Diamond Disc Recreations, Records and Artists 1910-1929,* Brooklyn, APM Press, 1985.

# Glossary

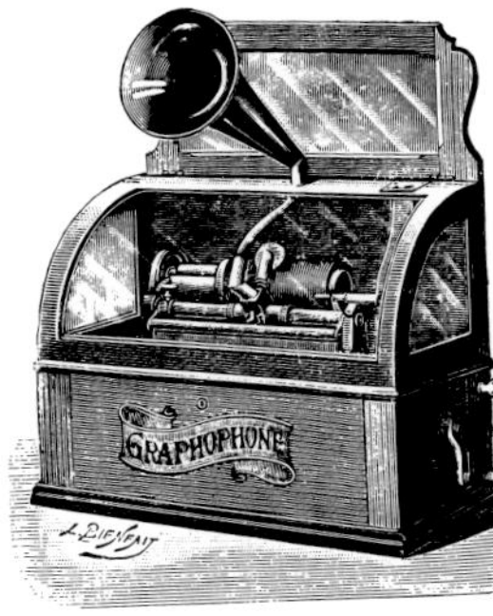


AMBEROL: The first four-minute cylinder developed by Edison, 1908-1912. These cylinders are black in color, made of especially hard metallic soap, and were usually sold in green and white containers.

AMBEROLA: The name denoting Edison's line of internal-horn cylinder Phonographs, 1909-1929.

BACK MOUNT: A term used to describe a talking machine which uses a back bracket which supports the horn and thus removes its inertia from the soundbox.

BEDPLATE: The plate (usually metal) to which the upper mechanism of a cylinder talking machine is mounted.

BLANK: A smooth, grooveless unrecorded cylinder.

BLUE AMBEROL: The blue celluloid four-minute cylinder sold by Edison, 1912-1929. The containers for these cylinders were blue until 1917, orange and blue thereafter.

CARRIAGE: The assembly which "carries" the reproducer of a cylinder talking machine across the recording.

CARRIER ARM: Edison nomenclature for the carriage. The half-nut and spring are attached directly to the carrier arm on nearly all Edison machines.

COMBINATION ATTACHMENT: Devices offered by Edison to convert pre-1908 Phonographs to play four-minute cylinders in addition to the two-minute variety.

CONCERT: Edison's trade name for the five-inch diameter cylinder and the Edison Phonograph designed to play it.

CRANE: The support used to mount horns of 15-inch length or greater to cylinder talking machines.

CYLINDER: A geometric form on which entertainment recordings were made, 1877-1929. The earliest sheets of tinfoil were followed by self-supporting cylinders of ozocerite-covered cardboard, stearic acid/paraffin, hard metallic soap, and celluloid. Advantages of the cylinder format included a constant surface speed and the ability to make home recordings.

DIAMOND DISC: Edison's line of disc records and machines, 1912-1929. The Diamond Discs were vertically recorded, and the Diamond Disc Phonographs were one of the very few disc talking machines to use a feedscrew.

DIAPHRAGM: The flexible, circular vibrating membrane of a soundbox or reproducer which converts mechanical energy to acoustic energy or sound waves. Mica, glass, compressed paper, copper and aluminum were commonly used as diaphragms in early talking machines.

ELBOW: The connection between the horn and the soundbox or tone arm of a disc talking machine. Earliest elbows are made of leather, gradually giving way to metal elbows after 1900.

ENDGATE: A swinging arm which supports one end of the mandrel on some cylinder talking machines. To mount or remove a cylinder it is therefore necessary to open and close the endgate.

FEEDSCREW: A threaded rod which usually drives a half-nut fixed to the carriage of a cylinder talking machine, thus guiding the reproducer across the record grooves. Certain disc machines used feedscrews to drive the soundbox across the record or to move the turntable beneath a fixed soundbox. Similarly, some cylinder machines used feedscrews to drive a mandrel longitudinally beneath a fixed reproducer.

FRONT MOUNT: A term used to describe a disc machine where the horn attaches directly to the soundbox, and the support arm (or mount) runs directly below and parallel to the horn. In such an arrangement the support arm points in the same general direction as the bell of the horn.

GRAMOPHONE: Originally the name by which Emile Berliner's disc talking machine was known, it became a generic term to denote any disc playing talking machine, but fell out of use in the United States.

GRAND: Columbia's trade name for the five-inch diameter cylinder and the various Columbia machines designed to play it.

GOVERNOR: The mechanical assembly in a talking machine motor which regulates the speed, usually by limiting the outward movement of spinning weights.

HALF-NUT: An internally threaded metal piece usually in the form of a nut which has been cut in half. The threads of the half-nut correspond to the threads of the feedscrew. As the feedscrew revolves, the half-nut will be propelled along it, thus driving the carriage of a talking machine.

LATERAL RECORDING: The type of disc talking machine recording where the information is encoded in the sides of the groove. (see VERTICAL RECORDING)

MANDREL: The tapered drum upon which the cylinder record is placed for playing.

NEEDLE: The point (usually steel) of the soundbox which rides the grooves of the recording and transmits vibrations to the diaphragm.

NEEDLE TIN: A container to store and dispense steel talking machine needles.

NEEDLE SHARPENER (OR CUTTER): A device for repointing disc talking machine needles of fibre, thorn or steel.

RECORDER: A device comprising a diaphragm and cutting stylus for recording cylinder or disc records.

REPEATING ATTACHMENT: A device for cylinder or disc talking machines which returns the needle or stylus to the beginning of the record after the selection has played.

REPRODUCER: The component comprising stylus, linkage and diaphragm, which reproduces the sound from the record grooves. This term is most frequently applied to cylinder machines. (See SOUNDBOX)

SHAVER: On a cylinder talking machine, a device which holds a knife in position to pare the recorded surface from a wax cylinder.

SOUNDBOX: The component comprising needle, linkage and diaphragm, which reproduces the sound from the record grooves. This term is most frequently applied to disc machines. (See REPRODUCER)

STYLUS: The point (usually sapphire or diamond) of the reproducer which rides the grooves of the recording and transmits vibrations to the diaphragm.

TONE ARM: A movable hollow tube which conducts sound to the horn from the soundbox.

TRUNNION: Rightly, the sleeve visible on either side of the carriage which slides over the feedscrew shaft on a Graphophone, but commonly used to denote the entire carriage.

VERTICAL RECORDING: The type of cylinder or disc recording in which the sound vibrations are encoded in the bottom of the groove. (see LATERAL RECORDING)

# Index

Use me often, you'll find
Your records will
WILLIAM J. MA
VICTROLAS AND
DUSTOFF
RECORD CLEANER
THE TALKING
97 Main St. Fr
BELL PHONE 3296
HOME PHONE 1766
FOR CLEANING ALL RECORDS
EITHER DISC OR CYLINDER
GILBERT'S RECCO BRUSH.
MADE BY
E. T. GILBERT MFG. CO., ROCHESTER, N. Y.
JERONIMUS
OLDEST VICTOR DEALERS
Duluth
10,000 Victor Records Always on Hand
Columbia Grafonolas and Records
C. S. HUSSEY,
GOWANDA, N. Y.
500
SUPERIOR STEEL
BRILLIANTONE
NEEDLES
MEDIUM TONE
MADE IN U.S.A.
Columbia Grafonolas and Records